From the Privileged to the Professionals

This book is concerned with the early years of the Football Association Challenge Cup – more commonly known as the FA Cup – examining events from its inception in 1871–2 to the beginning of the Football League in 1888–9. The work is underpinned by the figurational sociology of Norbert Elias, employing his ideas around the European 'civilising process', power and lengthening chains of human interdependency.

Most of all, the majority of the text has been compiled using primary source material, such as newspaper reports and the minutes of the Football Association, which encourages original and unique additions to the body of knowledge. There exist no comparable offerings on the time period involved, with the book providing a distinct perspective for scholars and non-specialists alike. The initial years of the competition were dominated by teams consisting mainly of upper-middle-class southern amateurs. However, by the early 1880s, they were supplanted by men who were initially covert – and eventually overt – professionals, many of whom hailed from Scotland, but mainly represented clubs from Lancashire and the West Midlands.

The FA Cup, despite losing some of its allure when compared to competitions such as the UEFA Champions League, still retains a magic of its own in the English football calendar.

Graham Curry was Head of Physical Education at Tuxford Academy, UK, for 30 years, gaining his PhD at Leicester University in 2001. He has written extensively on the sociology of association football, producing with Eric Dunning, *Association Football: A Study in Figurational Sociology* in 2015.

Routledge Soccer Histories
Series editors

Chris Bolsmann
Professor in the Department of Kinesiology at California State University Northridge, USA.
Dil Porter
Emeritus Professor of Sports History and Culture at De Montfort University, Leicester, United Kingdom.

Soccer's reach is global and the series is seeking to make a major contribution to the cultural and social history of the world game, embracing both men's and women's football. Topics covered include and will include histories of the game in particular countries and regions with an emphasis on its role in the formation of national, regional and local identities; histories relating to the development of women's football; explorations in transnational and international football history, including surveys of the development of the game across Africa, Central Europe, South-East Asia, North America, South America and other key regions; histories relating to the institutional framework of the global game, such as the Olympic movement, FIFA, its associated regional federations and national associations; cultural and social histories of soccer in cities worldwide which locate its development within a particular urban cultural context; deep historical explorations of significant moments in the history of the world game and their wider resonance; the history of the game as a mediated experience – journalism, television and digital media. The series also looks to accommodate reprints of classic texts which have made important contributions to our understanding of the history of association football with new critical introductions.

Regeneration through Sport: Football, Sport, and Cultural Modernization in Spain, 1890–1920
Andrew McFarland

Association Football and English Society, 1863–1915 (Revised edition)
Tony Mason

Female Football Spectators in Britain 1863–1939
A Historical Analysis
Robert Lewis

From the Privileged to the Professionals
The Early Years of the FA Cup
Graham Curry

From the Privileged to the Professionals
The Early Years of the FA Cup

Graham Curry

LONDON AND NEW YORK

First published 2024
by Routledge
4 Park Square, Milton Park, Abingdon, Oxon OX14 4RN

and by Routledge
605 Third Avenue, New York, NY 10158

Routledge is an imprint of the Taylor & Francis Group, an informa business

© 2024 Graham Curry

The right of Graham Curry to be identified as author of this work has been asserted in accordance with sections 77 and 78 of the Copyright, Designs and Patents Act 1988.

All rights reserved. No part of this book may be reprinted or reproduced or utilised in any form or by any electronic, mechanical, or other means, now known or hereafter invented, including photocopying and recording, or in any information storage or retrieval system, without permission in writing from the publishers.

Trademark notice: Product or corporate names may be trademarks or registered trademarks, and are used only for identification and explanation without intent to infringe.

British Library Cataloguing-in-Publication Data
A catalogue record for this book is available from the British Library

Library of Congress Cataloging-in-Publication Data
Names: Curry, Graham, author.
Title: From the privileged to the professionals : the early years of the FA Cup / Graham Curry.
Description: Abingdon, Oxon ; New York : Routledge, 2023. | Series: Routledge soccer histories
Identifiers: LCCN 2023001307 (print) | LCCN 2023001308 (ebook) | ISBN 9781032258997 (hardback) | ISBN 9781032259116 (paperback) | ISBN 9781003285595 (ebook)
Subjects: LCSH: F.A. Cup (England)--History. | Professionalism in sports--England--History.
Classification: LCC GV943.6.F25 C87 2023 (print) | LCC GV943.6.F25 (ebook) | DDC 796.3340942--dc23/eng/20230216
LC record available at https://lccn.loc.gov/2023001307
LC ebook record available at https://lccn.loc.gov/2023001308

ISBN: 978-1-032-25899-7 (hbk)
ISBN: 978-1-032-25911-6 (pbk)
ISBN: 978-1-003-28559-5 (ebk)

DOI: 10.4324/9781003285595

Typeset in Bembo
by SPi Technologies India Pvt Ltd (Straive)

Contents

List of tables		vi
Acknowledgements		vii
	Introduction	1
1	The 'making' of the FA Cup	11
2	The inaugural FA Cup	21
3	The beginnings of change	49
4	The rise of East Lancashire	68
5	Importations and the coming of professionalism	94
6	West Midlands supremacy and the advent of the Football League	115
	Conclusion	132
	Appendix 1 Football Association Challenge Cup Finals, 1871–2 to 1888–9	138
	Appendix 2 Football Association Challenge Cup entrants by region, 1871–2 to 1887–8	142
	Appendix 3 Tertiary education of southern amateur FA Cup finalists, 1871–2 to 1882–3	144
	Appendix 4 Schools of southern amateur FA Cup finalists, 1871–2 to 1882–3	145
	Newspapers, periodicals etc.	146
	Index	152

Tables

1.1	Champion House competitions of 1854 and 1865	16
1.2	Ties and results for the Youdan Cup, 1867	17
1.3	Ties and results for the Cromwell Cup, 1868	18
2.1	Initial FA Cup draw, 1871–2	23
2.2	First round FA Cup draw, 1871–2	24
2.3	Third round FA Cup draw, 1871–2	41
2.4	FA Cup semi-finals, 1871–2	41
4.1	The Darwen line-up, with occupations, for the first game in their trilogy of matches versus Old Etonians	76
4.2	The Blackburn Olympic line-up for the FA Cup Final, 1882–3	78
4.3	The Blackburn Rovers line-up for the FA Cup Final, 1883–4	84
5.1	Scottish football players based with English clubs, December 1884	99
6.1	Clubs involved in the FA Cup First Round Proper, 1888–9 (32)	123
6.2	Clashes between cup and league, 1888–9	124
6.3	Defeats suffered by Preston North End in the 1888–9 season	129

Acknowledgements

Judy Wright and James Cooper for proofreading.

Dil Porter for his encouragement and honing of the final draft.

Tony Brown for sharing his knowledge of the FA Cup.

Andy Mitchell for his much-appreciated advice and suggestions on all things connected with Scottish football history.

Keith Warsop for his encyclopaedic knowledge of the southern amateur FA Cup finalists.

Tony Collins, Keri Griffiths, Dominic Malcolm, Kevin Neill and Maxine Tivey.

Eric Dunning.

Introduction

The 2021–2 English football season represented the 150th anniversary of the advent of the FA Cup, or Football Association Challenge Cup to give it its formal name. Some club football competitions pre-dated it – I am thinking primarily of the Youdan and Cromwell Cups in Sheffield – but both of them only lasted for a single year. Without wishing to stray too far from a fairly strict academic perspective, the FA Cup does possess a certain romance and it is worth registering that fact. However, over the past 30 years with the beginning of the UEFA Champions League, 'the cup' has lost much of its allure, mostly due to not providing the winners with a pathway to that financially replete competition and the commercial benefits that would accrue. Unfortunately, such romance often brings with it only a passing recognition of the proven facts, hiding unwanted realities and becoming involved with too many emotional attachments leading to a lack of detachment. This is particularly true when dealing with the cup's early events, but these initial years suffer from a lack of serious, in-depth study and have too often been glossed over or dealt with in a fleeting, lazy fashion. The social historian's deterrent, of course, is that painstaking research is required into primary sources of events which have taken place one and a half centuries ago. Therefore, the aim of this book is to present an exhaustive pathway and 'drill down' into the first 18 years of the competition – the timeframe will extend from the initial season, 1871–2, to 1888–9, when Preston North End completed the 'double', winning both the first English League Championship and the FA Cup and, in the process, becoming the original 'Invincibles' – in an effort to test certain existing hypotheses, propose original ones and re-examine some of those prevailing beliefs.

Any reader expecting a conventional history will be disappointed; rather the approach is designed to test the early FA Cup story, that is, the opinions and beliefs surrounding it, perhaps revealing anomalies and inconsistencies, modifying them where appropriate, but also, conceivably, supporting some of the current received narratives. These, of course, will depend on the evidence accrued and the interpretation of such data.

Principally, an attempt will be made to answer the following significant questions:

DOI: 10.4324/9781003285595-1

2 *Introduction*

- Where did the idea and format of the FA Cup originate?
- What was the social structure of the competing sides throughout the timeline of the study and how did it change?
- Did the advent of professionalism in English football and the establishment of the Football League modify the processes and/or perceptions of the FA Cup?

Of course, tangents of interest will be explored, but the three bullet points above will be central to the book's narrative.

In terms of existing texts on the subject, other than primary sources, which this author has found most useful, the most exalted is probably Geoffrey Green's *The Official History of the F.A. Cup*, which was published as long ago as 1949. Clearly, it only transcribes events up to that date and necessarily omits occurrences in the years following the Second World War. Without being too critical, Green's text has surely outlived much of its usefulness, as so many studies on the subject have superseded its content and analysis since its publication. Despite the book's continued reputation, there are only a mere 34 pages which deal with the early history and, in doing so, Green is guilty of underplaying this era, something which this book seeks to rectify. Indeed, there is no other text that solely examines those initial years. Four further studies, however, are worthy of note. Keith Warsop has produced *The Early F.A. Cup Finals and the Southern Amateurs*, focusing on the first 12 finals – deliberately ending with the initial victory of a northern-based club, Blackburn Olympic – detailing the final ties, but also providing biographies of every southern amateur to play in those games. Warsop attempts some analysis – 22 pages out of 144 – but the vast majority of the book is taken up with team lists of the finals and finely detailed biographies of each finalist. The latter work represents an invaluable resource and the book is a good investment for this information alone. Indeed, it should be required reading. It would be remiss to leave out Rob Cavallini's superbly researched *The Wanderers F.C.*, which, as a resource item, is along the lines of Warsop's offering and is full of factual treasures. For those seeking the results of matches, they should go no further than Tony Brown's *The FA Challenge Cup 1871/2 to 2011/12* and, should one wish to consult the early minutes of the FA and newspaper reports appertaining to them, another of Brown's offerings, *The Football Association 1863–1883: A Source Book*, is an excellent source of information. As a primary source for this book, the original FA minutes have been consulted, though newspaper reports often provide much more detail than the minutes themselves.[1]

Of the major historical works on football, Dunning and Sheard's *Barbarians, Gentlemen and Players* deals with the subject more analytically than most, although, as with most writers, their interventions on the FA Cup are rather truncated. The pair briefly pose the view that the competition's foundation may have been connected to the formation of the Rugby Football Union in the same year.[2] Indeed, this hypothesis is taken up by Adrian Harvey in *Football: The First Hundred Years*, who strengthens the case for a link by noting that the codification of rugby outside of Rugby School took place on 26 July 1871, just six days after the FA had proposed the establishment of their competition.[3] Although this cannot be described as a clear causal link – the first mention of the FA Cup in the FA Minutes took place six days before rugby's codification – almost certainly, both sides were aware of the other's machinations and these events were simply part of an ongoing process of status and sporting rivalry between two competing football groups.

Harvey's section on the early FA Cup begins promisingly enough, but, at less than two pages in length, ultimately disappoints, though he echoes Dunning and Sheard in noting the increase in crowds at FA Cup Finals as more northern, working-class teams became involved.[4] Growing spectatorism was directly linked to class. Spectators paid an entrance fee and this was utilised to attract and reward better players. Of course, the idea of being watched was anathema to most former public schoolboys who participated for the game's sake, were almost embarrassed by people watching them and continued to wonder why spectators gained any benefit from what they would have described as a sedentary pursuit. Cup final crowds themselves did not exceed 8000 until the twelfth edition in 1882-3 when a team from the north enjoyed a first victory, as Blackburn Olympic defeated the Old Etonians.

Additionally, in *Barbarians*, Dunning and Sheard note the growing seriousness of sport in mid-to-late Victorian Britain, leading to an intensification of competition, of which the introduction of the FA Cup was a part. They also argue convincingly that this escalation, together with a trend towards sport becoming more culturally central, has led to 'a real increase in violence on and off the field of play'.[5] They quote Charles Alcock as he ruefully remembers 'the days when football had not grown to be so important as to make umpires necessary, and the "gate" the first subject of conversation'.[6]

The examples offered by Dunning and Sheard, as well as Adrian Harvey, present the reader with more food for thought than Tony Mason in *Association Football and English Society*, who makes a plethora of brief references to the FA Cup – there are 70 in the index – but proposes little in-depth analysis. Mason does present two useful maps which clearly represent the geographical locations of the entrants for the FA Cup in, firstly, 1871-2 and, secondly, 1883-4, the former being dominated by clubs from in and around the capital, while the latter shows the emergence of Lancashire, the West Midlands and the East Midlands.[7] Matthew Taylor in *The Association Game*, charting the link between the establishment of a national association and a subsequent cup competition, notes the civic pride and enthusiasm that cup competition evoked over 'friendlies', before listing the occupations of some of the early East Lancashire teams. It is unfortunate that he chooses to devote only five pages to the cup's first 12 years.[8] Indeed, Mason's and Taylor's treatment of those early years remains the biggest justification for this book, which concentrates in detail on the first 18 years of the competition. There is simply nothing remotely like it in terms of data, narrative and argument, and, particularly, the examination of new themes and individuals from a period which has attracted scant attention. The reader of the major texts has to sift the 'wheat from the chaff', and devise hypotheses of their own.

However, there is one specific article which tackles an event in the FA Cup head on. James R. Holzmeister's 'The 1883 F.A. Cup Final: working class representation, professionalism and the development of modern football in England' is a worthy attempt to use a footballing watershed for academic comment.[9] In truth the article focuses much more on the growth of football professionalism than it does the 1883 final. Holzmeister recognises that there were obvious class and geographic comparisons to be made between the two protagonists, Blackburn Olympic and the Old Etonians, but seeks to play down this obvious dichotomy.[10] However, as will be attempted in Chapter 4 of this book, this particular cup final and this particular team from Blackburn, not only emphasised working-class employment in their job descriptions, but 'employed' two professionals, who seemed to epitomise the cultural change taking place in the monetisation of certain football clubs in Lancashire. Most strange of all in his essay is that nowhere does he mention either Jack Hunter or George Wilson, the two professionals from Sheffield and Swinton (South Yorkshire), respectively, who were the star performers of the Olympic team. It is clear that his article is strong in terms of eloquent analysis and theory, however, from a sociological point of view, he rarely mentions people, the actors who shaped events. Hunter and Wilson represented the process of footballing professionalism itself and were also examples of importations from other areas. Holzmeister rightly concentrates on the events surrounding the advent of football professionalism together with the subsequent debate over its acceptability and, as the author of this book has discovered, it is difficult to divorce that discourse from any writings on the FA Cup. His attempt to connect the 1883 final with post-colonialism is rather weak and any real discussion on this subject only appears as an afterthought in the conclusion. This is unfortunate as the subject itself, the 1883 FA Cup Final, has more obvious sociological lessons to impart.

The figurational sociology of Norbert Elias[11]

In a book underpinned by the figurational sociology of Norbert Elias, it seems apposite to trace for the reader what is meant by this approach. Briefly, those key features of figurational sociology pioneered by Elias used in the text can be summarised as follows:

i   There is the shared conviction that human individuals and the societies they form can best be understood as long-term processes. That is, there is a commitment to examine the emergence of sociologically significant features over a period of time, rather than rely on static elements. There is no room for words such as 'invent', something which conjures up the work of a magician or alchemist, rather, the term 'develop' would be employed to suggest events over a much longer term. Those developmental processes have taken place as part of a series of figurations or interdependencies between people in those societies. Figurational sociology – or process sociology as it is also known – is a perfect way of studying and interpreting historical human actions. To understand football's complex history, its story should be treated as a long-term process, over several generations, beginning with a study of its 'mob' or 'folk' form, pausing briefly to examine types existing outside the public-school setting, noting its journey through the public schools and universities and, eventually, into the wider society.

ii That the processes undergone by societies have tended, up to now – especially in the longer term – to be mainly 'blind' in the sense of being the outcome of the largely unintended consequences of the aggregates of multiple individual acts. For instance, there was no deliberate strategy or plan to professionalise soccer, it was simply the end result of thousands of inadvertently connected human acts. No one could have imagined, in the middle years of the 19th century, that the game of football in all its subsequent forms would have been the subject of such global acclaim. The developments in the game, of which the early footballers were merely a part, were being conducted as 'blind' processes with unintended outcomes rather than purposeful acts with fixed aims and objectives. For Elias, human understanding of their social worlds is currently so limited that efforts to guide the future cannot be done with much accuracy. This, incidentally, is also part of the rationale for undertaking an historically sociological approach, as has been attempted in this book. Given the current imperfections in human knowledge, it is more reliable to make statements about past developments than to focus on the contemporary, ever-changing events.

iii That power is a universal property of human relations at all levels of social integration and is, arguably and certainly in this text, the most important aspect. Elias also argued that power is not explainable solely by reference to single factors, such as Karl Marx's ideas of the ownership of production or Max Weber's ideas of the control of the means of violence. Eric Dunning strongly believed that in mid-19th century England, a struggle was taking place between elements of the established social order, the aristocracy and upper classes, and the *bourgeoisie*. This struggle, he contended, manifested itself in various ways, most notably, for our purposes, in the codification of football rules and the administration of the newly created administrative bodies which were formed to organise the game. The 'battle' was ultimately won by high-status Old Etonians and, to a lesser extent, Old Harrovians, who were champions of a 'proto-soccer', a kicking and dribbling version of football, and was one reason why association and not rugby became the dominant football form. Furthermore, the perceived societal power – they had attended public school and/or university and were employed in jobs with high social *cachés* – of men such as Charles Alcock at the FA and Nathaniel Creswick in Sheffield ensured that their preferred forms of the game were adopted by their sporting sub-groups. Subsequently, in Alcock's case, his power and that of his companions in London football proved too strong even for relatively important provincial élites such as that of Sheffield.[12] Additionally, the social power and prestige of the southern amateurs was important in successfully avoiding a split in association football in the early 1880s, not only keeping the northern covert professionals under the control of the FA, but also maintaining their hold on the administration of the game. This latter subject will be analysed in more detail in Chapter 5 of this book. The power struggle evokes Elias's theory, with John Scotson, established in their work *The Established and the Outsiders*, where the former group is clearly dominant, while the other is plainly subordinate.[13] Alcock and the members of the FA were more advantaged in terms of wealth, income, occupation, education and – most significantly – social prestige and, therefore, imbued with a high degree of 'power'. Because of this status, the London footballing subcultural group was able to impose their will in the decision-making processes involved with the development of football. Yet Elias stressed the bi-polar nature of power because it exists not simply for one individual or group in a relationship, but for both. In other words, all individuals are powerful, but some are more powerful than others. Working-class players would have been powerful because of their footballing abilities, which were much prized, but in an administrative sense they would have possessed little influence on debates at the FA, for instance.[14]

iv That sociologists should see as their primary concern the accumulation of bodies of reliable knowledge. Elias suggested that in a piece of research the aim should be, first of all by means of what he called 'a detour *via* detachment', to build up as 'reality-congruent' a picture of what a process actually involves and how and why it is socially, psychologically and historically generated. Sport, in general, and football, in particular, are important parts of society and are worthy of academic inquiry.

v That there is a need in sociology to undertake a constant two-way traffic between theory and research. Theory without research, Elias used to argue, is liable to be abstract and meaningless; research without theory to be arid and descriptive. In this book Eliasian ideas have been followed in this respect, producing a synthesis of diligent primary research together with theoretical rigour which has generated a text of the highest academic standard. Holzmeister's worthy tome on the 1883 FA Cup Final, which is discussed earlier in this introduction, might be offered as a good example of an over-emphasis on the theoretical to the detriment of factual data.

vi That Elias's theory of 'civilising processes' constitutes what he called a 'central theory', i.e. a theory through which a variety of apparently diverse and separate social and psychological phenomena can be meaningfully studied. It is important to note that Elias did not use the concept or theory of 'civilising processes' in a moral or evaluative way. He usually enclosed the word 'civilisation' and its derivatives such as 'civilised' and 'civilising' in inverted commas in order to signal this. 'Civilising process' was for him a technical term. He did not intend to suggest by it that people who can be shown to stand at a more advanced level in a 'civilising process' than some others are in any meaningful sense 'better than' or 'morally superior to' people in the past. Rather, by 'civilising process', Elias referred to a long-term decrease in violence and aggression within societies. As societies became more internally pacified, so the personality and habitus structures of the majority of their peoples became more peaceful and this was reflected, among other ways, in what began around the seventeenth and eighteenth centuries to be called their 'sports'. The evidence suggests that this development in terminology began to take place firstly in England. Elias showed how, in the course of a 'civilising process', overtly violent conflicts tend to be transformed into relatively peaceful struggles for status, wealth and power. Laws in association football are designed not just to regulate play but, also, to protect participants from injury and create a relatively civilised environment.

Although Elias has come to be recognised as one of the most important sociologists of the 20th century, he only occasionally wrote on sport (although compared to other notable sociologists – perhaps with the exception of Pierre Bourdieu – he actually wrote a good deal). However, his most famous student, Eric Dunning, filled the gap. Dunning himself was one of the founding fathers of the sub-discipline known as the sociology of sport, where his passions were football and cricket, though he worked mostly on the former. Dunning developed a theory of status rivalry between the public schools of Eton and Rugby expressed specifically in their juxtaposed football forms. He believed that the two varieties were almost direct contrasts, with Etonians stressing kicking, limited use of the hands and scoring under the crossbar, while Rugbeians championed handling and carrying, almost boundless use of the hands and scoring over the crossbar. With Ken Sheard, he produced the incomparable *Barbarians, Gentlemen and Players*, a work which focused on the sociological study of the early development of rugby football. The book was first published in 1979 and, over 25 years later, in 2015, Graham Curry and Eric Dunning produced a similar tome, but dealt with the association game.

Research patterns and the organisation of the text

The vast majority of the research has taken place in online newspapers. This has the distinct advantage that they are regarded as a virtual primary resource. A figurational sociologist might argue that newspapers report past events and may well be a day or even a week old, so they are not a perfect primary point of reference – though this would be 'splitting hairs'! Additionally, the researcher should preferably be working from 'macro' to 'micro', that is, there is a need to be cognisant of the narrative of football history surrounding that particular snippet of opinion or reportage of fact which a newspaper article represents. This gives the investigator the advantage that she or he can 'read between the lines' and test hypotheses around a newly acquired piece of information.

However, the researcher must be aware of bias in terms of regional variations of opinion within the press and, of course, judging the impact on readership and opinion is a task for someone else at another time. For instance, London-based newspapers and periodicals such as *The Field*, *The Sportsman* and *Bell's Life* would almost certainly favour southern amateur viewpoints, while *The Athletic News*, for instance, being a Manchester publication, would openly support Lancashire clubs in their struggles with the FA over professionalism in English football. This is the main reason for utilising such newspapers as, for instance, the *York Herald* and the *Nottingham Evening Post*, which might take a more reasoned stance in important debates.

Mention of the latter title makes us aware of the first publication of evening newspapers. The *Nottingham Evening Post* began life on 1 May 1878, but did not begin immediately to carry football stories, results and reports in their Saturday editions. However, on 31 January 1880, the Nottingham Forest against Blackburn Rovers FA Cup third round game on Trent Bridge was said by a 'messenger' who had been forced, no doubt by publication deadlines, to have left 20 minutes before the end, that the home team was leading by 'five goals to love'.

Forest would end up winning by six goals to nil. Reports would be truncated, revealing scores and scorers, though more detailed accounts would still have to wait until Monday's editions.

There has been a conscious effort during the writing of this book to avoid secondary sources. Firstly, it was important that there should be no regurgitating of previously well-trodden narratives, which have a tendency to repeat other people's errors as well as covering old ground. A perfect example of this was the continual, lazy repetition by even the most renowned of football historians – Percy Young in 1968[15] and Eric Midwinter as late as 2007[16] – of the mistaken registering of the first two initials of the Blackheath representative at the early meetings of the FA as being FW Campbell. Work over the past decade has seen this amended to the correct form of FM (Francis Maule) Campbell. It is this author's belief that the error originates from Geoffrey Green's otherwise classic *The History of the Football Association*, with subsequent secondary source-obsessed writers compounding the mistake by not checking primary tracts.[17] Furthermore, while interned as an 'enemy alien' in Britain during the Second World War, Norbert Elias noted the lack of books as an advantage, probably not from any arrogance on his part, but more from the belief that debate within one's own thoughts and with colleagues was more productive than repeating the opinions of others.[18]

Secondly, no real in-depth study of what is approximately the first two decades of the competition exists. There are, of course, many studies of sections and particular actors of this time period, which include Rob Cavallini's recent *A History of Clapham Rovers*, very similar in scope and organisation to his book *Wanderers F.C.*, equally outstanding in terms of data, but lacking an analytical cutting edge. Another recent addition is Ian Chester's *Charles Alcock and the Little Tin Idol*, which concentrates on the first season of the FA Cup but 'is an attempt to use the historical information of the time to paint a picture of what it was like to play the game at its conception in Victorian society'.[19] The book is a series of apocryphal tales interwoven with some new data on individuals and teams following what must have been much hard research. The author's notes at the end of certain chapters are worthy of consultation. Certainly, as essential background for the latter stages of Chapter 6 of this book and the emergence of the Football League, Mark Metcalf's offering *The Origins of the Football League: The First Season* is as informative as anything that has been produced on that subject at the present time.

Other useful texts consulted have included Keith Booth's *The Father of Modern Sport: The Life and Times of Charles W. Alcock*, for obvious reasons mentioned in its title, and Mike Bradbury's *Lost Teams* series, which are complete curate's eggs – some brilliant leads but lots of understandable errors. The substantial tome produced by Terry Morris, *Vain Games of No Value?* is also worth a mention. His bibliography is rather light on previously published books and articles, but is replete with primary sources, especially newspapers, making this a largely original work and not a 'copycat' narrative of other people's thoughts. With apologies for labouring the point, secondary sources are, at best, a serious risk which should be treated with care and, at worst, incorrect in part and, therefore, unintentionally misleading. Eric Dunning's advice to check the primary source sounds simple but is absolutely crucial.

The text itself is organised chronologically, though certain events overlap more than one chapter in an attempt to add clarity to an ongoing storyline. Additionally, in tracing the careers of certain individuals, those narratives are dealt with in one particular section so that their stories are not split irretrievably in a plethora of places in the book. This will involve exploring dates falling outside a chapter's expected remit. For those looking for perfect symmetry in terms of chapter length, the reader will find that Chapter 1 is necessarily shorter as it relates solely the origins of the competition and little else. The author has found no other text which attempts to test in detail the claim that the cup was based on the Champion House football competition at Harrow School, where Charles Alcock was educated. There is also consideration given to the possibility that the idea came from Sheffield, which had hosted two such competitions before 1871–2. Chapter 2 tells the tale of the first season of competition, charting the original entrants, the 'Immortal Fifteen',[20] and looking in detail at their social composition. Just as interesting as the teams which entered are the clubs which did not participate, despite many being members of the FA at the time. Detailed reflection is offered for their negative responses. Chapter 3 concerns the beginnings of change in terms of the social composition of the players in the teams entering the cup. The competition continued to be dominated by the southern amateurs, but there began an eventual emergence of teams representing lower-middle- and working-class communities emanating from geographical areas from Lancashire, and also the appearance of strong combinations from the East and West Midlands. Of course, this was no simple dichotomy where each team was wholly representative of a particular class, but there was a significant trend developing. Chapter 4 notes the supremacy of East Lancashire clubs, which led to the transference of on-field hegemony from 'privileged to professional'. A feature of the section is an in-depth examination of the social composition of the three leading East Lancashire teams at that time: Darwen, Blackburn Olympic and Blackburn Rovers. The findings are again indicative of the social class of the participants being much more than a simple split between two sections of English society. Chapter 5 chronicles the acceptance of professionalism in English football, its overt emergence taking place following an FA Cup encounter between Preston North End and Upton Park, noting importation as well as payment for playing. Legalisation took place under 'stringent conditions', which enabled the southern amateur administrators to retain control of the everyday running of the game. The process was tortuous, but the compromise eventually reached almost certainly saved the association game from what may well have proved to be an irreconcilable, rugby-like split. Lastly, Chapter 6 traces the final season of Scottish clubs' participation in the cup and the fleeting dominance of West Midlands clubs. More importantly, it looks at the advent of the Football League, considering whether its arrival had any effect on participation and attendances in the FA Cup and, additionally, asks whether the magic of the cup, as alluded to at the beginning of this introduction, still exists. As if to re-emphasise that the real footballing power base in the country still lay in Lancashire, the final season under consideration in this book, 1888–9, charts Preston North End's 'double' triumph as they captured the first league title, unbeaten, and also won that season's FA Cup.

10 *Introduction*

The appendices are included for varying reasons. Appendix 1 gives a detailed synopsis of the first 18 finals; Appendix 2 provides a breakdown of entrants by region in the first 18 seasons; Appendix 3 notes the tertiary education of each individual southern amateur FA Cup finalist from 1871–2 to 1882–3; while Appendix 4 relates the schools of those same southern amateurs over the same time period. All four should be seen as helpful overviews to aid understanding.

Finally, in several places, endnotes appear in the middle of sentences. This is not lazy practice on the part of the author, rather some endnotes relate to specific newspaper articles on particular occurrences, usually match reports. A good example of this is in Chapter 3 when the career of Nottingham Forest player Mark Holroyd is traced and several footnotes are utilised within one sentence and refer to separate appearances by the player. It is the hope of the author that readers will be sympathetic to this way of precise referencing.

Notes

1. See *The Sportsman* report (18 October 1871) of the establishment of the FA Cup at the FA Committee Meeting of 16 October 1871. Of course, consultation of both sources is preferable.
2. Dunning and Sheard, *Barbarians*, 110.
3. Harvey, *Football*, 171.
4. Ibid, 171–2.
5. Dunning and Sheard, *Barbarians*, 244.
6. Dunning and Sheard, *Barbarians*, 158, quoting from Green, *History of the Football Association*, 97. Green himself is quoting from Alcock's *Football Annual* of 1882.
7. Mason, *Association Football*, 61–2.
8. Taylor, *Association Game*, 39–44.
9. Holzmeister, '1883 F.A. Cup Final', abstract.
10. Ibid, 219.
11. My thanks to Dominic Malcolm for his suggestions in this short piece on figurational sociology. See Elias, *Civilising Process* and, for its application to sport, Elias and Dunning, *Quest*.
12. Curry and Dunning, *Association Football*.
13. Elias and Scotson, *The Established and the Outsiders*.
14. Dunning and Hughes, *Norbert Elias and Modern Sociology*, 63–8.
15. Young, *History of British Football*.
16. Midwinter, *Parish to Planet*.
17. Green, *History of the Football Association*, 20.
18. Dunning and Hughes, *Norbert Elias*, 26.
19. Chester, *Tin Idol*, Foreword.
20. Green, *Official History of the FA Cup*, 18.

1 The 'making' of the FA Cup

Introduction

Modern forms of football were developed in Britain from existing mob/folk games. The latter were loosely organised local contests between teams of often unequal size which were traditionally played on holidays, such as Shrove Tuesday, New Year's Day or Easter Monday. Most historians of association football would not claim the sport to be a direct descendant of a handling, mauling form of mob/folk football, such as the one still being played in the early 21st century at Ashbourne in Derbyshire. This remains a distant cousin. A closer progenitor existed in the kicking games in Penistone and Thurlstone in South Yorkshire and, additionally, the match which took place in February 1827 near Derby, which was seemingly a curtain raiser to that year's Derby street football, the version being significantly described as 'kick-ball'.[1] Types of football existed in most countries: *la soule* is an example in France, but it would be in England where the game first blossomed into a modern sport. Local forms brought to England's leading public schools were codified and 'civilised' by the boys, with those former pupils of the major boarding institutions of Charterhouse, Eton, Harrow, Rugby, Shrewsbury, Westminster and Winchester being ultimately the most influential. Subsequently, these former public schoolboys debated the primacies of their football games at university, especially Cambridge, polarising opinion between kicking and dribbling or handling and carrying codes. However, their distinctive forms were not diffused directly from these schools into the wider society. Rather, former public schoolboys and university men made their preferences clear when they joined or re-joined communities where football, with more than a little encouragement from local populations already cognisant of some form of the game, was ripe to adopt its modern form. Boys at local grammar schools, best described as the educational stratum of society just beneath the public schools, also engaged in football and in some areas, notably Sheffield, were largely responsible for the creation of their own subculture. This group represented what might be termed a local sporting or footballing elite. Club football began in Sheffield with the formation of Sheffield FC in 1857, though there were soon similar processes taking place elsewhere in England, especially in and around London. In 1863, a number of metropolitan clubs came together to form the Football Association (FA) and, although this organisation struggled initially for widespread recognition, it was destined to

DOI: 10.4324/9781003285595-2

become a focal point for footballers, not only in the capital, but also, eventually, as the national governing body for the sport. For our purposes in tracing the early years of the FA Cup, it is necessary, initially, to examine events at Harrow School, where the future Honorary Secretary and Treasurer of the FA, Charles William Alcock, attended as a pupil. It is here that a football competition, the format of which the Football Association Challenge Cup may have been based on, was played.

This opening chapter aims to study the origins of the FA Cup. As well as repeating the rather trite statement that the cup's organisation was built around the Champion or Cock House football competition at Harrow, the beginning of the chapter delves more deeply into the exact nature of that competition and gives detailed examples on which to base more consistent judgements. The chapter's particular strength, and that of the whole book, is that it presents a succession of new data to move the body of knowledge forward and generally avoids repeating the standard evidence offered by the vast majority of secondary sources. Chapter 1 will delve briefly into the background of Charles Alcock, the man generally credited with being the instigator of the FA Cup, and rely heavily on events of Champion House football matches at Harrow, also considering events in Sheffield which may have had an impact on the FA Cup's beginnings. It is a short but succinct chapter, which will set the scene for the advent of the competition.

The origins of the FA Cup: the Harrow connection[2]

Charles Alcock was born on 2 December 1842 in Bishopwearmouth, then a separate entity but now part of the city of Sunderland. He adopted his middle name William much later, possibly in memory of his younger brother who had died at the age of 11 or under pressure from his attendance at a major public school where middle names were very much in vogue. His father was a shipbroker and the family was part of an emerging northern middle class. By the mid-1850s, they had moved to Chingford in Essex with Charles's father establishing himself in similar work. Both sons attended Harrow School: John Forster Alcock, Charles's elder brother, is recorded as beginning his studies in January 1855 and leaving in July 1857, while Charles began at Easter 1855 and left in July 1859.[3] The Alcocks chose not to go on to university and sought to earn a living, which they did in their father's recently established marine insurance business. John would eventually take over affairs, whereas Charles moved into other areas.

Along with his brother John, Charles played a prominent part in the formation of the Forest Football Club based in Leytonstone in 1859. The club has been presented as being founded by Old Harrovians and, though they were the most prominent and, consequently, most powerful members, they were not in the majority, with many players having been educated nearby at The Forest School or mentored privately. For its first two or three years, the club served as a meeting of like-minded friends to play their favoured sport and only expanded into fixtures against other clubs in March 1862 when Forest played Crystal Palace.[4] By 1864, another club by the name of Wanderers, who would win the FA Cup five times in the first seven seasons of the competition, appears to have been formed and ran concurrently with the existing Forest club. Essentially, it seems that the players involved with both Forest and Wanderers may have been some of the same individuals.

Towards the end of 1863, the FA was formed. At the first 'meeting of captains', Forest, Leytonstone were represented by their captain, John Forster Alcock, and secretary, Alfred Westwood Mackenzie, the latter having been educated at Walthamstow House School in Wood Street, Walthamstow.[5] The only Alcock present at the early meetings of the FA was John. As a firm believer in using the feet more than the hands, together with no hacking, he was to the fore in the heated arguments over the initial laws. Charles Alcock only attended his first FA meeting on 22 February 1866, when he was immediately voted onto the committee. There is no list of those present at that particular gathering either in the minute book or in a newspaper report, but from proposers and seconders it appears that only six people attended: Arthur Pember, Ebenezer Cobb Morley, George Twizell Wawn, Alfred Joseph Baker, Robert Watson Willis and Charles Alcock. Charles Alcock was, therefore, a late starter in football administration and it was his brother John who was one of those instrumental in framing the first laws and who helped to thwart the attempts of the pro-rugby faction at the FA in the latter months of 1863. As such, John perhaps deserves more credit than has been afforded him by football historians. Subsequently, at the AGM of the FA on 23 February 1870, Charles was elected Honorary Secretary. He would serve in that role until 1895 when he became Vice-President.

As a footballer, Alcock improved with age. However, often because injury precluded him from taking part, he only played and won one FA Cup Final, when Wanderers beat Royal Engineers by the only goal of the inaugural final. This seems to echo events at school when his constitution appears to have restricted regular physical exercise. The injury curse saw him miss the first international game, Scotland versus England, though he acted as umpire and took part in one international, a 2-2 draw against Scotland in March 1875, when he scored. Certainly, officiating was another strength and interest, refereeing the 1874–5 and 1878–9 FA Cup Finals. Alcock also gained representative honours for Middlesex against Surrey and Kent on 2 November 1867 and Middlesex against Surrey a year later on 14 November 1868. However, in representative terms he will probably be most remembered for initiating and continuing to support games between the London Association and their Sheffield counterparts, playing ten times in the fixture between 1866 and 1875, refereeing twice and umpiring three times.

Alcock was relatively accomplished at cricket, though he became more of a proficient administrator in that sport than a successful player. He was secretary of Surrey County Cricket Club from 1872 to 1907, being based at Kennington Oval, which he also developed into a football venue. Indeed, 20 of the first 21 FA Cup finals, not including replays, took place there,[6] together with the first 15 semi-finals up to and including the 1880–1 season.[7]

His eventual line of work saw him employed as a journalist, not only contributing to newspapers but also being the author of many books. Perhaps his most famous and influential set of works was his *Football Annual*, which spanned the years from 1868 to 1906. Other books included *Football: Our Winter Game* and

Football: The Association Game. He was also editor of *James Lillywhite's Cricketers' Annual* and sub-editor of *The Sportsman*. His true claim to prominence, as well as his longevity of service, lies in the initiation firstly of a competition and secondly a rivalry, both of which began within just over a year of each other. The first matches in the initial FA Cup were played on 11 November 1871, while the first official international match between Scotland and England took place on 30 November 1872. While it might be sociologically implausible to suggest that humans have an innate desire to compete, especially against others from further afield, it is easy to understand that competition between club members had a limited time span. Not only would different opponents break the monotony, they might also provide more problematic opposition for better footballers, especially in a representative scenario. Both the FA Cup and international games went some way to fulfilling this need.

Keith Booth, in his first class 2012 biography of Alcock, cites four areas which are important here.[8] Firstly, sports journalism, where much of what Alcock established in terms of the compilation of lists, the categorisation of information, factual accuracy and balanced opinion has been copied by future generations. Secondly, the establishment of the competitive device, where teams would play games as part of a larger competition, specifically on a knockout or sudden-death basis. Thirdly, the pioneering of international sport, specifically and initially England against Scotland at football, aided and abetted by vastly improved transport arrangements, as a forerunner to what, in 2022, might be described as the almost complete globalisation of soccer. Finally, the acceptance of professionalism and the recognition of sport, for some, as a job rather than a recreation.

However, it is Alcock's involvement in sport, specifically football, at Harrow, which is crucial to this opening section of the book. Physically Alcock was a late developer and he did not shine at sport in his early school days. However, although his biographer Keith Booth rather decries Alcock's sporting achievements at school, his two claims to recognition in that regard are accurate.[9] Firstly, it is correct that he represented his house, Reverend BH Drury's (most boys resided as a group in boarding houses run by a Master), at cricket. While this was an accomplishment, he did not earn selection to the Harrow XI. He played for Drury's against Oxenham's in May 1858,[10] when he batted at number 11 and scored nought and one not out, and the following year against Rendall's, when he scored one run and took three wickets in what went on to be a decisive victory.[11] Hardly a resounding personal success but involvement, nonetheless.

Of course, it was Alcock's connection with football at Harrow that is our most pressing concern. He is listed as playing in a Champion House game when Drury's easily beat Harris's in November 1858.[12] Subsequently, in the following month, Drury's defeated Dr Vaughan's by one 'base' (the equivalent of a goal in the association form) to nil to become Champion House at Harrow football. The game must have been of some significance as it was reported in *Bell's Life*, which noted that the scorer of the winning 'base' was Charles Alcock, the shot being described as 'a capital kick'.[13] The latter phrase would probably have been used to describe a score from 'yards', that is a free kick awarded following a 'fair catch', therefore the writer would have been attempting to describe a punt or drop kick from a considerable distance. But what did this mean? Was it of importance? The knowledge that we have regarding public schools and the value placed on games there around this time should lead us to conclude that it was of some significance. Not only did Alcock's team reach the final match, they won the game, and Alcock scored the 'base' with what seemed to have been an impressive 'shot'. Although he had achieved a notable feat, Alcock had not been included in Harrow's best 32 footballers when the First Twelve met the Next Twenty in November 1858.[14] Perhaps his winning effort had arrived too late to earn selection, but it must have spurred him on to continue playing after he left school.[15] More importantly, Alcock was just 16 years of age when he left Harrow and would have been competing against Sixth Form boys who were one or perhaps two years his senior, which made his exploit doubly impressive. It is surely worthy of mention that 1858 represented the only time that Drury's – or Mr. Holmes's as it became in 1865 – won the Champion House for football between the competition's inception in 1853 and 1890, making the triumph all the more striking.

Almost certainly, Charles Alcock would have been delighted to have scored the winning goal in the Harrow Champion House football final and the competition may well have provided the template for the FA Cup. Indeed, most authors suggest that the mode of organisation used in the FA Cup originated from the Champion House or Cock House – a schoolboy nickname for the contest – football competition at Harrow.[16] Below are the ties played in the Champion House competitions of 1854 and 1865, the format of which will allow us to compare it to that used in the early FA Cup. The layout and punctuation is shown in Table 1.1 as it appears in *Bell's Life*.

Alcock was not present at any of the matches, but it is the organisation of the competition that is now paramount. In the early 1860s there were nine 'Large Houses' and several smaller ones at Harrow, the latter called Small Houses which often combined to make one team. In each year of the examples in Table 1.1, there was an odd number of houses involved, but at no point until the final game was any attempt made to make this an even number. Indeed, there were byes or odd houses in each round all the way to the final. What is interesting is that a different house was always given a bye, which seems to have been deliberate. The obvious question is why did the organisers not try to create an even number of teams – 2, 4, 8, 16, 32 etc. – as soon as possible? To contemporary eyes it seems simple to resolve but knockout competitions in wider sporting society were in their infancy.

Yet this was the format, and the one eventually used for the early FA Cup closely resembled it. Obviously, Alcock's connection with Harrow strengthens the link between the two systems. However, other knockout competitions, for instance the Youdan Cup and the Cromwell Cup in Sheffield, preceded the first FA Cup in season 1871–2 and, although it is unlikely, it may have been that the national soccer competition leant heavily on those examples. It is to Sheffield that we now turn.

Table 1.1 Champion House competitions of 1854 and 1865

HOUSE TIES – 1854[a]

First Ties
Mr. Vaughan's beat Rev. Simpkinson's
Rev. Middlemist's beat Rev. Drury's
Dr. Vaughan's beat Rev. Rendall's
Mr. Harris's beat Rev. Oxenham's
Home Boarders, a bye

Second Ties
Mr. Harris's beat Homeboarders
Dr. Vaughan's beat Rev. Middlemist's
Mr. Vaughan's, a bye

Third Ties
Mr. Vaughan's beat Mr. Harris's
Dr. Vaughan's, a bye

Deciding Game
Mr. Vaughan's beat Dr. Vaughan's

HOUSE TIES – 1865

First Ties
Rev. Bradby's beat Rev. Westcott's
Rev. Butler's beat Rev. Middlemist's
Rev. Steel's beat Mr. Vaughan's
Rev. Rendall's beat Mr. Harris's
Odd House, Mr. Holmes's

Second Ties
Rev. Bradby's beat Mr. Holmes's
Rev. Rendall's beat Rev. Butler's
Odd House, Rev. Steel's.

Third Ties
Rev. Bradby's beat Rev. Steel's
Odd House, Rev. Rendall's

Last Tie
Rev. Rendall's beat Rev. Bradby's

a *Bell's Life*, 17 December 1854.

Sheffield: the Youdan Cup and the Cromwell Cup

Sheffield's legacy to the football world is usually judged by its primacy in terms of club formation, which began in 1857 with the founding of the world's first such organisation, Sheffield Football Club.[17] The footballing community in and around the city represented the most vibrant subculture of its kind in Britain in the years between 1857 and 1875. The city's penchant for innovation also extended into the organisation of the first club football competition in the form of the Youdan Cup, illustrating the desire among players to test themselves in a more stimulating environment than intra-club matches and friendlies and could, therefore, have played a part in influencing the format of the FA Cup, first played four years after the Sheffield example. The competition took its name from local theatre owner and impresario, Thomas Youdan. Twelve teams entered: Hallam, Heeley, Norton, Mechanics, Norfolk, Fir Vale, Broomhall, Pitsmoor, Mackenzie, Garrick, Milton and Wellington. Sheffield FC were not among the entrants as they had decided to play no further matches against local opposition.[18] The club was often styled as a gentleman's organisation and may have become disillusioned by the growing seriousness of competition in the city. It took until March 1888 for Sheffield FC to accept matches against local opposition again.[19]

The ties and results for the Youdan Cup are shown in Table 1.2.

Interestingly, the cup appeared to illustrate how such competitive matches (Eric Dunning would have categorised the development as the growing seriousness of sport) could elicit rough play causing injury. A report in the *Sheffield Daily Telegraph*

Table 1.2 Ties and results for the Youdan Cup, 1867

First Round	16 February 1867a			Venue
Mechanics	0 goals 0 rouges	Norton	2 goals 6 rouges	Norton
Garrick	0 goals 0 rouges	Mackenzie	1 goal 1 rouge	The Orphanage[b]
Hallam	2 goals 2 rouges	Heeley	0 goals 1 rouge	Sandygate[c]
Norfolk	4 goals 2 rouges	Fir Vale	0 goals 0 rouges	Norfolk Park
Broomhall	2 goals 0 rouges	Pitsmoor	0 goals 0 rouges	Ecclesall Road
Milton	5 goals 2 rouges	Wellington	0 goals 0 rouges	The Orphanage
Second Round	**23 February 1867**[d]			
Norfolk	1 goal 0 rouges	Broomhall	0 goals 0 rouges	Norfolk Park
Hallam	0 goals 0 rouges	Norton	0 goals 0 rouges	Norton
Mackenzie	0 goals 1 rouge	Milton	0 goals 0 rouges	The Orphanage
Replay	**25 February 1867**[e]			
Hallam	1 goal 0 rouges	Norton	0 goals 0 rouges	Unknown[f]
Semi-final	**2 March 1867**[g]			
Hallam	0 goals 4 rouges	Mackenzie	0 goals 0 rouges	Bramall Lane
Norfolk	Bye			
Final	**5 March 1867**[h]			
Hallam	0 goals 2 rouges	Norfolk	0 goals 0 rouges	Bramall Lane
Second place play off	**9 March 1867**[i]			
Norfolk	0 goals 1 rouge	Mackenzie	0 goals 0 rouges	Bramall Lane

a *Sheffield Daily Telegraph*, 18 February 1867.
b The Orphanage was a recreational ground which was formerly known as Cremorne Gardens on London Road in Sheffield. It was the home ground of the Milton club.
c Hallam FC's home pitch.
d *Sheffield and Rotherham Independent*, 2 March 1867.
e *Sheffield and Rotherham Independent*, 2 March 1867.
f As a replay, the game probably took place at Sandygate, home of Hallam FC.
g *Sheffield Daily Telegraph*, 9 March 1867.
h *Sheffield Daily Telegraph.*, 6 March 1867.
i *Sheffield and Rotherham Independent*, 12 March 1867.

noted a 'severe sprain' and two fractured shoulders,[20] as well as the attempt by the Norfolk, Milton and Mechanics clubs to establish funds on which incapacitated individuals could draw while unable to work. This would be the beginnings of the Sheffield Players Accident Fund established in 1867 and directly related to injuries caused in the Youdan Cup games.

Rouges were a differential scoring method to prevent a proliferation of drawn games. The practice was used most notably at Eton College where, if an attacker reached the ball first after it had been kicked behind the goal line, a rouge was awarded. In the early 1860s, it was also utilised in Sheffield and is mentioned in the 1869 Cheltenham College football rules. Rather than being a particular way of scoring or a single, unique rule, the rouge most probably represented the application in certain football forms of 'minor points' such as a drop goal or conversion in modern-day rugby.

18 The 'making' of the FA Cup

For our purposes in discussing the arrangements of the matches and any influence they may have had on the format of the FA Cup four years later, it is clear that Norfolk were awarded a bye to the final, while Hallam and Mackenzie played for the right to meet them, as the *Sheffield Daily Telegraph* announced on 2 March 1867. This is confirmed in a *Sheffield and Rotherham Independent* report, which noted that Hallam and Norfolk were playing off for the prize.[21] With the semi-final, second place play-off and final being staged at Bramall Lane, it was clear that the competition had some prestige in the eyes of the Sheffield footballing establishment. It also signalled the beginning of a successful formula for a knockout competition, with the most important match – the final – being held at the most prominent venue. Twelve original entrants meant that, at some stage, byes would be required and perhaps this was the key. There was only one team who required a bye in the semi-finals, which may have seemed preferable to awarding four teams a bye in the first round as would be the case today.

The format was strikingly similar to Harrow's Champion House system and there may be a suspicion that it spread from there to Sheffield. However, while one might expect such a top-down diffusion of ideas, there is no apparent socially prestigious individual or group in the city who might be identified as the receivers, carriers and implementers of such an innovation. There was very little direct influence on early Sheffield football from former major public schoolboys and, while men in the South Yorkshire city would have been aware of goings on at the likes of Harrow, it appears unlikely that the connection was strong enough for football competition formats to have been borrowed. Sheffield's footballing subculture was the first of its kind in the world and, therefore, events there – particularly those linked with competitions for prizes – are of interest. That the footballers of the city should initiate two such contests prior to the inception of the FA Cup makes it doubly so.

Perhaps disappointingly, the recently formed Sheffield Football Association, which began life in 1867, did not attempt to carry on with the Youdan Cup. However, another local theatrical entrepreneur Oliver Cromwell sponsored a second knockout cup, the eponymous Cromwell Cup. The competition was only for clubs who were less than two years old, and thus attracted only four teams:

Table 1.3 Ties and results for the Cromwell Cup, 1868

First Round	1 February 1868[a]	
Wednesday 4 goals 3 rouges	Exchange 0 goals 0 rouges	Mackenzie Ground Myrtle Road[b]
	8 February 1868[c]	
Garrick 0 goals 1 rouge	Wellington 0 goals 0 rouges	Mackenzie Ground Myrtle Road
Final	**15 February 1868**[d]	
Wednesday 1 goal 0 rouges	Garrick 0 goals 0 rouges	Bramall Lane

a *Sheffield and Rotherham Independent*, 4 February 1868.
b Westby lists Mackenzie's ground in 1868 as being on Myrtle Road in Heeley. *History of Sheffield Football*, 115.
c *Sheffield and Rotherham Independent*, 17 February 1868.
d *Sheffield Daily Telegraph*, 22 February 1868.

Wellington and Garrick, who had both entered the Youdan Cup, and Wednesday and Exchange, who had only been formed during that current season.

It is worth mentioning the Cromwell Cup, if only for the fact that it succeeded the Youdan Cup and preceded the FA Cup, so Charles Alcock would almost certainly have been aware of both Sheffield competitions. In terms of format, the Cromwell Cup does not really help in our quest for the inspiration for the FA Cup format, as only four teams entered which meant that it was simple to organise.

Conclusion

The organisation of the initial FA Challenge Cup competition leant heavily on the experiences of Charles Alcock at Harrow School, with the use of byes at any stage mimicking the Champion House football contest there. It is, therefore, interesting that the organisers of the Youdan Cup in Sheffield employed something similar, certainly in terms of a semi-final bye. The direct diffusion of footballing ideas and practices from public schools to Sheffield has been proved to be improbable, but in the unlikely event that those same Sheffield footballers could have been labelled as 'cultural dopes', they would have been aware of happenings in the public schools.[22] However, there is no suggestion that Sheffield 'borrowed' from Harrow, though as has been mentioned in the text, top-down diffusion was a possibility, and an interesting question for another time would be 'How did the organisers of the Youdan Cup choose their own particular format?' What is clear is that modern competition organisers generally frown on the use of byes in the latter stages of important events.

It is highly likely that Alcock organised proceedings based on the Champion House football tournament held at his school, Harrow. The similarities are too apparent to ignore, in particular the way that, often at each stage, one team was granted a bye or – in Harrow School parlance –were recognised as the 'odd house'. When this device was employed later in a competition, to modern eyes it clears a passage unfairly straight through to the final for one of the semi-finalists and smacks of demeaning the importance of that stage of the contest. However, to Alcock this was simply replicating what he had experienced at school, and after all, these were early days in terms of developing any sort of suitable, competitive mechanism. Subsequently, the last bye awarded in a semi-final in the FA Cup was granted to the Old Etonians in 1880–1, though, in 1884–5 the organisers still managed to confer seven byes in a fifth round of nine clubs. However, one cannot but be amazed that such intelligent individuals did not realise that to end with two competing teams in a 'final tie', previous rounds would have to be engineered so as to be multiples of two at the earliest stage possible. Working backwards from the final was the key. Of course, it may simply have been the case that it did not really matter that much to them. They just wanted to play football and the arrangements, at least in this first season, almost got in the way. In succeeding years, they learned from experience that there was a more efficient way of organising a knockout competition. For the moment, the organisation was rather *laissez-faire*.

Whatever one's views on 'watersheds' or 'great man theories', the 1870 AGM of the FA, where Charles Alcock was elected to serve as the association's secretary and treasurer, represented the beginning of a period in office of a single man who was to transform the fortunes of that organisation. Norbert Elias and Eric Dunning would have argued that 'all are "important", but some are more "important" than others', the sociological inference being that everyone in the football figuration had an impact, with some exerting more power – and therefore influence. Alcock did not work alone in establishing the FA Cup as a national football competition – for instance, the rules for the competition were drawn up largely by James Powell, Honorary Secretary of the Barnes club – but he could certainly be credited with the idea itself which, following detailed study of its origins in this chapter, clearly emanated from his experiences at Harrow School.

Notes

1. See Curry, 'Up'Ards, Down'Ards and derbies'.
2. Many thanks to Dale Vargas, former Second Master at Harrow School, 1956 Harrow Football XI, Master i/c Football 1970–74, House Master 1982–95, for his help on this section.
3. Welch, *Harrow School Register*.
4. Curry, 'Football in the capital'.
5. Curry and Dunning, *Association Football*.
6. The exception was in 1872–3 when the final was played at Lillie Bridge. The replay of the 1885–6 final took place at the Racecourse Ground, Derby, now the Derbyshire County Cricket Ground and the original home of Derby County FC.
7. This included one replay and six editions where a bye was awarded in to one of the three semi-finalists.
8. The most detailed and up-to-date book on Alcock's life and career is Keith Booth's *Father of Modern Sport*.
9. Booth, *Father of Modern Sport*, 28–9.
10. *Bell's Life*, 6 June 1858.
11. Ibid, 26 June 1859.
12. Ibid, 21 November 1858.
13. Ibid, 12 December 1858.
14. Ibid, 28 November 1858.
15. There has been speculation that he suffered from illness at that time (email communication with Dale Vargas, 5 June 2021).
16. Examples include Booth, *Father of Modern Sport*, 165; Green, *Official History of the FA Cup*, 10; Goldblatt, *Ball is Round*, 32.
17. For more on early Sheffield football see Curry, *Crucible of Modern Sport*; Harvey, *Football*; Westby, *History of Sheffield Football*.
18. *FCR 3*. Club minute book dating back to 1864 (Sheffield Football Club Records). These historically significant resources were a series of often original documents from the early days of Sheffield Football Club, which included the first rules of football in the city dated 1858 (*FCR 1*). In all there were 16 sections to the records, which were retained at Sheffield Archives in the city. In 2011, several items in the collection were sold for almost £1 million to an unknown buyer.
19. *Sheffield Daily Telegraph*, 26 March 1888.
20. 9 March 1867.
21. *Sheffield and Rotherham Independent*, 9 March 1867.
22. Curry, *Crucible of Modern Sport*; Harvey, *Football*.

2 The inaugural FA Cup

Introduction

This chapter will consider primarily the first season of the FA Cup. As well as noting the FA's attempts to popularise and organise it, the author will attempt to answer the questions 'Why did particular organisations enter the competition?' and, since the FA had not even been in existence for a decade, 'What motives would they have for becoming part of a contest set up by a fledgling body of fairly anonymous London footballers?' Conversely, 'Why did certain members of the FA decide not to enter?'

The social composition of each of the 15 clubs involved in the initial season of competition is important as it confirms the belief that, not only were the vast majority of teams at the time comprised of upper-class participants, but the entrants for the first FA Cup very largely reflected this view. This task will involve compiling short histories, which should be viewed as detailed and worthwhile investigations into the backgrounds of team members and individual clubs. 'Drilling down' into events will be the key and, hopefully, guard against what has often been an over-generalisation of inquiry in this area. This kind of information is particularly important because, over the period of almost two decades which the book traces, the social class of the participants in soccer in general and the FA Cup in particular changed drastically from the upper echelons of society to much more of a working-class base.

There will be a brief interlude of results and, in the conclusion, an assessment of the early impact of the competition on the rivalry between the two codes of football – association and rugby – existing in Britain at that time.

The 1871–2 Football Association Challenge Cup

Football in 1871 had developed in the 14 years since the formation of the first club in Sheffield in 1857 and was evolving slowly from the formation of the FA in 1863. However, the game itself would have seemed quite a different proposition to its modern form in terms of playing style and other practices. For instance, formations were different and seemingly more attacking, with the one used by Wanderers against Queen's Park on 9 October 1875 consisting of a goalkeeper, one back, two

DOI: 10.4324/9781003285595-3

half backs and seven forwards.[1] Handling was minimal, though before 1871, a throw-in was used to restart play after the ball had been kicked into touch, but only after this year was a goalkeeper designated and allowed to handle the ball to protect the goal. The general playing style in association football still remained a largely dribbling game, an individualised form popularised in the major public schools of England, while playing surfaces were of a poor standard. The reliability of players was very much open to question. Newspaper reports were awash with teams playing under strength because a number of their players had failed to arrive with getting lost, missing trains, and dealing with last minute emergencies all contributing to individuals simply not turning up. A perfect example of this 'misdemeanour' was exhibited by Charles Edward Burroughs Nepean (Charterhouse School 1861–9; St. Alban Hall, Oxford 1870–3; FA Cup winner with Oxford University 1873–4) when he failed to make an appearance at the first ever match between the North and the South on 17 December 1870 at Kennington Oval, which was probably used as a selection process for future England XIs. Nepean qualified for the North through his Scottish family links and was an excellent goalkeeper – the position he would have taken up had he played – but also a first-class centre forward. He was an outstanding cricketer, transferring his goalkeeping skills to wicketkeeping. It is unclear why he did not keep his appointment to play.[2] Participants were almost exclusively from the upper-middle class with a sprinkling of aristocrats, many of whom were familiar with mob football as played in their towns and villages, but also having played a more codified and organised type at their school and/or university.

It was in this climate that, at a committee meeting held at *The Sportsman* office in Boy Court on Ludgate Hill on 20 July 1871, those present

> Resolved unanimously that it is desirable that a Challenge Cup should be established in connection with the Association for which all clubs belonging to the Association should be invited to compete. The Secretary was instructed to communicate this resolution to the several clubs and to invite subscriptions towards the purchase of the Cup.[3]

There is some evidence that this proposal was largely the work of Charles Alcock.[4]

By the middle of October 1871, the FA was ready to host a meeting of interested parties for their new Challenge Cup competition, of which at least 11 attended – Royal Engineers, Barnes, Wanderers, Harrow Chequers, Clapham Rovers, Hampstead Heathens, Civil Service, Crystal Palace, Upton Park, Windsor Home Park and Lausanne – with, from afar, Queen's Park of Glasgow also expressing a desire to be involved.[5] The Glasgow-based club, though quite literally from another country, had, after all, been a *bonafide* member of the FA since November 1870.[6] Despite an objection suggesting a year's postponement of the cup as individual club fixture lists had already been compiled, the committee meeting, held on 16 October 1871, confirmed the establishment of the cup competition. However, Windsor Home Park and Lausanne withdrew, while Hitchin, Donington Grammar School (located at Donington, near Spalding, Lincolnshire) and Reigate Priory decided to enter. The initial draw is shown in Table 2.1.

Table 2.1 Initial FA Cup draw, 1871–2

Barnes	v	Civil Service
Hitchin	v	Crystal Palace
Upton Park	v	Clapham Rovers
Wanderers	v	Harrow Chequers
Queen's Park	v	Donington Grammar School
Royal Engineers	v	Reigate Priory
Hampstead Heathens (Awarded a bye)		

A sub-committee of five was selected to draw up a list of rules. This consisted of Charles Alcock, James Powell, Alfred Stair, James Kirkpatrick and Reginald Halsey Birkett, with all but Birkett present at a meeting of that sub-committee on 19 October 1871. Those rules, drawn up largely by James Powell, Honorary Secretary of the Barnes club, were presented a week later, some of which would be familiar to followers of the game today.[7]

- 11-a-side.
- 90 minutes per game.
- No individual to be allowed to compete for two different clubs.
- Regional ties for provincial clubs.
- Provision for replays.
- Medals 'of trifling value' to be presented to the winners, thus maintaining a participatory, amateur stance regarding rewards.
- Neutral officials.

The rule regarding playing for multiple clubs would be seemingly 'ignored' to accommodate Morton Peto Betts, a stalwart of the FA committee, who would go on to represent both Harrow Chequers and Wanderers. However, his original club – Harrow Chequers – never actually played a match in the competition, therefore Betts did not formally 'represent' them as they scratched in the first round, allowing Wanderers a walkover. Betts' switch of allegiance proved significant, as he scored the only goal of the final and was registered for the match under the pseudonym of AH Chequer (A Harrow Chequer), confirming that his true club loyalties lay elsewhere. However, representing two clubs in that same competition was not restricted to Betts. Cuthbert John Ottaway, eventually to become an England international and FA Cup winner with Oxford University in 1873–4, played for Marlow when they lost to Maidenhead in Round One and also for Crystal Palace in two later games, ironically beating Maidenhead in the first of them.[8] The scratching of Harrow Chequers was extremely fortunate for Wanderers in the long run. On 14 October 1871, they fought out a no score draw with Chequers at Kennington Oval, with their opponents including two of the Wanderers 1871–2 Cup Final side. Betts was absent on this occasion, but both Reginald Courtenay Welch and William Parry Crake played for Chequers and would go on to strengthen significantly the Wanderers XI in the final tie, though the former was involved on no fewer than 21 occasions for Wanderers in 1871–2 and, while he would pick Chequers when confronted with a choice, could be considered a Wanderers regular.[9] They were also assisted in other rounds by Robert Erskine Wade Crawford (Harrow School 1866–71) and Gilbert George Kennedy (Harrow School 1858–63; Trinity College, Cambridge 1864–8), Crawford being captain of Chequers and an important addition in the semi-final against Queen's Park. Kennedy was an athletics 'blue' at Cambridge and an accomplished rower who went on to play for Wanderers on a regular basis from 1866–74 as well as serving on the FA committee (1868–70).[10] This latter evidence appears to support the view that Wanderers were an all-star selection.

Further coaxing from Alcock in the press drew Marlow into the fray and, with them, their near neighbours and close rivals Maidenhead, who did not appear to have been members of the FA.[11] The revised draw for the first round of matches, all played on 11 November 1871, is shown in Table 2.2.

An additional anomaly was that both Hitchin and Crystal Palace were permitted to advance to the second round without a replay taking place, though this was covered in the original competition rule which stated, 'In the case of a drawn match, the Clubs shall be drawn in the next ties, or shall compete again at the discretion of the Committee'. This was amended in the following season to force clubs to replay and settle the issue.[12]

A quick scan through the 15 entrants reveals that two clubs, Windsor Home Park and Lausanne, who attended the original meeting to discuss arrangements for the cup in October 1871, were not included in the draw. A newspaper report on the FA meeting of 16 October 1871 may provide a clue to their omission. Part of it noted that 'an objection was entered against the establishment of the cup this season owing to the difficulty of deciding the ties in consequence of most of the fixtures of the several clubs having been already made'.[13] It may have been that these two clubs had already decided on a calendar of fixtures for the year and did not want to break promises made to valued opponents. The Windsor club, however, did not appear to have had any commitment on 11 November 1871 when the first round was played, though it did enter the FA Cup in the following season. Lausanne was a dual code club along the lines of Clapham Rovers and flirted with association and rugby rules. It had attended the 26 January 1871 meeting to form the Rugby Football Union (RFU) and would go on to opt for the rugby code. A report in December 1871 noted the sporting dichotomy of the club, describing how the rugby section of the 'Merry Swiss Boys' lost to Oakfield while the

Table 2.2 First round FA Cup draw, 1871–2

Barnes	v	Civil Service	2–0
Hitchin	v	Crystal Palace	0–0
Upton Park	v	Clapham Rovers	0–3
Maidenhead	v	Marlow	2–0
Wanderers	v	Harrow Chequers	Walkover Wanderers
Queen's Park	v	Donington Grammar School	Deferred to Round Two
Royal Engineers	v	Reigate Priory	Walkover Royal Engineers

Hampstead Heathens (Awarded a bye)

association members beat their Leyton counterparts.[14] It seems clear that their leading lights were at a crossroads in 1871 and decided to follow the rugby tangent and, though they were interested enough to attend discussions on the FA Cup, made up their mind to rebuff the soccer variety, indicating this by not entering. Significantly, the club was absent for the 1872–3 FA Cup competition, but was one of the original members of the RFU when that governing body was formed on 26 January 1871.

There were also several other possible entrants who did not take part in the initial competition. From attendees at the 1871 AGM held on 27 February, the following clubs failed to register interest in participating: Harrow Pilgrims, Nottinghamshire (Notts. County), Clapham Common Club (CCC), Westminster School, Brixton, West Kent, Forest and Chesterfield.[15] The Lausanne club was also present and has been dealt with, along with Windsor Home Park, in the previous paragraph. General contact had been made with Sheffield, where a significant footballing subculture had been thriving for over a decade, but the obstacle of two similar but sufficiently different sets of playing laws mitigated against complete amalgamation. South Derbyshire also represented a blossoming example of the early game, evidenced by a letter to the FA which appears in the minutes of the 20 July 1871 committee meeting. In reply to communications addressed to him from Alcock and Stair at the FA, their Secretary CW Houseman suggested a meeting between their recently formed association (8 March 1871) and the FA to be held in Birmingham. The London-based body replied rather tetchily that they were not interested in amending their laws and that the South Derbyshire men could send representatives to the next FA AGM at which, more encouragingly, amalgamation could be discussed. Perhaps understandably, as with relations with Sheffield, the FA were not happy to be seen to be accepting compromise in terms of law-making and they clearly wished to be considered the most prominent body in this regard.[16] Ironically, in a match played on the same day as the formation of the South Derbyshire FA, two players from Sheffield – one of them William Edward Clegg, who along with his brother Charles would play and administer the game in the South Yorkshire city for many years – were included in one of the teams. This proselytisation contrasted markedly with the FA's negative attitude. The latter's isolative approach no doubt deterred clubs from entering a national cup competition, but ultimately, in hindsight, it did not matter, though numbers could have been supplemented had the FA acted in a more conciliatory manner. In what might be seen as a gamble, the London body excluded perhaps 30 or 40 clubs from Sheffield and South Derbyshire alone.

Sheffield and South Derbyshire were alienated by the FA because of a disagreement over laws. However, the other non-entrants had differing reasons for their omissions. The Chesterfield club was busy following its formation in 1867 and had close links with Sheffield, just 13 miles to the north.[17] Nottinghamshire FC also fell under the Sheffield aegis, though perhaps less so than Chesterfield.[18] However, both had the excuse of 'tyranny of distance' for showing disinterest in the cup and neither would enter in the first campaign. Notts. would become involved in 1877–8, but Chesterfield only entered from 1892–3 under its reincarnation as Chesterfield Town.

As for the Clapham Common Club, widely known as CCC, this was almost certainly defunct from the end of the 1870–1 season. It may have played its last match against Sydenham on 18 March 1871, which, just as the game of football was blossoming and a national cup about to begin, was unfortunate timing.[19] Fleeting glances briefly appear in the press of individuals at athletic sports under the CCC name,[20] but there are no more footballing references.

It is important to accept the practice of individuals playing for a plethora of clubs in the early 1870s. For instance, Charles Alcock is listed as representing Harrow Pilgrims when his name is noted as gaining selection for England in the unofficial international against Scotland on 25 February 1871.[21] In the cases of Pilgrims, Forest (presumably the club rather than the school) and West Kent, there was a substantial overlap of personnel, created largely because regular fixtures were hard to come by and those wanting to play once or even twice a week were forced to join several teams to satiate their football appetites. Certainly, Forest almost certainly disbanded following the 1871–2 season – one of the last references in the press is on 27 March 1872 when they are noted to have a fixture three days at home to Crystal Palace[22] – and must have been in the final throes of their existence, so did not seek to become involved. Alcock was an example of representing multiple clubs, but so were Morton Peto Betts and Edgar Lubbock, who were listed under West Kent for the same game against Scotland. The probable reason why all three clubs did not enter was that they would be battling each other for players and, although in this first season it was seemingly circumvented, there did exist the rule that no one could represent more than one team in the FA Cup.

There is no hard evidence for Westminster School's absence from the first FA Cup. However, term-time limitations and the time-honoured reluctance of the schools to involve themselves fully in the business of wider society, might be proffered as possible reasons. Certainly, the major public schools had been slow in their support for the nascent FA in the autumn of 1863 and an inflexible fixture list could have added to their disinclination to participate. They may also have been exhibiting an attitude of status rivalry, regarding the men who had formed the FA as distinctly socially inferior.

Finally, came Brixton. As with many amateur clubs around that time – and indeed today – Brixton Football Club leant heavily on one man. John Cockerell, born in Camberwell in 1846, was a clerk in his uncle George's coal merchants and a fine athlete who competed for South Norwood Athletic Club[23] and the socially exclusive London Athletic Club,[24] which had been formed as long ago as 1863. Captain of Brixton, he was noted as serving on the FA committee in 1871[25] and played in the second (9 November 1870) and third (25 February 1871) unofficial internationals for England against Scotland. Cockerell also represented Surrey and Surrey and Kent.[26] As well as Brixton, he also played football for Crystal Palace (1865–8), and Barnes and South Norwood's disputed first fixture against Windsor Home Park on 23 November 1872 and in the replay a fortnight later.[27] As for the Brixton club itself, it seems to have folded in the summer of 1871, as the athletic sports of May 1871 is the last mention in the press for some time,[28] though there is a tantalising reference to Brixton holding an athletics sports with a Clapham club, so the possibility of amalgamation might not have been out of the question.[29]

The fact that the club re-formed three years later is probably supportive of the disappearance in 1871 of the first Brixton club. The first annual dinner of its second coming was reported in May 1875, so it is safe to assume, with several speakers mentioning the 'previous season', that this particular organisation began in 1874.[30] The number of clubs entering the cup was disappointing, especially when 49 were listed as members of the FA in the summer of 1871. However, this figure may have been slightly misleading as it included 17 from Sheffield who, apart from Sheffield FC, would find the distance from most of the other contestants too far, making it impractical to participate.[31]

While the bulk of entrants came from in and around London, two clubs came from outside that geographical area and provided vastly contrasting narratives. If 26 October 1863, the first meeting of the FA, was one of the defining dates in the history of English football, then 9 July 1867, the forming of Queen's Park Football Club, marks the genesis in club form of an organised, modern proto-soccer variety in Scotland. The phrase 'proto-soccer' is used because it is unclear and probably unlikely that Queen's Park would have adhered to the exact laws of the FA in distant London during its initial games of football. However, it almost certainly engaged in a type of loose association form, with kicking to the fore. By June 1868, the club was lauded in the local press, being described as 'the most influential in numbers, well organised and respectable', but opponents were initially hard to find and Queen's Park was forced, as was the case elsewhere, to resort to matches within the club.[32] However, by 1 August 1868, it had discovered its first adversary, the 'Thistle' club. Thistle was defeated and eventually the club began to champion the association code with great vigour, having written to John Lillywhite, the sole publisher, for a copy of the laws of the FA. Queen's Park enjoyed a period of phenomenal success, not conceding a goal between its formation in 1867 and January 1875 and not losing a match until February 1876. The club was so influential in the Scottish game that, when the first international match was played between Scotland and England on 30 November 1872, it was Queen's Park with whom Charles Alcock of the FA conducted negotiations for the fixture, no Scottish FA existing until March 1873. The Scotland team for that first *bona fide* international soccer fixture was made up entirely of Queen's Park members.[33]

The Queen's Park versus Donington Grammar School tie found its way into the second round as the two clubs were 'unable to decide a date for their first encounter owing to the short notice received'.[34] The Scottish club's record in the FA Cup became a curious mixture of good results and 'scratching' from the competition. From the first season, 1871–2, up to and including 1884–5, the club entered on nine occasions, reaching the final twice where they were beaten on both occasions by Blackburn Rovers, 'scratched' without playing a game four times, reached the semi-finals without playing a match twice and the third round once. For a club with such a pedigree of success, this is a strange tale. 'Tyranny of distance' certainly played its part, but, ultimately, the quest to win the English Cup proved to be a step too far for Queen's Park. With this relative failure, did the Scottish club fail to secure a truly lasting legacy of real success in the early story of the game?

The exact reasons why Donington entered still remain a mystery, though we can perhaps surmise that an individual or group within the school had been enthusiastic about the game. Indeed, Langton Samuel Calvert, second master at Donington, probably fits the bill. Calvert was born at Hoby, near Melton Mowbray in 1845 and studied at Trinity College, Dublin, before being listed in the 1871 England Census as Second Master at Donington. To add to his athletic credentials, in later life he was a devoted alpinist and rambler. Additionally, his brother Walter Henry Calvert was also present at Donington as assistant master with both of them a good age for physical exertion, as the only other possibility – the headmaster Dr William John Rawson Constable – was by that time 51 years old. However, Constable, who served as headmaster from 1853 to 1880, was blessed with a footballing pedigree. He was born on 8 July 1819 and received his schooling at Glasgow University, where it was common for students to start in their early teenage years or even younger. Constable actually began there in 1833 when he was aged 14. He spent some of his early years, therefore, in a city which would become steeped in a culture of the kicking and dribbling style of football. More tellingly, after completing his MA at Aberdeen, he went on to Clare College, Cambridge, between the years 1841 and 1845 at the very beginning of discussions on a compromise form of football for undergraduates and others from various schools. He was thus placed in two of the most important centres of the game's early history and diffusion. In truth, there is as yet no direct evidence that Constable was involved with his school's entry into the first FA Cup, though he must have been aware of its inclusion. The only reference of him to date in connection to sport is a mention in a newspaper article in 1871 noting Constable as President of the school cricket club, which was an active institution in Donington around that time.[35] Additionally, by 1871, the school already employed a Sergeant Lomas as a drill instructor, testament to a belief in physical fitness which may have had a bearing on their entry into the national football competition.[36]

Subsequently, when Langton Samuel Calvert left the school in 1876, a newspaper report noted him as the captain and driving force behind the aforementioned school cricket club.[37] It only requires a small leap of faith to imagine the Calvert brothers being the catalysts for the FA Cup entry. As for the match itself, Queen's Park's reputation, the long distance involved and the overbearing financial burden of completing such a fixture, appeared to conspire against Donington's continued participation, so they withdrew and Queen's Park was awarded the tie.[38] Disappointingly, Donington's name is not listed in local newspapers in the late 1860s or early 1870s as playing football matches in their locality. Furthermore, what is also mysterious is that there appears to be no direct link with the FA in London. One might have expected to uncover some kind of connection between a staff member at the school and, for instance, someone on the FA committee, but none has so far appeared.

Meanwhile, in London, a club made up of what would have been considered the pick of the southern amateurs, was making a name for itself. It began life in the suburbs of North East London under another name. An organisation by the name of Forest Football Club was founded in 1859 at Snaresbrook on the edge of Epping Forest, basing its games on a version of the minimal handling tradition of football and included in its number Charles William Alcock, later to be Secretary of the FA.[39] By 1864 another club, this one accorded the name of Wanderers, which would win the FA Cup five times in the first seven seasons of the competition, appears to have been formed and ran concurrently with the existing Forest club. Essentially, it seems that the players involved with both Forest and Wanderers may have been the same or similar individuals in both cases. Wanderers was one of the leading teams of the 1870s, enlisting the foremost southern amateur players of the day in what often amounted to a select XI of London footballers. In fact, just prior to the 1871–2 FA Cup Final, Wanderers were described as being able to 'muster in their greatest strength' as 'in other ties they have been liable to lose for the occasion some of their best men, whose first allegiance may have been to their local club'.[40] The inference was that they were virtually a select XI who cherry-picked the best players from other clubs for specific matches, such had become their allure. They had almost become a forerunner of the Corinthians, who would, from the 1880s, tempt the best former public school and university association performers.

Does the evidence support Wanderers' policy of choosing the best players in the London area? Five of the 1871–2 cup-winning team had appeared in six or fewer games for the club in that season. Edgar Lubbock played sporadically for Wanderers over his career, which spanned the late 1860s and early 1870s when he was, as an Old Etonian, to be found in Old Etonian teams of the period.[41] As previously mentioned in this chapter, William Parry Crake was a Harrow Chequers player, playing against Wanderers in October 1871.[42] But perhaps the most obvious example of their cherry-picking approach to enlisting the best talent was the use made by Wanderers of Charles Henry Reynolds Wollaston (Lancing College 1862–8; Trinity College, Oxford 1868–71), who was only to be found in three of their selections that season, all of which came towards the end of their fixtures. Wollaston played in the semi-final of the FA Cup versus Queen's Park on 4 March 1872, one 'friendly' against Clapham Rovers on 9 March 1872, and the final itself. Emphasising his allegiance to clubs elsewhere, on 13 March 1872, he represented Clapham Rovers at Charterhouse, just three days before the final.[43] Wollaston, however, was still designated as an Oxford University player when he represented London against Sheffield in January 1872.[44] He was clearly not a Wanderers regular and had been invited for specific, significant matches only. He was, however, to play at least 75 games for them in the next nine seasons.[45] Robert Walpole Sealy Vidal (Westminster 1867–72; Christ Church College, Oxford 1872–6), nicknamed the 'Prince of Dribblers', played in an intra-school game for Queen's Scholars against Town Boys at Vincent Square, marking the end of the Westminster football season on 6 March 1872, just ten days before the 1872 FA Cup Final, which in effect meant that he was still an 18-year-old schoolboy when he won the FA Cup.[46] Vidal, a teenage footballing prodigy, had made his debut for Wanderers against Old Etonians at Kennington Oval on 23 October 1869, aged just 16 years.[47] The final example of the Wanderers' policy of recruiting the best men for the most important matches provides a contradiction. Edward Ernest Bowen (Trinity College, Cambridge 1854–8; master at Harrow School 1859–1901) only played six games for them during that first FA Cup season but was to become a mainstay of the team for 19 years, playing his last game in December 1883 at the age of 47. However, he only made 46 appearances during those seasons, though one reason for this may well

30 The inaugural FA Cup

have been that he was a fine all-round sportsman, who 'excelled at rowing, athletics, shooting, skating, cycling and mountaineering'. As well as his teaching duties, he managed to fit in standing unsuccessfully at Hertford in a General Election.[48] Certainly for the 1871–2 FA Cup Final against Royal Engineers, the Wanderers pulled out all the stops in recruiting many of the best footballers available and, although one might frown on such a strategy, it paid dividends in terms of the success they achieved in the competition.

It would be simple to repeat the usual narrative involving the eventual winners of the first FA Cup, but this will not be attempted. However, just one original point is worthy of note. Wanderers and, indeed, their predecessors, Forest Football Club, have been presented as organisations of Old Harrovians, former pupils of Harrow School. They were not: in fact, neither club was.[49] In Forest FC's first fixture, against Crystal Palace on 15 March 1862, only four of the 15 players were Old Harrovians. In the 1872 FA Cup Final, there were again four who had been educated at Harrow, three at Eton, one at Charterhouse, one at Westminster, one at Lancing and, finally, one at King's College, London. Seven had not attended university, and, of the four that had, two attended Trinity, Cambridge; one Christ Church, Oxford; and one Trinity, Oxford. The Harrow connection was real but was perhaps over-emphasised by the fact that some of their most influential members – the Alcock brothers and Morton Peto Betts – were schooled there. However, to complicate matters, during the parade before the 1972 FA Cup Final to celebrate the centenary, each of the 37 clubs who had won the trophy at that time provided a representative. Because Wanderers was by then defunct, its place was taken by a member of the Old Harrovian Association Football Club.

The existence of just two clubs who did not reside in the south of England in the first season underlines the fact that the FA Cup began as a London-based competition. Donington would not play a game in the tournament and Queen's Park just the one, but in actively recruiting members from the rest of England, and indeed Scotland, the FA had almost certainly made the decision to canvas national support and did not wish to be regarded simply as a footballing organisation for the capital area. As the next section will illustrate, the rest of the clubs were very much from that geographical area and consisted of players and administrators from the upper-middle-class stratum of society.

The other entrants

It is important to register the histories of the participating clubs in the opening season and note the backgrounds of their players, as this affords an insight into the social class of the people involved in the game at that time. Because football was in an initial phase of its development, it is likely that the men involved exerted a disproportionate influence on its progress and, if we are interested in why the game grew in a particular way, then the past experiences of these individuals are central. Furthermore, the classifying of entrants for the FA Cup hopefully presents the reader with an overview of the type of organisation which was tempted to compete; it suggests geographical and perhaps social trends in terms of participation. It is possible to incorporate the remaining 12 teams into sections: the 'small town social élite' (4 clubs), occupational (2), pre-existing sporting clubs (3), former major public-school old boys (2) and a cross-code club (1).

The 'small town social élite': Marlow, Hitchin, Maidenhead and Reigate Priory

Four clubs – Marlow, Maidenhead, Hitchin and Reigate Priory – represented a 'small town social élite' on the edges of the capital. They proved to be competitive, though none of them threatened to win the trophy at any stage. Marlow FC was formed on 22 November 1870, with teams from Windsor, Wycombe, Uxbridge and Maidenhead providing their initial opponents. By the time they were ready to play their first FA Cup tie against the latter, they had secured the services of Cuthbert John Ottaway, the first England international soccer captain and future FA Cup winner with Oxford University in 1873–4.[50] Ottaway attended Eton (1863–9) and Brasenose College, Oxford (1869–74) and was studying at the latter at the time of the cup match. He was a superb all-round sportsman, perhaps the leading exemplar of his generation, and gained 'blues'[51] at Oxford in football, cricket, real tennis, athletics and racquets.[52] Arthur Cowling Faulkner was the captain of Marlow, and, indeed, the cricket club, and he was probably the person who, as a fellow Old Etonian, enlisted Ottaway's assistance. Faulkner had attended St. John's College, Cambridge (he began in 1855, but seemingly did not complete his degree)[53] and became a wealthy man, being noted as retired by the time he was 44 and 'lived by his own means' for the rest of his life. However, his educational career is sketchy, with only a very brief notation in the Eton College register.[54] As noted elsewhere in this chapter, Ottaway represented both Marlow and Crystal Palace in the FA Cup's first season, though he was conspicuous by his absence in any other reports of the Marlow club's fixtures, leading one to believe that he was recruited especially for the cup tie against Maidenhead. The game has been humorously labelled the 'Battle of the Brewers', as each town possessed a major brewery at the time – Nicholson's at Maidenhead and Wethered's at Marlow – both of which were involved with the football clubs.[55] Despite Ottaway's presence, Maidenhead won by two goals to nil.

Maidenhead Football Club was formed for the 1870–1 season and played its first fixture against Windsor Home Park on 17 December 1871 at the York Road site used by Maidenhead United today. The first round of the FA Cup against Marlow gave the distinct impression of being an enthusiastic, rather parochial affair, arousing a good deal of spectator interest. Included in the Maidenhead team were the Reverend Arthur Henry Austen-Leigh (Radley College 1851–2; Cheltenham College 1853–5; Balliol, Oxford 1855–9) and William Goulden, the captain and local schoolmaster.[56] The next round away to Crystal Palace gave clues as to the status of a club such as Maidenhead both on and off the field. Despite losing by three goals to nil, Maidenhead dominated large portions of the match especially in its early stages, which must have come as a shock to their more celebrated opponents. It was also noted that Maidenhead were suffering their first recorded defeat on that day, though it should be said that they had only been in existence for a year. Claims were made by the vanquished that the reversal was aided by the fact that they were more used to a much larger playing area, though an element of 'sour grapes' cannot be ruled out. Maidenhead had hoped to arrange a return fixture at their ground, but would leave disappointed, the home team perhaps considering a rural Berkshire side to be below their normal socially exclusive adversaries in the capital. For the next ten seasons, Maidenhead had some success in the cup. They registered 12 victories against the likes of Reigate Priory, High Wycombe, Hitchin and Ramblers, but, when confronted with one of the more established clubs such as Oxford University, Old Etonians or Royal Engineers, they succumbed heavily. Nevertheless, at the very least, Maidenhead can fairly be described as the 'best of the rest' around that time.

The Hitchin club was founded on 24 November 1865, probably by Francis Shillitoe – its first captain, a freemason and keen rower, who served as Hertfordshire coroner – and William Tindall Lucas, who would become a banker.[57] The Reverend John Pardoe was chosen as Secretary and the opening game would be played between members on Saturday 25 November 1865. Pardoe had attended Harrow School (1853–8) and Trinity College, Cambridge (1858–62), being present at the university when rules debates were at their height; with his educational background, he would have been a confirmed disciple of kicking and dribbling codes. He had also been one of the founders of Forest FC, Wanderers' predecessor, while Shillitoe played four games for Wanderers in 1868 and 1869 and had obviously been identified as a more than useful footballer. The first round FA Cup tie with Crystal Palace, played on 11 November 1871, identified a further connection: Hitchin's captain, despite the presence of Shillitoe and William Lucas, was Cecil Frederick Reid, Old Harrovian (1855–61) and former student at Christ Church, Oxford (1861–5). A noted cricketer, he was also a partner in Reid's Brewery, which in 1898 became Watney, Combe & Reid. Interestingly, he played well over 40 times for Wanderers, including games in the FA Cup's inaugural season when he would have been heavily involved with Hitchin.[58] There were clearly links between the two clubs, after all Pardoe, Reid and Charles Alcock were all Old Harrovians and contemporaries there, thus explaining Wanderers' visits to Hertfordshire. For the tie against Palace, Hitchin lined up with two clergymen, two army lieutenants, a brewer, a banker, a solicitor, a maltster, a gun salesman, a farm labourer and the son of an auctioneer.[59] The team was an eclectic bunch, with room for local lads of working-class origins.

Reigate is a town in Surrey with a 13th century priory. A flourishing cricket club already existed in the town and most authorities give 1870 as the date of the football club's formation. However, there was a football organisation called simply Reigate playing in 1869 which in early January of that year lost narrowly to Crystal Palace.[60] Names such as surveyor Ralph William Clutton (Harrow 1858–62; Trinity, Cambridge 1862–6) and James Nightingale, a solicitor, overlapped from the cricket XI to suggest a connection, as did the fact that by February 1871, home matches were being hosted at Reigate cricket ground. In the first round of the 1871–2 FA Cup, Reigate Priory was drawn away to the Royal Engineers but scratched with the Engineers going through on a walkover. It would remain a club, like several others – Harrow Chequers, Hitchin and Civil Service being examples – which enthusiastically took part before realising that they were overreaching themselves.

The existence and thriving nature of these clubs strongly suggests that the game was not restricted to more centrally placed parts of the capital, though the social class of participants is fairly similar. Realistically, however, judged on results, playing standards were below those of clubs such Wanderers, Crystal Palace and Clapham Rovers.

Occupational: Civil Service and Royal Engineers

The Civil Service club was undoubtedly active by the 1863–4 season as it is recorded as one of the attendees at the early meetings of the FA, being represented by George Twizell Wawn of the War Office. His affiliation to the War Office is explained by the fact that it was, apparently, then as now, not uncommon for the team's players to use their work address or department when describing themselves. GT Wawn is duly recorded in the War Office staff lists from 1863–1905. He had graduated from Durham University and entered the War Office in June 1860 as a temporary clerk and worked there until June 1871 before serving in Africa with the commissary service.[61]

The club led a rather nomadic existence in terms of where it hosted its home matches, being found at the Civil Service Cricket Ground at Battersea Park in 1865,[62] Middlesex Cricket Ground in Islington[63] and Battersea Park[64] in 1868 and, by at least 1870, Lillie Bridge, the home of the Amateur Athletic Club in West Brompton and FA Cup Final venue in 1873.[65] Interestingly, the club grounds are listed in Alcock's *Football Annual* of 1871 as being Kennington Oval and Lillie Bridge, though the fixture list for the 1870–1 season shows them scheduled to play 18 matches of which seven were home fixtures, with five being played at Lillie Bridge and two at Kennington Oval.[66] In terms of the first season of the FA Cup, Civil Service did not last long. In the first round, they were defeated by Barnes by two goals to nil, a not unsurprising result on the day as Civil Service were shorthanded 'as usual' playing eight men against 11. This may have been linked to the fact that their rugby side was engaged on the same day against Clapham Rovers, both of whom were multi-sports clubs, which necessitated taking 13 men to Clapham to play against 15 of the home club. It was a bad day all round for the Service as they were defeated in both matches.[67] At this time, the club's Secretary was John Hardinge Giffard, who also served as captain in that first round cup game. Giffard worked as a clerk in the Admiralty and lived comfortably in Twickenham. Also present in the cup team was James Kirkpatrick, a colleague of Giffard's at the Admiralty, who would go on to win the cup with Wanderers in 1878. Both of them played a further part in the story of the inaugural FA Cup, when they served as umpires in the final – Giffard for Royal Engineers and Kirkpatrick for Wanderers. Indeed, Giffard would umpire both the 1874–5 final and the subsequent replay for the Engineers. This development was part of the growing increased seriousness of competition when the days of gentlemen amateurs settling their own disputes were at an end. It is interesting that the FA should have recognised this at the outset of the FA Cup and ensured that it appeared clearly in the rules. Presumably the parent body sensed that, even with so-called fair play enthusiasts taking part, it was wise to provide neutral decision-makers.

The 'Sappers', as the Royal Engineers are known, were one of the early powers in the game. They seem to have been founded formally in 1863, though there is evidence that they had begun as early as 1842, playing on the open fields of 'The Lines' at Chatham, no doubt holding games within their own club.[68] Letters were presented at the fourth and sixth meetings of the FA in autumn 1863, both from Lieutenant Henry Cecil Moore of the 'Royal Engineers, Brompton Barracks, Chatham'. Interestingly, although they joined, they did not send a representative to any of the very early meetings of the FA and, consequently, there is barely any further mention of the club in the initial FA minutes, until a recognition of membership in 1868.[69] The next tangible reference to them appeared at the 1871 AGM, when Captain Francis Arthur Marindin (Eton College 1851 – he only appears to have attended the school for that year; Royal Military Academy (RMA), Woolwich 1852–4; Royal Engineers, entry 1854), eventually to become an influential figure in the development of the game, was elected to the committee. He would play in two FA Cup Finals but end up on the losing side on both occasions. He is better known for refereeing the final on nine occasions and serving as President of the FA from 1874 to 1890. Marindin was present at the meeting when it was decided to offer a Challenge Cup for competition to member clubs. The side appeared to be restricted to officers, indeed the XI for the 1871–2 cup final defeat to Wanderers consisted of two with the rank of captain, one of which was Francis Marindin, and nine lieutenants. The educational backgrounds of the team indicated their links to England's major public schools: two each from Eton, Harrow and Cheltenham, while one each went to Kensington School[70]/Addiscombe College (Croydon), Bruce Castle (Tottenham, London) and Marlborough; two were tutored at home. All but one, William Merriman, attended the RMA at Woolwich. Merriman was educated at Kensington School and Addiscombe College, the latter being the East India Company's equivalent of the RMA at Woolwich.[71]

For all the dissatisfaction at their performance and disappointment following the result, the Royal Engineers had enjoyed a very successful season. *The Field* reported that they had 'played twenty foreign [games against opposition from other clubs] matches and have lost one – the final tie for the Association Cup v. Wanderers – drawn four and won fifteen. They have kicked fifty four goals and [had] three goals scored against them'.[72] Widening the results spectrum, over four seasons from 1871–2 to 1874–5, the 'Sappers' posted the remarkable record of Played 86, Won 74, Drawn 9, Lost 3, Goals for 244, Goals against 21.[73] The three games they lost were in FA Cup ties, two of them in finals. In the first seven years of the cup, they would be losing finalists three times, eventually winning the trophy in 1874–5 after a replay.

Pre-existing sporting clubs: Crystal Palace, Barnes and Upton Park

Crystal Palace played its first game against Forest FC, the forerunner of Wanderers, on 15 March 1862.[74] The probability is that the club was formed in 1861 and became a founder member of the FA in 1863 with representatives varying at the early meetings, but including the following: Francis (Frank) Day (owner of the

Black Eagle Brewery), James Turner (FA treasurer 1864–8, wine merchant), Theodore Lloyd (stockbroker, refereed England versus Scotland in 1873), Lawrence Vivian Desborough (accountant, travelled and worked widely), John Louis Siordet (indigo merchant, from a Swiss family) and Frederick Urwick (wine merchant), providing Palace with an eclectic mix of influential individuals.[75] The club clearly grew out of an existing cricket club, which both Turner and Day played for against the Gentlemen of Kent in July 1864,[76] representing an organisation which had been in existence since the mid-1850s. Two important facts are mentioned in the newspaper report. Firstly, Frank Day was the Honorary Secretary of the club and, as such, would have been the likely driving force behind any formation of other sporting arms in the organisation. Secondly, it was noted that the club had 'nearly 200 members', a very respectable number. The football and cricket sections came under the Crystal Palace umbrella, but rarely did their selections contain the same names. Other than Day and Turner, various team lists of the early 1860s did not seem to indicate much overlap of personnel. Perhaps the most important figure in those early FA Cup encounters was Douglas Allport, who was elected to the committee of the FA at the 1871 AGM and had considerable input into the organisation of the FA Cup. Born in Peckham, he is described as a West India merchant in the 1871 England census, Palace's membership generally reflecting jobs in the mercantile sector.

Barnes Football Club grew from existing cricket and rowing clubs of similar names. Certainly, leading figures at the FA who represented the Barnes club had rowing backgrounds. Ebenezer Cobb Morley, first Secretary of the FA (1863–6), and his two successors, Robert Watson Willis (1866–7) and Robert George Graham (1867–70), were all keen oarsmen and played for the Barnes club at football. It is no exaggeration to describe the FA at this point as 'The Barnes Football Association',[77] such was the preponderance of their players and administrators in the organisation. The first mention in the press occurred following their game against Richmond at Barn Elms Park on 30 November 1862,[78] though the enthusiastic rowers would, as was the case with other clubs, probably have been engaged in matches between their members for some time before this. In the first FA Cup, Barnes won their opening match against Civil Service with some ease, aided by the fact that the latter were only able to muster eight men. They were subsequently defeated by Hampstead Heathens in the second round following a replay, though only by a single goal.

The Upton Park club emanated from another organisation called the South Essex Football Club, which in turn had been founded by members of a cricket club of the same name.[79] In what may have been South Essex's final football fixture against the London Hospital in March 1867, no fewer than 11 names coincided with another 15-a-side match for Upton Park at Forest School a month later on 6 April 1867.[80] This latter match almost certainly represented Upton Park's initial encounter – the two organisations were, in fact, the same club under a different name. They toyed with rugby rules in the spring of 1868 before eventually settling on association[81] and it was around this time that Alfred Stair began to take more of a role in the football side of the club, having been a member of the cricket section. Stair was head of the Inland Revenue Services and part of the Civil Service where both Giffard and Kirkpatrick were broadly employed. As with Giffard and Kirkpatrick at Civil Service FC, Stair would earn recognition more as an official than a player and would referee the first three FA Cup finals plus the England versus Scotland international of 1875. He would also serve for a time in the early 1870s as FA treasurer and Assistant Secretary. Stair did not play in Upton Park's FA Cup debut, however, when they were comprehensively beaten three goals to nil by Clapham Rovers despite having home advantage. In terms of the social composition of their players, Kerrigan notes that most of its players at this time 'belonged to a prosperous, local middle class. Several were engaged in the law, in insurance or the Stock Exchange or were…the sons of successful local business men'.[82]

Former major public-school old boys: Hampstead Heathens and Harrow Chequers

Clearly, with 'Heathens' as an epithet, the Hampstead Heathens club stood out as worthy of further research. The club had seemingly adopted its name from a phrase used to describe a literary group led by John Keats, who lived and met around the heath in the early 19th century. The title had been bestowed on the latter in 1861 in an article on Keats' life and poetry by David Masson, the editor of *Macmillan's Magazine*.[83] Taking inspiration from literature around that time was a common occurrence and football was no exception. (The founders of the Dingley Dell club had clearly been reading Charles Dickens' *The Pickwick Papers* when they began in 1858). It is tempting to describe the Heathens as a primarily Old Wykehamist (former pupils of Winchester College) side. However, although the team was usually, at least in large part, made up of Winchester old boys, it was not exclusively so and a number of young men had received an education at Highgate School – or Sir Roger Cholmeley's School at Highgate, to give its full title – which appears to have produced a good many association players, leading this author to believe that its own brand of football was almost certainly a kicking and dribbling affair. Of the ten Hampstead Heathens who faced Barnes in the FA Cup Second Round on 23 December 1871, six had been educated at Winchester College, two of which had also attended Highgate; two went to Highgate School alone; while one was at Marlborough. The tenth member was the Hon. Albany Mar Stuart Erskine. Educated at home, Erskine was born in Edinburgh on 24 February 1852, lived in Knightsbridge while he played for Heathens, moved to the West Country, before passing away at Reading in 1933. His father was the Earl of Buchan, but unfortunately for him he was the second son and never succeeded to the earldom. It is highly likely that the R Barker listed in the team line up was Robert Barker, usually of Hertfordshire Rangers but also of Wanderers, drafted in to strengthen the Heathens as his former side had not entered the 1871–2 competition. Barker was an accomplished all-round footballer, having attended Marlborough College where he played rugby and became a goalkeeper, the position in which he began for England against Scotland in the first ever recognised international in 1872, though later in the game he moved to the forwards where he had also been engaged by his various clubs. The organisation was, therefore, typical of London football teams at that moment in time – upper class, ex-public school and often ex-university. Heathens was awarded a bye in the first round of the 1871–2 FA Cup and then drawn against Barnes in the second.

The game against Barnes finished 1-1 and went to a replay, which the Heathens, despite again playing ten against 11, won 1-0 with Barker once more in their side. In the third round of the cup, Heathens played the Royal Engineers at the latter's ground in Chatham. Despite having Barker, they lost easily by three clear goals.[84] This game is believed erroneously by many to have been their last match. On 10 February 1872, Heathens, with just eight men, played out a rather drab no score draw in a friendly at Hertfordshire Rangers, with Robert Barker absent for both teams.[85] By 1873, several former players were to be found in the ranks of Meteors,[86] while towards the end of the year others were part of the Old Wykehamists.[87] Whether failure in the cup was a reason for ending matters is doubtful, but it appears strange that what was a relatively successful XI should simply cease to exist mid-season. The Hampstead Heath Act of 1871 ensured that the area was freely open to Londoners, and this may have led to a lack of a guaranteed, extensive area to play football, though the bill itself was not passed into law until 29 June 1871. The cessation was so abrupt that one is left wondering at the explanation.

Harrow Chequers was probably founded in 1864. The clearest indication for not suggesting an earlier date comes from the fact that the club was not involved in the early discussions at the FA. Indeed, it only gathered momentum in terms of fixtures late in 1865 and January 1866, when it played the likes of Civil Service, Crystal Palace, NN Kilburn, Westminster School, Reigate, Crusaders and Charterhouse School. The club was able to call upon the services of Charles Alcock – he had, after all, attended Harrow School – and it established a competitive reputation. Foremost of the early players was Charles Lewis Tupper, who attended Harrow School from 1861–6, where he was in the football XI, and went on to Corpus Christi College, Oxford (1866–70). Tupper is mentioned as captain in the game against Civil Service on 14 December 1866,[88] before entering the Indian Civil Service, arriving there in November 1871. However, Chequers disappeared from view around the 1867–8 season, only to re-form for the 1871–2 season, a note being published in *The Sportsman* telling of the club's re-establishment under the secretaryship of Morton Peto Betts, the Old Harrovian who scored the winning goal in the FA Cup Final that season under the pseudonym of AH Chequer. They played their first match following their revival against Wanderers on 14 October 1871,[89] but it may well have been the lure of the FA Cup which began their recovery. The club merged with and into Old Harrovians and, despite entering the FA Cup in three of the first five seasons, it scratched on each occasion, never actually completing a fixture. The fact the club was drawn away from home on each occasion may have affected its participation.

Former public schoolboys and university men were spread around early London football clubs, though some were controlled by influential friendship groups from one particular establishment: Harrow Chequers was dominated by Old Harrovians, while Hampstead Heathens was under the direction of Old Wykehamists.

Cross-code club: Clapham Rovers

Clapham Rovers' formation date is often quoted as 10 August 1869, the prime movers being Robert Seymour Whalley and William Edward Rowlinson. Francis Marshall claimed that the club 'was formed on the 10th August 1869. The circular calling the meeting was issued by WE Rawlinson who, on the formation of the club was elected Hon. Secretary'.[90] However, it is possible to challenge this date as there are distinct references to Clapham Rovers in the 1868–9 season when they played Universal Humbugs and Alexandra (twice).[91] The match against the Humbugs looks to have been a hybrid type of football with touchdowns and 12 players on each team. The Rovers team that day was as follows: E Tayloe (Captain), AH Batten, AW Bentley, JE Bentley, WM Clark, F Luscombe, JH Luscombe, AE Dixon, S Dixon, A Cooper, R Kerr, H Humphrey. One name of note for the Humbugs was John Edward Tayloe. He was born on 1 January 1848 and lived on Clapham Common. Tayloe had attended Westminster School from 1861 to 1864, had also played for the Clapham Common Club[92] and would be the driving force in the first couple of years of Rovers' existence. His last game for the club was on 5 March 1870 against Wanderers, after which time he moved to Calcutta, before living in South Africa. He died on 19 January 1919 in New South Wales, Australia.

The games against the Alexandra club from Croydon were played on 2 and 9 January 1869 on Clapham Common and ended in defeats for the Rovers. The evidence points to at least the initial encounter being a kicking and dribbling variety, with the report noting that an Alexandra player 'succeeded in running past the Rovers' goalkeeper and scored a goal'.[93] However, Alexandra were clearly playing a rugby form against Dagnall House on 12 December 1868 with touchdowns and 15 players per side and so appeared to be a 'cross-code' organisation.[94] But the laws employed are largely, though not totally, irrelevant in terms of Rovers' date of formation, as they played both soccer and rugby. They cannot even be accused of not playing inter-club matches because they were playing intra-club games, as Sheffield FC may well have done from 1855 and Notts. County almost certainly did from 1862. Rovers was, in fact, involved in formal fixtures by late 1868 and represented an organised club by at least 26 December of that year. For those seeking to establish Clapham Rovers as an existing organisation in late 1868, it is surely significant that they were clearly using that name in print. The club was probably only organised in a formal way in August 1869, but had been playing very sporadically around Christmas and New Year eight months previously.

Rovers was drawn away to Upton Park in the inaugural FA Cup, the two meeting on 11 November 1871. The opening goal of that game by Jarvis Kenrick was the first ever scored in the FA Cup and helped his side to a 3-0 win. *The Field* noted that, after an even first quarter of an hour, 'Kenrick, with a good piece of play, obtained a goal'.[95] Kenrick was born in Chichester, attended Lancing College and went on to play for Wanderers and win the trophy in three consecutive years, scoring in two of those finals. He was a solicitor by profession and succeeded Alcock as Secretary of Wanderers in 1875.[96] Rovers was one of those rare clubs which organised separate teams that followed the association and rugby varieties of football. However, for historians seeking performers who crossed codes, thereby supporting the hypothesis that the two forms had barely diverged, the evidence is unsupportive. Of six games – three association, three rugby – played by Clapham Rovers between the beginning of October and the end of December 1870, only five players represented the club at both codes. These were Reginald Halsey Birkett, formerly of Lancing College; Louis Birkett, Reginald's brother and formerly of Haileybury College (both of these became England rugby internationals); the previously noted John Edward Tayloe; GJ Harman/Harmar; and G or C Bergman – denoting just five individuals from 45 different players in six team lists. In reality, Clapham Rovers was operating two virtually separate teams within one club, though its soccer section was a refuge for former public schoolboys from the kicking and dribbling establishments. Examples include Reginald Birkett and Jarvis Kenrick from Lancing; Robert Ogilvie; George Holden and Alexander Andrew Ellis Nash from Brentwood;[97] and John Tayloe from Westminster. The association code was probably perfect for Clapham as it represented a compromise for their members who were drawn from an eclectic list of schools.

Why did these particular clubs enter? Of the 11 represented at the inaugural meeting of the FA on 26 October 1863, only four – Barnes, Crystal Palace, Civil Service (War Office) and Forest (Wanderers) – played in the first season of the FA Cup eight years later. These clubs might be classified as stalwarts of the FA. After all, Barnes provided the association's first three secretaries and Forest/Wanderers was the club of Charles Alcock, the FA Secretary from 1870 to 1895 and prime instigator of the FA Cup. It should, therefore, come as no surprise that these teams were present. The rugby adherents who left the organisation at an early stage in its development – Blackheath, Blackheath Proprietary School, Perceval House and Kensington School – clearly had no interest in supporting the venture. The other three clubs – Crusaders, Surbiton and No Names, Kilburn – were no longer members of the FA in 1871.[98]

Crusaders had been relatively active during the 1860s[99] and were still playing in 1871–2, with a record of Played 13, Won 7, Drawn 1, Cancelled 4.[100] A new club of the same name had been established in January 1872, but it was announced that it would follow rugby rules.[101] The Crusaders association team was, however, one which relied heavily on players who represented multiple clubs and, as such, was constantly scratching around for replacements.[102] The team was recorded in the first round draw for the 1872–3 FA Cup, but never made it to the field of play, being replaced in the competition by Windsor Home Park.[103] Ironically, with the beginning of the FA Cup, players were forced to become more circumspect with regard to which clubs they would represent as they could turn out for only one in the competition. This may have had the effect that some folded as they were compelled to face the reality that they could rarely put a full side onto the pitch. Theodore Bell of Surbiton had attended the first meeting of the FA on 26 October 1863, but was not seen again. The club itself had been out of existence for some years by the time the FA Cup began. As for No Names, the final mention in the FA minutes was at the meeting on 23 February 1870. Arthur Pember, the driving force, had departed from the FA by 1868[104] and, as with many organisations, No Names lost its impetus. It left the scene just as the association game, with the advent of the cup and international matches, was about to take some significant steps forward.

Yet there were 49 clubs which, according to Alcock's *Football Annual* of 1871, were members of the FA, although 37 did not enter.[105] Seventeen were from in and around Sheffield, where they were probably of the opinion that their code of the game was superior to that of London and would not have wished to become part of a competition where different 'foreign' rules were employed, a situation which would have hampered their chances of success. 'Tyranny of distance' may well have prevented the participation of such provincial clubs as Bramham College (York), Chesterfield, Lincoln, Marlborough Club, Newark, Nottingham and Oxford University, but there was less excuse for Essex Rifle Volunteers (21st) and Windsor Home Park, though the latter, as Chapter 3 will note, did enter in the cup's second campaign. As for the former, there is nothing extant in the press concerning any football activity around that time.

However, 11 of the 'metropolitan' clubs were absent. The three schools – Charterhouse, Forest and Westminster – could be forgiven for having their minds on their own internal football; Forest Club was in a downward spiral with most of its members and better players opting for the Wanderers, with the two athletic organisations, Amateur Athletic Club and London Athletic Club, perhaps pre-occupied with their main sport; Lausanne, as previously explained in this chapter, was increasingly leaning towards the rugby camp; this left Brixton, Clapham Common Club, London Scottish Rifles and West Kent, with little indication why these last four opted to remain on the sidelines, though the latter, as also noted in the conclusion of this chapter, may well have suffered from many of its players being involved with multiple clubs.

The social make-up of the first FA Cup was extremely interesting and was largely, though not exclusively, 'southern amateur'. Hitchin, Reigate Priory, Marlow and Maidenhead represented a 'small town social élite' responding to the footballing tentacles of nearby London. The latter club was the most competitive despite its claim of participation over winning, but at this point, none of the clubs from distinctive towns outside the capital threatened the footballing hierarchy of London. Civil Service and Royal Engineers gave sporting opportunities to their personnel, while Barnes sprang from rowers who wanted to expand their sporting horizons, with Upton Park and Crystal Palace repeating the exercise, though this time for cricketers. Hampstead Heathens and Harrow Chequers were formed from former public schoolboys and acquaintances, though Clapham Rovers was an almost unique example of a cross-code organisation, initially playing association one week and rugby the next. If nothing else, as with the advent of the Football League in 1888, the cup was a way of improving a club's fixture list and this may have proved attractive. Certainly, there was little to lose as it became clear that those teams who 'scratched' when faced with an inconvenient draw would not be penalised. However, as well as football, one thing brought each club together: all of them were replete with individuals from the upper middle class.

The closing stages of the inaugural FA Cup

The rest of the inaugural competition progressed apace, with some of the second round ties being decided before Christmas. Wanderers squeezed through in a close

Table 2.3 Third round FA Cup draw, 1871–2

The third round:				
20 January 1872	Wanderers	v	Crystal Palace	0-0
27 January 1872	Royal Engineers	v	Hampstead Heathens	3-0
Queen's Park awarded a bye				

Table 2.4 FA Cup semi-finals, 1871–2

Semi-finals:				
17 February 1872	Crystal Palace	v	Royal Engineers	0-0
4 March 1872	Wanderers	v	Queen's Park	0-0
9 March 1872	Crystal Palace	v	Royal Engineers	0-3 (Replay)
	Wanderers	v	Queen's Park	
Walkover Wanderers				

encounter against Clapham Rovers by a single goal, Maidenhead blamed their defeat at Crystal Palace on the fact that the ground was half the size of the one to which they were accustomed and Royal Engineers trounced Hitchin by five goals to nil, with the latter only playing with eight against 11.

With five clubs remaining making an odd number of sides, echoing Harrow's Champion House competition, Queen's Park went through to the semi-finals without playing a match. The decision, taken at an FA committee meeting on 5 January 1872 attended by Charles Alcock (Wanderers), Douglas Allport (Crystal Palace), John Hardinge Giffard (Civil Service) and Alfred Stair (Upton Park), followed one of the rules of the competition. This stated, 'In the case of Provincial Clubs, it shall be in the power of the Committee to except them from the early tie-drawings, and to allow them to compete especially against Clubs in the same district, except in the case of the final ties'.[106] Because the rules were so open-ended, giving the committee the power to allow almost anything, both Wanderers and Crystal Palace, following a draw, went through with the Scots. This had been decided at the FA meeting of 7 February 1872, when letters were received though not disclosed from Captain Francis Marindin (Royal Engineers), Charles William Stephenson (Wanderers), Douglas Allport (Crystal Palace) and Robert Watson (Barnes) regarding the drawn game between Wanderers and Crystal Palace and a discussion took place as to whether they should replay. Unfortunately, neither the details of the letters nor the particulars of the discussion are revealed, but ultimately it was decided to allow both clubs to advance.[107] Again, this followed a competition rule allowing for a replay or, at the discretion of the committee, the clubs would be drawn (usually together again) in the next round. The latter instance had already taken place with the Donington School–Queen's Park tie and the Hitchin–Crystal Palace drawn match.

The first Crystal Palace–Royal Engineers match was uneventful and scoreless, but the 'Sappers' overwhelmed the London side in the replay by 3-0, two of the goals being scored by Henry Waugh Renny-Tailyour (Cheltenham College 1859–67; Royal Military Academy, Woolwich 1868–70; Royal Engineers entry 1870),

Scottish rugby international (1872), soon to be Scottish soccer international (1873) and talented cricketer.

The Wanderers versus Queen's Park encounter was a clash between what were probably the two best sides in Britain at that time. The fixture gave the impression of being more akin to a real test of strength at association football between the two countries than the five pseudo-internationals between England and London-based Scotsmen from March 1870 to February 1872. Interestingly, admission was free to the match, which represented the first visit of a Scottish side to London. The Glasgow club used two players resident in the capital – the Smiths, Robert and James, who by now were both playing for South Norwood – and started the stronger. However, it was Wanderers which finished the match on top, though a draw (no score for both teams) was thought to be a fair result. The report of the game in *The Sportsman* noted that the London side suggested extra time, a proposition which was surprisingly turned down by Queen's Park, despite this meaning that their probable inability to return to London meant they would have to withdraw from the competition.[108] Presumably the Scottish XI was aware of the consequence of their action, though it was equally true that the information may have been reported by Charles Alcock, who worked on that newspaper and may have been creating mischief. Is it perhaps significant in this regard that the suggestion of extra time was not mentioned in the *Glasgow Herald*?[109] The same newspaper also felt that Queen's 'pressed their opponents pretty severely, both at the beginning and close of the game', but 'retired from the competition in favour of the Wanderers, as they found that to possess the cup would necessitate repeated visits to London… to play the clubs of the metropolis on their own ground'.[110] Interestingly, two Queen's Park players – David Wotherspoon and Robert Gardner – remained in London and assisted Wanderers in a friendly game against Clapham Rovers, in which they were said to have done 'most of the charging for their side'.[111] It was almost certainly during this extended stay that arrangements were tentatively agreed with Alcock for a full international fixture between England and Scotland.

Final: 16 March 1872, Wanderers v Royal Engineers, 1-0

On the day of the 1871–2 final, the *Morning Post* talked of the Royal Engineers in terms of 'working together', 'understanding', 'cohesion' and 'co-operation' and expected a final of contrasting styles between the individual brilliance of the Wanderers and the 'well-oiled' collective of the 'Sappers'.[112] Indeed, much has subsequently been made of the use made by the Engineers of combination play, where passing was employed rather than dribbling. As well as the 'Sappers', several other teams have been credited with the introduction of this method of play, including Sheffield FC, Lancing College (West Sussex), Old Carthusians and Queen's Park, though the Engineers are noted as demonstrating it on their northern tour in late 1873, when they beat Sheffield, Nottingham and Derbyshire to leave what may have been an indelible impression.[113] The adage of military teamwork sounded somewhat clichéd at the time, as it perhaps still does now, yet some of the press of the day and historians of the modern era seem to have employed the description of the Engineers' playing style fairly readily.

The *Morning Post* report of the game noted how 'perfectly one-sided' it was in favour of the Wanderers, while the 'Engineers could never get within many yards of their opponents' quarters'. The ease of victory was certainly not reflected in the score, with just a single goal separating the two sides. This is reiterated by Keith Warsop in his excellent *Early F.A. Cup Finals*, where he notes that the Engineers only made two chances, despite being favourites. Wanderers had the advantage of playing on their home pitch, Kennington Oval, where they had already hosted 18 matches during their successful season.[114] The cup was formally presented by EC Morley to the captain of the Wanderers – presumably Alcock – at the club's annual dinner on 11 April at the Pall Mall Restaurant in Charing Cross.[115]

Conclusion

Entries for the first playing of the FA Cup would probably have slightly disappointed the organisation's hierarchy. However, it was a start and, although it could not have been predicted, signified an important step forward particularly in relation to the rugby code, whose own national governing body, the RFU, would only be formed in 1871. Perhaps, as has been suggested in the Introduction to this book, the two events were connected, and the establishment of a cup competition by the FA was a response to the RFU's formation. One further point on entries. As has been mentioned, at a time when players turned out for a plethora of teams, having to opt to represent just one of them rather contracted the pool of talent available. Morton Peto Betts, the scorer of the winning goal in the 1871–2 final, was a good example. He played for West Kent in the previous season, 1870–1,[116] though seems to have transferred his services to Harrow Chequers – he was noted as their captain in November 1871[117] – for the 1871–2 campaign, with sporadic appearances for the Wanderers.[118] He was also listed as a member of the Crystal Palace club in October 1871.[119] He could, no doubt, have played for any of these in the competition, but his choosing, at least initially, of Harrow Chequers, may have contributed to West Kent not being present. Betts himself seemed to be an inveterate switcher of allegiance, or perhaps he was, in a time when games for each team were irregular, simply a man looking for a game.

In terms of the social backgrounds of the playing participants, the original 15 entrants in the 1871–2 FA Cup were overwhelmingly upper middle class with more than a sprinkling of aristocrats. Though the Hitchin club utilised a farm labourer, of all the contestants the players of Queen's Park were probably the least socially exclusive. Robert Smith was educated at the Fordyce Academy in Banffshire and went on to have various jobs, working in publishing and as a cashier. His brother James followed Robert to London in 1871 to become a commercial representative for an artists' suppliers, before tragically dying in 1876 following a stroke at the age of 32. Captain and goalkeeper James Gardner was originally a grain salesman and latterly a contractor's clerk on the Forth Bridge construction.[120] Queen's Park was hardly working class, but certainly decidedly from the lower-middle stratum of society. Donington School supplied a provincial anomaly, while the others provided examples of former public schoolboys and university students forming their own teams from existing friendship groups. This information indicates that the first season of the competition consisted of participants from the upper echelons of English society, though Scotland's representatives were certainly less so.

There is little doubt that the instigation of the FA Cup stimulated the association game. Indeed, in a letter to *Sporting Life* in January 1875, a writer bemoaned the fact that there was no similar trophy for rugby, noting that 'Since the Association Challenge Cup has been established, the interest shown in the game [soccer] has increased tenfold'.[121] Up to that point, the rugby form – particularly in London – had made great strides in the struggle for footballing supremacy. In terms of timing, Alcock may well have proposed a national cup in direct response to two events connected with the development of rugby in 1871, notably the formation of the RFU on 24 January and the holding of the first Scotland versus England international rugby fixture on 27 March. There is no extant 'smoking gun' of intention in this regard, but it would surely be naive to believe that rivalry did not exist between the two fledgling codes of football at that point. It should also be remembered that the members of the FA committee had only so far organised unofficial internationals between the two countries and were still some 16 months away from holding the first formally recognised encounter between Scotland and England, which took place on 30 November 1872. It is true that the inception of international fixtures in the early 1870s also helped to popularise association football, but because rugby had also embraced games between national representative sides, this new development would apply to both of the competing codes. The rugby game's seeming reluctance to embrace almost any form of competitive principle did not help the game to compete with what was becoming a soccer juggernaut. A further aid to the association game's eventual supremacy was that the rugby form was increasingly regarded by the wider society as being dangerous. A debate in *The Times* in November and December 1870 following a letter from 'A Surgeon' highlighting a list of injuries resulting from 'hacking' – the wilful kicking of an opponent who may or may not have possession of the ball – brought the violence of the game into the public domain.[122] While this did not immediately influence the wider nature of the sport, it may have had an influence on the banning of 'hacking' at the formation of the RFU a year later. However, as Eric Dunning and Kenneth Sheard argue in *Barbarians, Gentlemen and Players*,

> With its earlier, more comprehensive reduction of physical violence, soccer was a game better suited to Britain's temper in the third quarter of the nineteenth century. Rugby was less compatible with the dominant trends in a society where the most powerful and prestigious groups were coming to regard as odious and distasteful forms of violence accepted by earlier generations as normal. Even the abolition of 'hacking' was insufficient, by itself, to placate their conscience.[123]

Tony Collins appears to offer some support to Dunning and Sheard's argument. He notes that 'the disrepute that such publicity brought to the game was clearly beginning to undermine its legitimacy'.[124] The discussions over rugby's acceptability sowed a seed of doubt in people's minds regarding its safety and, along with soccer's introduction of a national competition in the form of the FA Cup, probably in the long run represented two mortal blows to the rugby game's relative popularity.

Yet, despite these varied stimuli to the association game's repertoire, *Bell's Life*'s summation of the recently completed 1871–2 season ended with a gloomy forecast for soccer's future ambitions, noting 'that their system…can ever rival the Union game in public estimation can hardly be hoped by its most sanguine admirer'.[125] Indeed, the writer would be supported by the existing evidence on participation. In October 1871, 16 association match reports compared to 33 for rugby were carried by *The Sportsman*. During the month of October 1872, the beginning of the season following the first FA Cup competition, there were just 13 association football reports in *The Sportsman* compared to 34 for the rugby code. This may well represent a narrow view of soccer's – or at least some form of kicking game's – popularity in Britain during that time, as London's partial rejection of that code was not mirrored in much of the country. However, it appears to show that, at least initially, association football lacked widespread popularity, despite the FA showcasing a new competition, though with hindsight it still seems possible to suggest that the FA Cup aided soccer's comparative status when compared to rugby. During that same month, Sheffield reported 29 fixtures of their own 'association-like' form, Sheffield Rules Football, while noting no matches under rugby rules in their vicinity. In Sheffield, of course, the kicking and dribbling game was the undisputed king. However, the beginning of the FA Cup cannot be seen as an instant watershed in soccer's ultimately victorious march to football predominance, but it was an important step in the right direction and immediately presented the sport with an excitement-generating possibility, which meant that rugby was perceived as less stimulating, over-complicated and also more dangerous and so, as a consequence, its own popularity declined. Finally, though historians frowning on 'great man' theories may take a different view, rugby did not possess a leader of the calibre of Charles Alcock. His biographer Keith Booth's epithet of 'Father of Modern Sport' seems to be quite appropriate.

Notes

1. Cavallini, *Wanderers*, 45.
2. Curry, *Making of Association Football*, 99–100.
3. FA Minutes.
4. Fabian and Green, *Association Football*, 34.
5. FA Minutes, 16 October 1871.
6. Robinson, *History of Queen's Park*.
7. There is precious little information on Powell. The author's best guess is that he was a close friend of Ebenezer Cobb Morley, first secretary of the FA, as indicated in an article on hare and hounds, a cross-country athletic paper chase, held at Roehampton in October 1871. Powell, an enthusiastic but average athlete, competed as a member of a team by the name of Morley's Beagles (*Sporting Gazette*, 4 November 1871). He was probably a trusted administrator of Morley's at Barnes and the FA. See also a further report on the 'beagles', a nickname for runners, with Powell as 'huntsman' in *Sporting Gazette*, 13 January 1872. He does not gain a mention in football team lists and even disappears from a list of Barnes FC committee members by 1874 (*The Sportsman*, 31 March 1874).

8   Warsop, *Early F.A. Cup Finals*, 111.
9   Cavallini, *Wanderers*, 128–9.
10 Mitchell, *First Elevens*.
11 *Bell's Life*, 21 and 28 October 1871.
12 FA Minutes, 3 October 1872.
13 *Bell's Life*, 21 October 1871.
14 *The Sportsman*, 23 December 1871.
15 Chesterfield was not mentioned in the FA Minutes of the AGM, but the name appeared in the report of the meeting in *The Sportsman* of 1 March 1871.
16 FA Minutes, 20 July 1872. See also *Derby Mercury*, 15 March 1871 for the formation of the South Derbyshire FA and Curry, 'Stunted Growth' for a detailed account of early football in South Derbyshire.
17 Curry, 'Clodhoppers'.
18 Curry and Dunning, 'The "origins of football debate"'.
19 *The Field*, 25 March 1871.
20 *Bell's Life*, 5 October 1872.
21 Ibid, 25 February 1871.
22 *The Sportsman*.
23 Ibid, 14 June 1870.
24 Ibid, 23 May 1871.
25 Ibid, 3 Mar 1871.
26 Mitchell, *First Elevens*, 110–1.
27 *Morning Advertiser*, 25 November and 9 December 1872.
28 *The Sportsman*, 27 May 1871.
29 Ibid, 10 August 1872.
30 *South London Chronicle*, 22 May 1875.
31 Brown, *The Football Association*, 52.
32 *Glasgow Evening Citizen*, 6 June 1868.
33 Robinson, *History of Queen's Park*.
34 FA Minutes, 23 October 1871.
35 *Morning Post*, 5 December 1871.
36 *White's Directory of Lincolnshire*, 1871.
37 *Lincolnshire Chronicle*, 4 February 1876.
38 Welbourne, 1972. However, one hundred years later, on 13 May 1972, Donington School, by then The Thomas Cowley High School, and Queen's Park eventually fulfilled the fixture, when the two teams met at the New Lesser Hampden Ground, the Scottish XI being victorious by six goals to nil.
39 Green, *History of the Football Association*: 17.
40 *Morning Post*, 16 March 1872.
41 Ibid, 15 December 1873.
42 *The Sportsman*, 17 October 1871.
43 *Morning Advertiser*, 29 January 1872.
44 *The Field*, 16 March 1872.
45 Cavallini, *Wanderers*, 66.
46 Ibid.
47 Ibid, 124.
48 Warsop, *Early F.A. Cup Finals*, 66.
49 See Curry, 'Football in the capital'.
50 It is worthy of note that both Marlow and Maidenhead are almost as close to Oxford as they are to Central London. In fact, Marlow is closer by four miles, meaning that, particularly in that club's case, it was able to utilise footballers from the university.
51 Awards for special ability in a particular sport.
52 He died tragically young at the age of 28.
53 Venn, 1940.
54 Stapylton, *Eton School Lists*, 247.

55 Chester, *Little Tin Idol*, 145.
56 *Reading Mercury*, 18 November 1871; England Census 1871.
57 *Hertfordshire Express and General Advertiser*, 25 November 1865. The local newspaper reported that 'A meeting of gentlemen, convened by private circular, was held in the National School-room on Friday evening, for the purpose of establishing a Foot-ball Club. Hubert Delmé Radcliffe, Esq., [the local Justice of the Peace and owner of Hitchin Priory] presided, and about twenty-five gentlemen were present'. Although it seems at first improbable that the newspaper was reporting events of the previous evening with such clarity, the *Hertfordshire Express* was published in Hitchin, so this may have been possible. If that is the case, it means that Hitchin was formed on 24 November 1865 rather than the previous week on 17 November.
58 Brown, *Cecil Reid*.
59 Chester, *Little Tin Idol*, 127.
60 *Sporting Gazette*, 16 January 1869.
61 Personal communication between Graham Curry and Neil Ward of the Civil Service FC, dated 1 February 2012.
62 *The Sportsman*, 16 December 1865.
63 *Morning Post*, 10 December 1868.
64 *Pall Mall Gazette*, 26 March 1868.
65 *Morning Post*, 24 November 1870.
66 *Sporting Life*, 19 November 1870.
67 *The Sportsman*, 15 November 1871.
68 Bancroft, *Early Years of the FA Cup*, 10–11.
69 FA Minutes. List of members, 1 January 1868.
70 It is surely of interest that Kensington School was one of the founder members of the FA on 26 October 1863.
71 Smart, *Wow Factor*, 332.
72 *The Field*, 30 March 1872.
73 Williams, *Code War*, 46.
74 Cavallini, *Wanderers*, 15.
75 Brief biographies taken from Andy Mitchell's excellent website, *Scottish Sport History*.
76 *Sporting Life*, 16 July 1864.
77 This phrase was first used by Smart, *Wow Factor*, Chapter One.
78 *Bell's Life*, 7 December 1862.
79 *The Sportsman*, 18 December 1866.
80 Ibid, 9 April 1867.
81 Ibid, 11 March 1868.
82 Kerrigan, *East London*, 5.
83 Masson, 'Keats', 4.
84 *The Field*, 3 February 1872; *The Sportsman*, 3 February 1872. Occasionally, the result of this game has been reported as being Royal Engineers 2, Hampstead Heathens 0. However, both the aforementioned sources say 3-0 to the 'Sappers'.
85 *The Field*, 17 February 1872.
86 Ibid, 4 January 1873.
87 *The Sportsman*, 16 December 1873.
88 Ibid, 16 December 1865.
89 Ibid, 17 October 1871.
90 Marshall, *Football*, 349.
91 *Illustrated Sporting News and Theatrical and Musical Review*, 2 January 1869. The game against Universal Humbugs was played on Boxing Day, 1868. The Humbugs was almost certainly a scratch side which had a very short existence. See *The Sportsman*, 13 January 1869 for both Alexandra games.
92 *Essex Herald*, 12 November 1867.
93 *The Sportsman*, 13 January 1869.
94 Ibid, 15 December 1868.

48   *The inaugural FA Cup*

95   *The Field*, 18 November 1871.
96   Cavallini, *Wanderers*, 72.
97   Also present in the Brentwood School team at the same time as Ogilvie, Holden and Nash was Robert Sandilands Frowd Walker, who would play in three of the pseudo-internationals for England against Scotland in the early 1870s.
98   Alcock, *Football Annual*, 1871.
99   See report of a game against Wanderers. *Illustrated Sporting News and Theatrical and Musical Review*, 18 December 1869.
100 *The Sportsman*, 13 April 1872.
101 Ibid, 6 January 1872.
102 See the game against Merton College, Oxford in 1870, when the club was helped out by 'several of their university members'. *Illustrated Sporting News and Theatrical and Musical Review*, 19 February 1870.
103 *The Sportsman*, 24 August 1872.
104 Smart, *Wow Factor*, 87.
105 I have not included the Sheffield Football Association, which was listed separately though it did not constitute an actual individual club.
106 FA Minutes, 28 October 1871.
107 Ibid, 7 February 1872.
108 *The Sportsman*, 5 March 1872.
109 *Glasgow Herald*, 5 March 1872.
110 Ibid, 20 March 1872.
111 *The Sportsman*, 16 March 1872.
112 *Morning Post*, 16 March 1872.
113 *Sheffield and Rotherham Independent*, 27 December 1873.
114 Cavallini, *Wanderers*, 128.
115 *The Sportsman*, 13 April 1872.
116 *Morning Post*, 27 February 1871.
117 *The Sportsman*, 4 November 1871.
118 *The Field*, 14 October 1871. According to Cavallini, he made six appearances in 1871–2 (*The Wanderers*, 128–9).
119 *The Sportsman*, 4 October 1871.
120 Mitchell, *First Elevens*.
121 *Sporting Life*, 23 January 1875. Strictly speaking, the correspondent to *Sporting Life* was not entirely correct, as the London teaching hospitals had agreed to compete for the United Hospitals Cup from 1874.
122 For an excellent summing up of the debate, see Dunning and Sheard, *Barbarians*, 98–104.
123 Ibid, 110.
124 Collins, *Social History of English Rugby Union*, 19.
125 *Bell's Life*, 20 April 1872.

3 The beginnings of change

Introduction

Chapter 3 will trace the competition from its second season in 1872–3 to 1881–2, a full decade of development. For the first six seasons, the cup changed very little. Entries were dominated by sides from the London area and, even when provincial teams decided to take the risk, they amounted to two or perhaps three clubs who rarely achieved any significant success. However, from the 1878–9 campaign, provincial XIs Sheffield, Shropshire Wanderers and Panthers began to make a real impact on the later stages of competition and, certainly in terms of the social make-up of participants, things were beginning to change.

However, these developments should only, at this time, be regarded as a first phase of a transformation as, in short, the southern amateur, upper-middle-class player remained dominant. The first 11 editions of the 'English Cup' effectively marked their ascendency, with Wanderers generally prevailing and going on to win the trophy five times. Five other southern-based teams would triumph in the contest. They were Oxford University, Royal Engineers, Old Etonians (twice), Clapham Rovers and Old Carthusians (Former pupils of Charterhouse School). Additionally, every beaten finalist in the first ten finals was also a southern amateur XI. Clubs from the south enjoyed an unrivalled supremacy in the early FA Cup, consisting as they did of former public schoolboys, ex-university men and players generally from the upper reaches of British (especially English) society. This hegemony would eventually be broken by a team from England's north-west.

The narrative was complex. Many of the teams involved were simply organisations created in various locations by returning local aristocrats or members of the upper middle class when they finished their schooling and/or university and reverted to their roots. This was particularly the case in and around London, where competing clubs almost solely consisted of men from the upper class. No doubt they enjoyed 'keeping in touch' with school and/or university friends through their shared leisure activity, though this type of club formation made up of relatively transient participants created organisations with a limited time span. Indeed, Charles Alcock's club, Wanderers, was a good example of this. Formed largely by former pupils of Harrow School and Forest School, the club, of course, won multiple FA Cups. However, though it began life as Forest Football Club in 1859 and transformed into Wanderers in 1864, it would end any regular involvement in

DOI: 10.4324/9781003285595-4

50 *The beginnings of change*

fixtures in the 1880–1 season[1] and disappear by 1888, when it played its final game in the annual match on 18 December against Harrow School at Kennington Oval.[2] The leading members had ended their playing careers and dispersed, leaving the club leaderless and with little reason to continue its existence.

However, though the teams of the Home Counties were still winning on the field of play, in the rest of the country clubs were being formed from other strata of society. Working-class members of various communities were clearly cognisant of the game, and it would not have been difficult to encourage them to join in. Although this is thought by some to be a rather simplistic explanation of club formation,[3] it was surprising how often it took place and examples will be given later in this chapter to support the contention. Towards the end of the 1870s, clubs with what might be termed a lower-middle-class intake emerged: a previously unheralded Nottingham Forest side reached the semi-finals, and eventually working-class teams initially from the West Midlands – particularly Stafford Road from Wolverhampton – and Darwen from East Lancashire. By 1880, at the beginning of a new decade, although footballers were unaware, the sport was ushering in a new era involving an almost entirely different class of players and, in some locations, even administrators. The working man, at least on the pitch, was about to take centre stage.

The 1872–3 competition

In line with the original concept of being a 'challenge' contest, Wanderers, as the holders, was granted a straight passage to the final round and also, interestingly, allowed to select the venue. Sixteen teams entered, one more than the previous year, which saw little change from the first season, with the cup still a small-scale competition of interest mainly to the FA and some of its member clubs. Hitchin withdrew without meeting Clapham Rovers in Round One, while soon to be perennial 'scratchers' Queen's Park were granted byes to the semi-finals where they allowed Oxford University a clear route to the final tie. New entrants included Windsor Home Park, South Norwood and 1st Surrey Rifles and, of these three, the team from Windsor is worthy of more detailed study because of its fascinating early history.

Windsor Home Park was and is part of the green space which partially surrounds Windsor Castle, with the wider area itself providing several entrants – Maidenhead and Marlow were significant others – in the early seasons of the cup. Interestingly, an advertisement for those 'desirous of joining a club' to play football, to meet two days each week at Home Park, was carried by the *Windsor and Eton Express* on 12 November 1853. One of the gentlemen mentioned in the advert was George Bambridge, noted in the 1851 England Census as being a schoolmaster. Furthermore, a year later, Home Park Football Club, along with the Prince of Wales and the 'Young Gentlemen of Eton College', were announced as the patrons of the Windsor Michaelmas Fair.[4] With the college in such close proximity, one might wonder whether masters, pupils or former pupils of Eton contributed to the forming of the Home Park club. Significantly, it was in 1853, the year in which a football club may have been formed there, that Queen Victoria opened 100 acres of the park for the recreational use of the public. There is evidence, however, to suggest that the club did not enjoy continuous existence from 1853 to 1870, when a newspaper report in the latter year noted that 'The Windsor Home Park Football Club played their first match on Saturday last [3 December 1870] at St. Stanislaus College, Beaumont, Old Windsor'.[5] If this is correct, it would be that organisation which would enter the second edition of the FA Cup. Interestingly, a report of a match against Marlow on 7 February 1871, remarked on a healthy number of spectators, 'among whom we noticed several old football players',[6] which seems to indicate a lasting tradition in the town before that date.

When they defeated Reigate Priory in the first round of the 1872–3 competition, the Windsor club turned out a strong XI, including the Heron brothers, Frank and Hubert, two future FA Cup winners with Wanderers, who would also represent England. They were joined by George Frederick Bambridge and his brother, Ernest Henry, who was also an England international in waiting. Both Herons and the latter Bambridge would go on to enjoy future success as players for the Swifts, an offshoot club seemingly formed by William Samuel Bambridge, the father of the aforementioned men.[7] There were two other brothers, Edward Charles and Arthur Leopold, who would along with Ernest Henry represent England. South Norwood, having disposed of Barnes, were Windsor's next opponents, with the former having procured the services of James and Robert Smith from Glasgow who were still members of Queen's Park FC in Glasgow, but had moved recently to South London. The brothers had played in the first recognised international against England in November 1872 and Robert would also take part in the second in March 1873. The FA Cup encounter at Kennington Oval ended in a most unsatisfactory manner as, with South Norwood leading by a single disputed though ultimately awarded goal, Windsor claimed an equaliser, which, in turn, was disputed by their opponents.[8] Subsequently, the FA committee ruled that there should be a replay and Windsor summarily dispatched South Norwood by three clear goals. Both the Glaswegians were present in the first game for South Norwood, but only Robert in the replay, while both Herons played for Windsor in each of the games, as did William Samuel and Ernest Henry Bambridge. Significantly, Charles Alcock acted as umpire for both sides in the second game, recognising it as an encounter which might create controversy.[9] The third 'new face' in the competition, the 1st Surrey Rifles, was a volunteer unit formed in 1859 whose headquarters was situated at Camberwell in South London, where they defeated Upton Park in the first round by two clear goals. The *Morning Advertiser* report seemed to suggest that the Rifles raised their game beyond previous levels, adding a common military metaphor, describing them as 'keeping well together, as riflemen should do'.[10]

Maidenhead reached the fourth round where they lost to Oxford University, who advanced to the final due to the withdrawal of Queen's Park. The latter found it impossible to agree a semi-final date which became complicated because of the England versus Scotland international at Kennington Oval on 8 March 1873, for which Queen's would provide the bulk of the Scotland XI. This reasoning, however, seems skewed. The university had defeated Maidenhead as early as 3 February 1873 and it appears inconceivable that a date between then and the final on 29 March 1873 could not have been found. Admittedly, Queen's played Vale of Leven in a prestige fixture on 15 February[11] and again on 1 March,[12] commitments probably made some months before and which they would have been eager to keep.

52   The beginnings of change

There did exist the usual problem of 'tyranny of distance' and Queen's would exhibit a tendency to 'scratch' in future years. Indeed, of the first 13 FA Cup competitions, Queen's scratched seven times, did not enter on four occasions and withdrew once. All this preceded the 1883–4 competition when they were awarded five consecutive home draws before their semi-final against Blackburn Olympic at Nottingham and the cup final at Kennington Oval, where they lost to another Blackburn side, Rovers.

The previous season's winners, Wanderers, awaited Oxford University in the challenge round. There were other sporting contests in future years which employed that format: for instance, the Wimbledon Men's Singles title was decided from 1878 to 1921 in a challenge round, as was the Ladies' Singles from 1886 to 1921. As well as the challenge round facility, Wanderers, as holders, chose the venue – the Lillie Bridge Ground, West Brompton – and warmed up there with a game against Gitanos 17 days before the final itself.[13] The location was the home of the Amateur Athletic Club, but the ground also hosted sports as diverse as cricket, boxing, wrestling and cycling, so was not altogether a surprise selection. The FA Cup Final was due to be played on the same day and at the same time as the Boat Race and, therefore, because it was clearly at that point the lesser of the two sporting occasions, its kick-off time was moved to 11.30 a.m.[14] It was thus possible to view both events as, no doubt, many Oxonians did, as Lillie Bridge was relatively close to the River Thames at Hammersmith Bridge, about a third of the way along the course, being perhaps 25 minutes' walk away. The weather on the day began particularly poorly – so much so that the Boat Race itself came under threat of postponement – with fog and haze until just after midday, when conditions cleared, and the afternoon was partly sunny and unexpectedly warm. However, the elements at 11.30 a.m. as the football kicked off remained disappointing, resulting in a low attendance, one newspaper assessing the spectator numbers as low as 150.[15] This was in stark contrast to onlookers for the rowing from the banks of the Thames, which was noted as the largest ever for the event and started at 2.21 p.m. precisely.[16] Allowing time for changing ends etc., the FA Cup Final would have finished around 1.15 p.m., so there would just have been time to decamp to the river, with a ride in a hansom cab the preferred option. Wanderers were victorious by two goals to nil, but the contest was described as being relatively even, with Kinnaird for the victors and Arnold Kirke Smith (Cheltenham College 1863–9; University College, Oxford 1869–73), the university captain, being the standout performers.[17] Smith was from Sheffield, where he played for Sheffield FC and the Sheffield FA representative side before being capped by England in the initial encounter with Scotland in 1872. As for the Boat Race, Oxford completed a miserable day as Cambridge won by three lengths.

1873–4 to 1877–8: provincials and Panthers

The next five seasons followed a similar pattern, except that the challenge round was abandoned. There were only two clubs from the provinces who entered regularly – Sheffield FC and Shropshire Wanderers. The possibility of having to travel to London, where most of the clubs in the cup were based, was probably still an important constraint, though the FA retained the right to draw provincial clubs together in the early rounds, thereby motivating entries from further afield. Unfortunately, this meant that Sheffield and Shropshire Wanderers were paired together in three consecutive seasons, though they only actually met in 1873–4, with the away side withdrawing on the other two occasions. With its primacy in club formation and early links with and support for the nascent FA, Sheffield was the obvious candidate to participate and the tie in that season produced an interesting conclusion when, after two drawn games, it was decided on the toss of a coin in a local hotel. The first game, played at Bramall Lane on Thursday 30 October 1873, ended in a 0-0 draw. The replay, on Monday 17 November, was played in a field adjoining Shrewsbury racecourse – Shrewsbury was, from around 1870, an enthusiastic centre of early club formation – and also ended in no score.[18] The match was quite physical and the home team's robust play contributed to the visitors playing the closing stages with only nine fit players. Shropshire also had the services of their captain, John Hawley Edwards, who had not featured in the first game. Hawley Edwards was a fascinating character. He was the first dual international, playing for England in 1874 and Wales two years later. He became an FA Cup winner with Wanderers in 1876 and was representing that club when he gained his Welsh cap in the same year. In the match report of the replay it was noted that, 'After the match the players dined together at the "Raven",[19] where it was agreed to toss which should be considered victorious and the Sheffield captain (Mr. Chambers) won'.[20] Sheffield would enjoy some success in the competition, but were usually beaten around the quarter final/fourth round stage, often at the hands of the Wanderers (for instance, in the 1875–6 and 1877–8 seasons). Their lack of success was somewhat understandable as their rules did differ from those of the FA, with practically no offside rules in South Yorkshire leading to long kicks from defence to forwards waiting near the opposition goal, a tactic of little use when a stricter offside law was employed.

Another interesting club, Panthers, entered for the first time in 1874–5. One might assume that this was another example of an exotically titled London organisation, such as Pilgrims (Clapham), Ramblers (Walthamstow), Trojans (Leyton), Saxons (Brixton), Remnants (Slough) or Minerva (Ladywell), all of whom briefly entered the cup in its early days. However, the Panthers were, in fact, from Sturminster Marshall in Dorset and were formed in autumn 1873, with their first newspaper reference being the report of their *return* game with Blandford School on 13 December of that year.[21] The original encounter must have pre-dated that match, though it went seemingly unreported, hence the broad foundation date. The club was the creation of Edward George Farquharson, who was born in 1847 at Buckland Newton in Dorset and attended Eton College from 1862 to 1865, his grandfather James John (Edward's father was also called James John) having made his money as an East India Company shipping merchant.[22] It is of little surprise that Edward, having received his education at Eton, championed a kicking and dribbling form of football similar to the Eton Field Game. Farquharson represented the classic club formation path of a local boy returning from public school to encourage a particular form of the game in his native town or village. A good number of current football academics, probably influenced by Adrian Harvey's publication of *Football: The First Hundred Years* in 2005, tend to minimise the notion that the early game was developed by ex-public schoolboys returning to their home towns and villages to inspire the establishment of organised clubs and teams in those areas. As this particular example shows, diffusion of this nature *did* happen, and it is surprising how often it occurred. Farquharson is listed as an ensign in the 22nd Regiment in the 1871 Census but eventually followed his father in becoming Justice of the Peace for the county and would almost certainly have been instrumental in the club joining the FA and entering the cup.

Another significant Old Etonian, the Reverend George Richard Dupuis, moved to Sturminster Marshall in 1875 to become the local rector. From Eton, Dupuis had won a scholarship to King's College, Cambridge, starting in 1854 and eventually becoming a fellow there. Although he only remained in the village for two years, he would have strengthened the Eton football connection and, even though he was by this time 40 years of age, Dupuis still managed to play in goal for the Panthers. Additionally, he was a fine cricketer and enthusiastic coach. Two other local families were involved in the club – the Caves and the Richards – both being farmers with large acreages and employing a good number of men just outside the village.

Panthers' first game in the 1874–5 FA Cup was against a strong Clapham Rovers side. However, they were not required to travel the long journey to London, as the match took place at Winchester College, conveniently around halfway between the homes of the two clubs, though Panthers, perhaps unsurprisingly, still lost by three clear goals. The following season, 1875-6, saw them again utilise Winchester's offer to host a game against a London suburban team, when they defeated Woodford Wells.[23] There are no extant team lists for the game against Clapham, but it is probable that the Winchester go-between for Panthers on both occasions was Montague John Druitt, who played against Woodford and had just left Winchester to follow the traditional path to New College, Oxford.[24] The victory had been sealed with a single goal scored by a gentleman named RWJ Vidal[25] and it appears that this may have been the 'prince of dribblers' himself, Robert Walpole Sealy Vidal, who was noted in Chapter 2 as winning the cup in its inaugural season with Wanderers. Despite still attending Oxford University, RWS Vidal did not represent them in any of their games in the FA Cup in 1875–6, which makes it more likely that he was the man who distinguished himself for Panthers, being used for a single, important encounter. Indeed, the goal was obtained by a fine piece of dribbling, though slight suspicions are aroused that it may not have been the 'prince' as he lined up as a half back. It was probable that this was, indeed, the 'prince' and the newspaper had printed his third initial in error as 'J' rather than 'S'. In another report of the Panthers–Woodford Wells game, Edward Farquharson was praised for playing 'remarkably well in the trial matches at The Oval last year', which seems to indicate that he was a performer of some skill and renown.[26] Unfortunately, Panthers scratched when faced with the Royal Engineers in Round Two.

In the 1876–7 edition of the cup, Panthers easily beat Wood Grange at Upton Park in East London and then entertained Pilgrims at Sturminster Marshall. Intriguingly, a newspaper report mentions the presence of 'several old Oxonians of note' and, indeed, the name 'Panthers' seems to suggest that they were very much a 'select' XI rather than a representation of Sturminster Newton. The Reverend John George Brymer, at this point a rector in Child Okeford, Dorset, just 10–15 miles north of Sturminster Marshall, was indeed one of those former Oxford men, having attended Christ Church College from 1867 to 1871. Giving an idea of the time required to fulfil this fixture, Pilgrims were said to have 'left for Southampton on Friday night, going on to Wimborne on the following morning'[27]; Sturminster Marshall is five miles west of Wimborne. The 1877–8 campaign, with the FA continuing to encourage the policy of neutral venues approximately halfway between the locations of the two clubs involved, saw Panthers outclassed by nine goals to one at Sandhurst/Farnborough[28] by a star-studded Wanderers side including internationals Hubert Heron, John Wylie, Henry Wace and Arthur Kinnaird. The Dorset side entered in the next two seasons and limped on through the 1879–80 campaign but, perhaps under pressure by the founding of rivals in nearby Wimborne, gave up pushing against an ever-increasing tide and folded. Interestingly, at least as early as January 1880, Edward Farquharson was playing for Wimborne, which may indicate that Panthers' FA Cup scratching against Birmingham Cricket and Football Club (no relation to the Birmingham City of the present day) in the 1879–80 season was the organisation's last act. By the following year Farquharson was captain of what appeared to be a thriving Wimborne club which turned out regular sides at both the association and rugby codes.[29]

★★★

There were new names on the cup in the 1873–4 and 1874–5 seasons. Oxford University and Royal Engineers were winners, while Wanderers managed to add three more titles to their already impressive two between 1875–6 and 1877–8, so by the end of the timeframe, the status quo had been maintained and the southern amateurs still reigned supreme, though there was as yet no one to provide an effective challenge as the competition remained of little interest to all but a quite narrow circle of gentlemen amateur teams based in and around London. Numbers entering the competition increased, but only very steadily. By 1876–7, the number of clubs involved in the Scottish equivalent stood at 81 and was well beyond the 37 involved in the English counterpart. Even the Sheffield FA Challenge Cup competition, in its first season, had 25, a creditable figure. Of those 37 teams in the FA Cup, 30 were based in and around London plus seven provincial teams, which included the two universities.

However, while there were new entrants, the clubs all consisted of men from the upper strata of society until Darwen tried their luck for the first time in 1877–8, beating Manchester Association but losing narrowly to Sheffield in the second round. Manchester Association - a name adopted to distinguish themselves clearly from the city's dominant rugby club – were, on paper, no pushovers and included in their ranks Stuart George Smith, who had emphasised the need for universal football rules in a letter to *The Field* in 1877.[30] Born and brought up in Nottingham, he attended Uppingham School, which meant that his early life had been spent in two bastions of the kicking and dribbling form of football. Also involved was James Strang, a former Queen's Park man who had moved to the area and joined the club.[31]

For their first round match in the 1877–8 season against Nottinghamshire – soon to be Notts. County – Sheffield FC had secured the services of the Nottingham-based England international, Arthur William Cursham. Indeed, the practice of representing one team in friendly fixtures while 'choosing' an entirely different club for cup ties was perfectly legal at the time. However, not only were they importing a player from another district, their opponents in the tie were none other than the club for whom Cursham had already played regularly in friendly games in that same season. It seems doubtful that Cursham's prime reason for preferring Sheffield to Nottingham was based on money, as both clubs were controlled by upper-middle-class gentlemen generally thought to be upholders of amateur sporting values and eschewers of payment for playing. Cursham's brother, Henry Alfred (HA or Harry), later represented the Corinthians Football Club, a team consisting of ex-public schoolboys and former university students, indicating that the family were of a relatively high social standing. However, the possibility of some kind of reward should not be dismissed entirely, but it was very unlikely.

There were, in fact, two games between the clubs, the first ending in a 1-1 draw. In a report on the first fixture, a reporter for a Sheffield newspaper noted that Cursham's appearance in the Sheffield XI elicited 'some slight expressions of disapprobation (which were quite improper) from the Nottingham people'.[32] However, to rub salt into already open wounds, Cursham scored all Sheffield's goals in the two matches, gaining a hat-trick in the second, deciding the encounter in Sheffield's favour by three clear goals. Despite the practice of players representing multiple clubs being an almost accepted part of 1870s football, this particular custom of importing the best talent from elsewhere for important cup encounters was nevertheless much frowned upon in local football communities. The whole process is indicative of the importance that clubs were beginning to place on FA Cup success, with Sheffield willing to incur the wrath of Nottingham by pursuing Cursham to play him in the competition. It is ironic, therefore, that in December 1877[33] and February 1878,[34] Cursham lined up for Nottingham *against* Sheffield in two friendly matches.[35]

However, despite all the previous prose, after careful research into former pupils of Sheffield Collegiate School, there appears to be a strong and clear connection to the city for the Cursham family, making it more understandable that 'AW' should decide to represent a Sheffield side at some point. Indeed, his father William George Cursham had been a pupil at Sheffield Collegiate in April 1838,[36] where he would have been a contemporary of the brilliant scientist Henry Clifton Sorby, whose family would be heavily involved in the beginnings of Sheffield football and Sheffield FC in particular. Arthur attended Oakham School and he turned out fairly regularly for Thursday Wanderers, a club formed in Sheffield of mainly Sheffield FC players who wished to play additional fixtures in midweek and enter local cup competitions. He had actually played for the latter club as recently as mid-October 1877.[37] Therefore, it should come as less of a surprise that Cursham might choose to play for a Sheffield-based side as he would no doubt have been on friendly terms with the majority of the players. Although this new evidence goes some way to explaining his decision, his actions might be described as being somewhat insensitive, though the fact that Sheffield were drawn against Nottinghamshire was particularly unfortunate for Cursham.

Following their victory after a replay over Nottinghamshire, Sheffield entertained Darwen in a close affair on a waterlogged pitch, which was only decided five minutes from time when Sheffield scored a disputed goal and, with the two umpires disagreeing, the referee came down in favour of the South Yorkshire side.[38] Interestingly, in the two matches, Darwen included six of the players who would draw 5-5 with Old Etonians in February 1879, by which time they had incorporated the important additions of Fergus Suter and James Love, both professional importations. Their three epic struggles with the Old Etonians would come to represent the emergence of new stronghold of the association game, East Lancashire, which would break the stranglehold of the southern amateurs on the national competition. It would also, as will be illustrated in Chapter 4, herald the beginning of professionalism in English football, thereby threatening to split the sport into two competing camps. However, there were important developments elsewhere, which have not been accorded the same coverage as those events, one of which involved Nottingham Forest.

★★★

It was the 1878–9 campaign which would prove to be the real watershed for provincial sides and, though the exploits of Darwen from East Lancashire have come, in a fit of historical romanticism, to overshadow the deeds of Nottingham Forest, it was the latter who had the more impressive run all the way to the semi-final. Subsequent football historians have, of course, seized on Darwen's working-class links and, rather than credit more middle-class organisations and their successes, have been inclined to glamorise the lower stratum of society.

Forest's path to that semi-final stage was incredibly difficult. They beat local rivals Notts. County, followed by Sheffield FC, Old Harrovians and Oxford University, both the latter two fixtures being at Kennington Oval, before falling to eventual winners Old Etonians by the odd goal in three. Most surprisingly, when the team sheets for the semi-final are consulted, Tommy Bishop from Chesterfield and a renowned player for local side Spital, was included in the Forest ranks. However, research into North East Derbyshire football reveals a link between Forest and Spital which, at least once, involved three Nottingham men helping out their Chesterfield counterparts.[39] Sam Weller Widdowson,[40] Arthur Copeland Goodyer and Arthur Hubert Smith, the first two being England internationals, aided Spital in a Sheffield FA cup victory against Derby Town in November 1878, with Goodyer scoring the winner. The three players had nominally represented Spital against Forest earlier in the season in order that they might be regarded as members of the Spital club. A Derby objection was overturned, but this might be termed 'sharp practice' by the Chesterfield-based organisation. Returning to the events of the semi-final, the absence through illness of Frederick William Earp may have led to Forest feeling that one of their most effective performers could only be replaced by someone approaching Earp's skill level and, certainly, Tommy Bishop was a player of the highest calibre. Bishop regularly represented Spital but was not averse to 'helping out' more ambitious clubs. Indeed, in the late 1870s and early 1880s, he appeared for Wednesday FC in Sheffield in several locally prestigious cup ties. However, with Bishop working principally in Mason's tobacco factory in Spital, he would surely not have refused remuneration for playing or, at the very least, expenses for travel, accommodation and meals. As an importation, Bishop would have been frowned upon in most quarters, but no doubt he was a tenuous member of the Forest club, thereby legitimising his appearance. The practice of importation, regularly used by East Lancashire clubs in the early 1880s, was linked to the early professionalisation of the game and is dealt with in Chapter 5 of this book. It is important to remember that, at this time, it was still not uncommon for a player to represent multiple clubs, though this had generally been stamped out in cup competitions. Regular fixtures every Saturday afternoon were rare for any team and players went wherever they could find a game in order to take part in their favoured recreation. For the more skilful and effective, it helped if their temporary club was offering an inducement. Despite these reservations, the Nottingham club's achievement was all the more praiseworthy as it was its first venture into national competition.

Forest repeated their semi-final feat in the 1879–80 season and, although their initial path through the early rounds was similar to their original experience – they despatched local rivals County in the first round – there then followed two matches against sides from the emerging footballing subculture of East Lancashire. If Turton and Blackburn Rovers were expected to give Forest a true test, neither did so and both were easily beaten by six clear goals, with none conceded, demonstrating that a gulf still remained in football terms between what one might have described as middle-class teams and those emerging from the working classes. Though their previous ties were uneventful, the fourth round against old rivals Sheffield FC proved to be full of controversy. Coming back from two goals in arrears, Forest finished the game much stronger and were keen to play extra time. However, when the Sheffield captain declined, the referee – none other than Charles Alcock – felt that there was little point in him remaining, even though the rules stated that the extra half an hour should have been played, and set off to catch his London train.[41] The FA ruled that the game should be awarded to Forest, prompting a good deal of acrimony in Sheffield, but righteous concurrence in Nottingham.[42] The FA Cup was clearly becoming a national competition and, judging by the reaction of both the Sheffield and Forest clubs, it was also a focus for expressions of local identity. The fact that Alcock travelled from London to referee also shows its significance, but not so significant that he felt able to miss his train!

But were Forest a Midlands representation of their London counterparts in terms of social class? Sam Weller Widdowson's story has been well documented.[43] He was regarded as an innovator in football terms, being involved with the first mention of a referee's whistle in Forest's match against Sheffield Norfolk in 1872 and introducing shinguards in the form of what must have been shortened cricket pads in 1874.[44] Widdowson, like many others in Nottingham, worked in the lace trade and eventually became a director of lacemakers Thomas Adams and Co. But what of his teammates? As well as Widdowson, the occupations of the other ten players who opposed Old Harrovians on 28 January 1879 in the third round of the FA Cup, included four lace salesmen, two others involved in the lace trade, a tailor, a railway clerk, a stationer and a hosiery warehouseman.[45]

With limited space available, only two detailed biographies of those additional players must suffice. Arthur Hubert Smith and Mark Holroyd were the most difficult to trace and, consequently, the information gleaned may be of help to future researchers. Smith was born in 1855 in Long Eaton. His father Thomas was a lace manufacturer and owner of the High Street Mills factory in Brown's Lane, Long Eaton. Arthur was described as a 'lace maker' and worked in the family business, though 'lace manager' was probably a better title.[46] As previously mentioned in this chapter, Smith was one of the three Forest players who helped Chesterfield club, Spital, against Derby Town in November 1878. Holroyd was born in 1859 and played for Forest from 1878 to 1881. His father was a grocer and, before his Forest days, Holroyd represented several junior teams in the Nottingham area. These included Thomas Herbert & Co., a local lace manufacturer in March 1874;[47] Trinity Institute, based at the Trinity Church on Mansfield Road, in December of the same year;[48] Broadway, an area near the Lace Market in the centre of the city, in 1876;[49] and St. Andrew's Presbyterian, the church being opposite the Forest Recreation Ground where they entertained opponents, in 1876.[50] His Forest debut came against Sheffield Wednesday on 26 January 1878[51] and he remained the club's regular half back (midfield player) until 1881 – his last mention in that year is in October[52] – when he moved to London. There he represented Dreadnought against Old Foresters at Walthamstow in the opening round of the FA Cup.[53] He seems to have returned briefly to Nottingham in late 1884 and turned out for Notts. Wanderers, with Forest and Long Eaton Rangers also competing for his services, though it appears that they were unsuccessful in convincing him to play for them.[54]

The team represented Nottingham's growing middle class, built, as exhibited in several of the above occupations, on lace manufacturing in the city. The industry had grown in the first three decades of the 19th century, though real impetus had occurred during the 1840s when permission was obtained to build on open fields close to the city, which enabled large factories using steam-powered machines to be constructed in easily accessible areas. Forest, however, were somewhat closer to the southern amateur XIs who had dominated the FA Cup in its opening years than they were to the emerging working-class sides from East Lancashire. They would have exhibited more of the former's sporting values and rejected covert professionalism and a 'winning at all costs' mentality which many working-class players might have more readily accepted. Indeed, it was County rather than Forest that first embraced paying players in Nottingham. It is interesting, however, that Forest should entertain a close relationship with Spital FC, as mentioned earlier in this chapter, a decidedly working-class organisation in Chesterfield. In short, Forest represented a provincial halfway house between patricians and plebeians. Forest had established a reputation as one of the better teams in England but fell agonisingly short in the early FA Cup. The following two campaigns, 1880–1 and 1881–2, saw them beaten by a rising Aston Villa, before again reaching the semi-final stage in 1884–5, but losing to Queen's Park after a replay. Nevertheless, the club had made its mark in the cup, without quite winning the trophy.

★★★

In the 1880–1 FA Cup, a new name and region came to the fore – Stafford Road from Wolverhampton in the West Midlands. Outclassing Lincolnshire side Spilsby in the first round at the neutral Trent Bridge in Nottingham, the club then drew with Grantham, who were 'assisted' by the England international Arthur William Cursham in the first game but not in the replay, when he refereed. Cursham has, of course, been mentioned on a previous occasion in this chapter, opting to play for Sheffield in a cup encounter against Notts. County, his preferred club for most of his career. His involvement in the FA Cup is a good example of the informality of the competition – he played for two different clubs and even refereed a replay, personifying gentleman amateur behaviour in football around that time. As regards the second instalment, the game was easily won by Stafford Road by seven goals to one. Following a bye in Round Three, they drew local rivals Aston Villa in an away tie. That Stafford Road emerged victorious by three goals to two was, considering the game was played at Aston Villa's home ground, a mild surprise, though the winners were known as a more than useful combination and had forced Villa to a replay in the FA Cup of the previous season. The game was described by the reporter from *The Field* as being 'one of the most obstinately disputed matches in the present series of Cup ties',[55] a real local 'derby' of intense rivalry and vigorous play. The next round saw Old Etonians travel to Wolverhampton in what must have been a culture shock, but the game itself was an anti-climax for the home team and their supporters, with the southern amateurs winning by two goals to one. The old boys were two goals to the good when the home side scored just three minutes from time, leaving them with little time to equalise. The Stafford Road goalkeeper, Ray, 'kept goal splendidly', which probably indicates the London team's ascendency.[56]

Who were Stafford Road? The team consisted of workers from the Stafford Road Railway Works just north of the centre of Wolverhampton. Although railway-related work existed on the site from 1849, it was not until a decade later that large-scale repairs were carried out and new locomotives built on site. The 1870s and 1880s saw an economic recession and it was feared that the works might have to close altogether.[57] However, the depression was weathered, and the works became noted for its organisation of sporting activities and facilities for its workforce. These included a library, gymnasium, seaside excursions, a fishing lake and – eventually – a sports ground, as well as cricket, fishing, athletics and (importantly for our purposes) a football team. By the early 1870s these were joined by a football club founded by Charles Crump, who worked there and was described in the 1881 England Census as being a railway clerk, though this probably understated the position he held at Stafford Road, which might more correctly be described as Chief Clerk for the Northern Division of the Great Western Railway. Crump became President of the Birmingham County FA at its inception in 1875. He was absent from Stafford Road's game against Spilsby but captained the side in the remaining FA Cup ties of the 1880–1 season. By this time, he was 39 years of age and would continue playing into his 40s. He served on the FA Council from 1883, eventually holding the positions of Vice-President and Senior Vice-President on the governing body, and came to be regarded as one of football's ablest administrators.[58]

Crump was a noted opponent of football professionalism and spoke against its acceptance at the FA special general meeting to discuss the subject in January 1885. He opposed Charles Alcock's motion urging its establishment, arguing that 'a professional would do no work, but sell himself to the highest bidder in the football world. After five years there would be an end to honest rivalry in play. The rich clubs would buy up the best talent'.[59] Crump did not represent a lone voice and found supporters in Sheffield in particular, but ultimately payment for players was recognised. Perhaps most of all, he embodied the characteristics of a muscular Christian, not only encouraging sport in other people but serving for over 40 years as Superintendent of the Darlington Street Wesleyan Sunday School in Wolverhampton. On ending his playing career, he took up refereeing and officiated at the FA Cup Final in 1883 between Blackburn Olympic and Old Etonians, together with the international between Wales and Scotland in 1891. He died in 1923.

★★★

In the four seasons from 1878–9 to 1881–2, the southern amateur clubs continued to dominate the competition as they had done since its inception, despite the increased entries from the north and Midlands.[60] Those campaigns saw three different winners in Old Etonians (twice), Clapham Rovers and Old Carthusians. As one of the original entrants, Clapham Rovers has already been examined, with the driving force behind its success being Robert Andrew Muter Macindoe Ogilvie. He made his debut against Forest School on 11 October 1870 and would play in each of the next 12 seasons before retiring from the game at the end of the 1882–3 campaign. Born in London on 20 October 1852, he attended Brentwood School – a kicking and dribbling stronghold – where he played football regularly for the school team. Following the 1879–80 final and Rovers' success, *The Sportsman* reported that 'a special demonstration was given to Ogilvie and Lloyd-Jones, and to the former, who has worked so energetically for the Rovers over the last eleven years, the success of his side must be most gratifying'.[61] It was Clopton Allen Lloyd-Jones who had scored the only goal of the final just six minutes from time to win the cup. He was born in Shropshire and had been educated at Trent College, near Nottingham, being a talented all-round sportsman in athletics, cricket and bowls, as well as a keen angler and useful rifle shot.[62] Rovers had gone close the previous year when they fell to the Old Etonians by a single goal in an uninspiring final, but they were just good enough to gain their own single goal victory against Oxford University and secure their only FA Cup triumph in a game described as being played throughout with great sportsmanship.[63]

The composition and backgrounds of the Clapham Rovers team are of some interest. Two were involved in the Stock Exchange, and two in the legal profession, with one each working as a hide broker, insurance underwriter, accountant, hotel manager, city clerk, indigo broker and architect.[64] Other than Norman Bailey at Westminster, the Clapham Rovers XI which won the FA Cup in 1879–80, could not be classed as emanating from any of the 'great' public schools. However, if one were to mention public schools of the second rank or slightly below the Clarendon schools in terms of status, Lancing (Reginald Halsey Birkett and Edgar Field), Malvern (Harold de Vaux Brougham), Forest (Felix Barry), Repton (Arthur John Stanley), Brentwood (Robert Andrew Muter Macindoe Ogilvie), Trent College (Clopton Allen Lloyd-Jones) and King's, Rochester (Francis John Sparks) provided the educational institutions of eight of the team and would form part of that subsidiary list. There existed, however, an embryonic soccer tradition in each of the seven named institutions and there may well have been a good deal of rivalry when the likes of Birkett, Ogilvie and Field opposed the Old Etonians, the latter representing more prestigious institutions and perhaps exhibiting a sense of superiority over less aristocratic and more middle-class institutions.

The semi-finals in the following season summed up the strange way, to modern eyes at least, that the national association organised the competition, probably indicating that, with the same people involved in the organisation, the same methods of working were still being practised. Unsurprisingly, there was an odd number of teams – three to be exact – and consequently Old Etonians were awarded a bye which meant that Old Carthusians played Darwen. This was a Darwen side which was now without its Scotsmen, Suter and Love, for differing reasons (Suter had 'transferred' to Blackburn Rovers, while Love had joined the army), but who had, in 1879–80, captured the prestigious Lancashire County FA Cup in its inaugural season. The establishment of local knockout football competitions may well have been as a direct result of the FA Cup providing a successful role model for such contests. Indeed, both the Sheffield FA Challenge Cup and the Birmingham FA Challenge Cup began in 1876–7, while the Berks & Bucks FA Challenge Cup started life in 1878–9. However, the Old Carthusians were opponents who had to be taken seriously and had, in James Frederick McLeod Prinsep and Edward Hagarty Parry, two first-class performers. Indeed, despite scoring first, Darwen were 'very wild in their play at the outset' and 'showed little form in any part of the game', the Old Carthusians running out 4-1 winners to the delight of their followers. The victor's supporters mimicked those of Clapham Rovers as 'At the finish Parry and Prinsep were heartily cheered' though they still had the Old Etonians to contend with if they were to fulfil their ambitions.[65] The 1880–1 final was the only one of its kind to be fought out by two old boys clubs. The early stages were dominated by the Old Carthusians and, though their opponents revived somewhat in the second half, 'the pace of the game had by this time begun to tell visibly on their efforts' as the Old Etonians faded badly, probably lacking fitness.[66] This comment, coming, as it did, just before the emergence of a more professional approach to the game, probably illustrates one of the drawbacks of taking the game less seriously, as fitness levels were clearly below those that would be achieved from players who trained full time. The game was as one-sided as the scoreline suggests – 3-0 to the Old Carthusians – and, as one newspaper report noted, at the conclusion of the match, 'to judge by the ovation that greeted each member of the winning team on his return to the pavilion, the Carthusians have the satisfaction of knowing that their victory was essentially a popular one'.[67]

Charterhouse was one of the great upholders of football as a kicking game in the public schools. Originally, there were basically two football games at the school, Cloisters and Under Green. These were played at the old school site in

Smithfield, London but when Charterhouse moved to Godalming in Surrey in 1872, Cloisters football ended. Under Green – or Green as it became known – continued and, because it was played outside on a field, it aided the adoption of the association form.[68] The school has close links to soccer: it was the only public school to send an observer, Bertram Fulke Hartshorne, the school's captain of football, to the first meeting of the FA on 26 October 1863; along with Westminster School, it championed what might be described as limited or compromise offside, with the two schools only acceding to joining the FA on the condition that the governing body did not operate a strict rugby-type offside; furthermore, a former pupil, Charles Wreford Brown, while attending Oriel College, Oxford and following a Victorian fashion of adding '-er' to certain words, such as 'brekker' for breakfast and 'rugger' for rugby, is said to have coined the word 'soccer' as a shortened form of the word 'association' to describe the code first fashioned at the FA.

Parry was the first man born outside the British Isles to captain a team in the FA Cup Final, when he did so for Oxford University in 1876–7 in a losing cause against Wanderers. With Old Carthusians in 1880–1, he became the first to captain a winning side, though he was by no means the first man born overseas to play in the showpiece. In the first ever final in 1871–2, Wanderers had William Parry Crake (Madras, India), while in the Royal Engineers XI there were no fewer than four – Colonel Edward William Cotter (Valletta, Malta), Colonel Edward William Creswell (Gibraltar), Colonel Henry Waugh Renny-Tailyour (Mussoorie, India) and Lieutenant Alfred George Goodwyn (Roorhir, India). In 1880–1, the Old Carthusians had five players born overseas as well as Parry, which meant that there was a majority not born in the British Isles. With Lewis Matthew Richards having been born in Wales and Alexander Hay Tod taking his first breaths 'at sea', there were, in actual fact, only four English-born men in the side.

It was surely fitting that both Clapham Rovers and Old Carthusians should eventually win their only FA Cups just as the torch of élite football was about to be passed to men from a very different subculture. It was doubly appropriate that the likes of Birkett, Ogilvie and Field along with Prinsep and Parry should gain their cup winner's medal – Birkett the double international, Ogilvie and Field the great servants, Prinsep of such a young age and Parry the inspirational leader. They managed it just in time, for the winds of change were coming to English football, a change which would appear as a precipitous revolution when the old guard of southern amateurs made way for the new wave of northern professionals in what proved to be an irreversible *coup d'état*, albeit unintentionally executed. The scene was set for the game to take the next step in its development.

Conclusion

Chapter 3 represents the dominance of the FA Cup by the southern amateurs, largely made up of ex-public schoolboys and former undergraduates – and, indeed, postgraduates and staff – from Cambridge and Oxford Universities. Within a couple of seasons, a sprinkling of provincial clubs became involved – Sheffield and Shropshire Wanderers are the primary examples – though each was comprised of players who were overwhelmingly middle class. Only towards the end of the decade would teams from a different social stratum begin to make even the slightest of impacts. The cup, even though it was marketed on a national basis, did not instantly – or even within a few seasons – stimulate interest in the game much further afield than the Home Counties. The 1877–8 season began a more widespread geographical process with teams entering from Lancashire, Lincolnshire, Scotland, Dorset, Wales, Shropshire, South Yorkshire, and Nottinghamshire, together with the two universities. One continued disappointing aspect for the FA would have been the total number of clubs involved in the cup, which lagged behind in popularity to its Scottish counterpart.

This chapter has explored several different storylines which provide original data about the FA Cup. The real origins of Panthers have been revealed, providing evidence of top-down diffusion from former public schoolboys returning home with an intention of continuing to play football. These considerations have echoes of the 'origins of football debate' which began around 20 years ago and, in a nutshell, represented a polarised view of the development of the game between 'orthodox' and 'revisionist' opinion, the former willing to accept that former public schoolboys had, indeed, been most influential while the latter believing that their influence should be diluted. Over the years, the two camps have become accepting of the other's interpretations, though the debate's most significant contribution is that new research and writing has been carried out with the consequence that the overall body of knowledge has been increased.

In terms of diffusion by returning public schoolboys to their original communities, there remains a distinct realisation that something more than this kind of stimulation was responsible for the rapid rise of football in the pantheon of preferred sporting activities in the latter part of the 19th century. The game clearly already held a foothold in lower-class society in a more regular form than the set piece mob/folk games held on festival days. This deep consciousness almost certainly added to any encouragement provided by returning or incumbent old boys and, although former public schoolboys coming home and teaching the local working class how to play football may smack of the partially discredited orthodox history of the game, it *did* happen to a considerable degree and is exhibited most frequently in local studies based around North East England, London, Nottinghamshire, South Derbyshire, Shrewsbury and Lincolnshire.[69] This is not to place the former public schoolboys on a footballing pedestal whereby they were condescendingly instructing locals in a game with which the latter were unfamiliar. However, football *had* been moved on in the major public schools and the version that former public schoolboys were attempting to inculcate *was* more rational, more organised and more 'civilised', in that it was safer and less physical and so could be played more regularly, though it was not an entirely new sport. The latter point may explain why versions of the game spread so quickly in the 1860s and 1870s. The Panthers' origins would not have been wholly public-school oriented, though being the most socially powerful, their founders provided a suitable example of this kind of sports diffusion.

Nottingham Forest's unheralded path to relative success has been unearthed, showing a middle-class membership based mainly in the lace trade, springing from a social class similar to those footballers and administrators in Sheffield; Stafford Road's story, along with a brief tribute to Charles Crump, has been undertaken, illustrating what the future held for the game – talented middle-class administrators organising a gifted (in football terms) lower-class workforce. If Sheffield and London had provided the game with their earliest clubs, the East and West Midlands would, prior to Lancashire's rapid leap forward, afford football its second phase of organisational development. This evidence represents fairly new ground, but the next stage of the competition's narrative would see the sport digress almost completely from its previous path – a shift to working-class supremacy on the pitch leading to the acceptance of professionalism as a result of the worst kept secret being revealed in the FA Cup.

Notes

1 Cavallini, *Wanderers*, 140.
2 *London Evening Standard*, 19 December 1888.
3 Harvey, *Football*.
4 Bradbury, *Lost Teams of the South*, 324.
5 *Windsor and Eton Express*, 10 December 1870.
6 Ibid, 11 February 1871.
7 The first born of the six Bambridge children (there were five brothers and a sister) similarly called William Samuel after his father, was also a footballer and the author of one of two letters to *The Field* on 10 March 1877, which championed a national code of rules for football in England and Scotland.
8 *Bell's Life*, 30 November 1872. At that point, the officials would include a neutral referee and two umpires, one from each club. If one umpire was of the opinion that a goal should be disputed, the decision was referred to the referee, who would adjudicate. Clubs also disputed goals after the match had finished and games were replayed if their objection was upheld. For instance, the 1886–7 fifth round tie between Lockwood Brothers from Sheffield and West Bromwich Albion.
9 *Morning Advertiser*, 9 December 1872.
10 *Morning Advertiser*, 28 October 1872.
11 *North British Daily Mail*, 17 February 1873.
12 *Glasgow Herald*, 3 March 1873.
13 Cavallini, *Wanderers*, 130.
14 Some accounts have the kick-off as 11.00 a.m. For instance, Williams, *Code War*, 44.
15 *London Daily News*, 31 March 1873.
16 *Morning Post*, 31 March 1873.
17 *Daily News* (London), 31 March 1873.
18 For early Shropshire football, see Curry, 'Early football in and around Shrewsbury'.
19 The Raven Hotel was on Castle Street in Shrewsbury until the early 1960s when it was replaced by a Woolworth's store.
20 *Sheffield and Rotherham Independent*, 19 November 1873.
21 *Bridport News*, 19 December 1873.
22 Interestingly, Farquharson married in New Brunswick, Canada in 1871.
23 *Southern Times and Dorset County Herald*, 13 November 1875.
24 Wainewright, *Winchester College Register*. Druitt came originally from Wimborne, entered the law profession, but tragically drowned at Chiswick in 1888.
25 *The Field*, 13 November 1875.
26 *Sporting Gazette*, 13 November 1875. Unfortunately, the nature of these trial matches has been impossible to discover. Nevertheless, the point about Farquharson's high level of football ability seems well made.

66   The beginnings of change

27 *Lloyd's Weekly Newspaper*, 10 December 1876.
28 *Bell's Life* gives the former venue while the *Sheffield Daily Telegraph* (12 November 1877) says the latter, though the two locations are just seven miles distant from each other.
29 *Salisbury and Winchester Journal*, 16 April 1881.
30 *The Field*, 10 March 1877, 281.
31 James, *Emergence of Footballing Cultures*, 89.
32 *Sheffield and Rotherham Independent*, 5 November 1877.
33 Ibid, 21 December 1877.
34 Ibid, 25 February 1878.
35 Arthur Cursham played his last game for the Nottingham club in April 1884. He promptly emigrated to Florida where he died of yellow fever in December of the same year. See Brown, *Official History of Notts. County*, 14–5.
36 Wallis, *Sheffield Collegiate*.
37 *Sheffield and Rotherham Independent*, 22 October 1877.
38 The *Manchester Courier and Lancashire General Advertiser* (31 December 1877) felt that Darwen had just about merited the win while the *Sheffield and Rotherham Independent* report of the same date argued that Sheffield deserved the victory.
39 See Curry, 'Clodhoppers'.
40 Widdowson's first name on his birth certificate was 'Sam'.
41 *Sheffield and Rotherham Independent*, 20 and 25 February 1880.
42 *Sheffield Daily Telegraph*, 27 February 1880; *Nottingham Evening Post*, 28 February 1880.
43 Wright, *Forever Forest*, Chapter Three.
44 The former episode was thought to have taken place in 1878, but recent research by Keith Warsop has found that the match in question, Nottingham Forest versus Sheffield Norfolk, happened as early as 9 March 1872 (*Sheffield Daily Telegraph*, 11 March 1872). Ten days later (*Sheffield Daily Telegraph*, 19 March 1872), William Brown, one of the founders of Forest, was reported as having made the suggestion that 'each umpire should be furnished with a whistle, which he should blow in case of granting an appeal for a foul'. Interestingly, Forest's secretary/treasurer, Walter Roe Lymbery, is recorded as buying an umpire's whistle for the club in his accounts book in December 1872. The report of 11 March mentions the dispute but has nothing on a whistle. Warsop has written an unpublished article entitled, 'The Referee's Whistle: Another Football "Myth" Clarified'. Conversation with Keith Warsop, 10 January 2022.
45 *Sheffield Daily Telegraph*, 29 January 1879. There is no hard evidence of Mark Holroyd's occupation, though playing for a team from a lacemaking factory, Thomas Herbert & Co., he did probably work in that industry. 'Lace salesman' is the educated guess of Tony Brown.
46 My thanks to Tony Brown for this biography.
47 *Nottingham Journal*, 17 March 1874.
48 Ibid, 12 December 1874.
49 Ibid, 25 January 1876.
50 *Nottinghamshire Guardian*, 13 October 1876.
51 Ibid, 1 February 1878.
52 *Nottingham Evening Post*, 31 October 1881.
53 *The Sportsman*, 12 November 1883.
54 *Nottingham Journal*, 6 December 1884. By 1891 he had married Elizabeth Richards Bateson in Chingford, Essex, remaining around the east of the capital until 1906 when he passed away in West Ham.
55 *The Field*, 26 February 1881.
56 *Sheffield and Rotherham Independent*, 21 March 1881.
57 *Midland Examiner and Times*, 2 June 1877.
58 Bradbury, *Lost Teams of the Midlands*, 315–21.
59 *Glasgow Herald*, 20 January 1885.

60 Two possible points of misunderstanding in terms of club names should be clarified. The Kildare club, which entered the FA Cup from 1879–80 to 1882–3, has been thought to be from Ireland. This was not the case. It consisted of employees from William Whiteley's retail company and department store in West London, with newspaper reports recording it as playing at Kensal Green. The name Kildare came from Whiteley's residence at Kildare Terrace, Bayswater. It was a multi-sports club offering rowing, athletics – its 1876 sports attracted nearly 3,000 people to Lillie Bridge – and cricket, together with a noted brass band and Rifle Corps, all provided by William Whiteley, who gained a reputation as a philanthropist and muscular Christian. The Rangers club which was involved in 1880–1 and 1881–2 was not the Scottish side of the same name. They were southern amateurs who played home games on Clapham Common.
61 *The Sportsman*, 12 April 1880.
62 Warsop, *Early F.A. Cup Finals*, 96–7.
63 Cavallini, *Clapham Rovers*, 46–51.
64 Ibid, 115–32. Also, Warsop, *Early F.A. Cup Finals*.
65 *Sheffield and Rotherham Independent*, 28 March 1881.
66 *Sheffield Daily Telegraph*, 11 April 1881.
67 Ibid.
68 Bailey, *From Cloister to Cup Finals*.
69 Curry, 'Football in the capital'; Joannou and Candlish, 'Football hotbed'; Curry, 'Stunted growth'; Curry and Dunning, 'The early development of the game in Nottinghamshire'; Curry, 'Early football in and around Shrewsbury'; and Curry, 'Early football in Lincolnshire'.

4 The rise of East Lancashire

Introduction

This chapter is about transition: the evolution of a national football cup competition from one which was dominated by teams from the upper strata of mid-to-late Victorian English society to a far more serious series of contests eventually largely inhabited and controlled – at least on the field of play and at the élite level – by working-class professionals.

The 1882–3 season saw the FA Cup won for the first time by a team from outside the southern amateur sphere of influence. Much has been written about Blackburn Olympic's triumph and, while it would be wrong to ignore it completely, this book is much more concerned with bringing to the reader's attention those developments which have only received scant recognition up to this point. Despite no southern amateur XI being ultimately victorious after this point, they did not disappear from view completely. In 1884–5, Old Carthusians were semi-finalists, though their passage in three of the previous rounds had been sprinkled with victories over lesser lights such as Marlow, Grimsby Town and Acton. However, they had recorded a fine single goal success at Church in East Lancashire in the sixth round. The home team that day included James Beresford from Staveley in Derbyshire – a noted covert professional – and it may have been interesting to have observed the southern club's reaction had they lost the game. A fuller rendition of his story will appear in Chapter 5. Professionalism had not been legalised by this time and it was the likes of Beresford, playing for money and, additionally and more contentiously, an importation, that rankled with those still determined to uphold amateur values and stamp out remuneration and its generally undesirable, over-serious side effects. These win-at-all-costs attitudes were, indeed, generally anathema to southern amateurs, but it might be worthy of note that they produced some positive effects, such as maximising skill levels through extended periods of practice and much improved fitness from prolonged physical training. Old Carthusians fielded a strong team which included Percy Melmoth Walters and his brother Arthur Melmoth Walters together with their captain Edward Hagarty Parry, all England internationals.[1] The semi-final found them out, as they were soundly beaten 5-1 by eventual winners Blackburn Rovers.

In the following season, 1885–6, another southern amateur team attempted to recreate past glories when Swifts reached the penultimate stage of the competition.

Despite only losing by two goals to one, the London team was outclassed, again by eventual winners Blackburn Rovers, notwithstanding the presence of Edward Charles Bambridge for Swifts, a character mentioned in Chapter 3 and an England international. Swifts were regarded as a scratch side and, though they defended gallantly for most of the match, were plainly out of their depth.[2] So, the odd incursion aside, amateur combinations from the south and their involvement in the final ties of the cup was at an end. A new generation of clubs was largely made up of a different class of people with contrasting attitudes who hailed from other geographical regions of the country. Darwen's exploits did not, however, open the floodgates for provincial sides – it was to be a much more slow-moving process – as, in the 1879–80 season, only Blackburn Rovers from East Lancashire reached the third round. In terms of number of entries, provincial clubs made up over half by the 1882–3 season, which, coincidentally, was the first year that an XI from the provinces was victorious in the cup, emphasising that the campaign was a turning point in more ways than just the winning of the trophy by Olympic. The draw, however, remained skewed for as long as possible, with regional ties being deliberately sought, which was an understandable step to take despite more efficient transport links. Had this not been so, it may have been that one or two geographical regions, probably either East Lancashire, the West Midlands or a combination of both, may have dominated proceedings had the draw been open nationally much earlier.

This beginning of the transference of footballing supremacy is adequately demonstrated in a list of FA Cup winners from the 1882–3 season onwards (see Appendix 1), but this should not be seen as a complete annexation of success, an instant passing of the torch or even an inevitability. The old boys certainly did not think of themselves as a total lost cause at the time, as no one could have predicted that teams representing their social class had won their last FA Cup. It was unfortunate for subsequent football historians that no southern amateur combination even reached an FA Cup Final following the 1882–3 season, as the results suggest that it was some kind of watershed moment, when supremacy passed instantly from one social group to another. The appearance of a 'precipitous revolution' noted at the end of Chapter 3 was exactly that. Christopher Andrew marks Olympic's triumph as 'the conquest of Patrician by Plebeian' and 'the victory of the emergent professional over the declining amateur',[3] which is far too simplistic. There were subtleties of class distinction within the Olympic XI as will be demonstrated later in this chapter. Andrew's explanation encourages sociologists or historians searching for simple dichotomies; the narrative was far, far more complex. Yet, at first glance and to the untrained eye, it is hard to dispute the evidence. Following the 1882–3 triumph of Blackburn Olympic, no southern amateur team would again come close to lifting the trophy.

Having set the scene regarding events on the field, this chapter will quickly concentrate on an examination of early professionalism in English football. The process was covert at this point, though it was a poorly kept secret, with firm evidence of payment for playing and importation emanating from the Sheffield area. The narrative will also note the exact backgrounds of players in three successful early Lancashire-based XIs – Darwen, Blackburn Olympic and Blackburn Rovers

– and focus on an over-romanticisation of the socio-cultural mix of these clubs, which has suffered from a generalised misrepresentation in football history over the years. The latter two clubs won the FA Cup, but along with Darwen, were indicative of the contradictory privileged and professional milieus which were operating in football at that time. In other words, simply because a team represented a working-class community, it did not necessarily mean that its players were solely from that section of society. However, perhaps the most significant story will be the one related about George Wilson, who accepted the offer of a substantial amount of money to play football for Blackburn Olympic and moved from South Yorkshire to East Lancashire in 1882. Most football history connoisseurs will be well acquainted with Jack Hunter, who undertook a similar journey around the same time, but although usually rating a mention in contemporary accounts, there has been little if any research attempted on Wilson. The chapter draws to a close with the 'professional cat being let out of the bag' in an FA Cup tie, the formation of the British Football Association to rival the FA and real fears of a schism in the game being expressed over the disagreements regarding professionalisation.

As described in the Introduction to this book, concepts in the figurational sociology of Norbert Elias will now be employed to tease out intricacies involved in the professional debate.

★★★

The professionalisation of English football is a good example of what Elias would have characterised as a long-term process. It would have been linked to growing seriousness in sport, where the importance of winning had grown throughout the 19th century and was reflected in the importance of the outcome – that is, the result – of the match or encounter. This process developed alongside the increasing complexity of societal interdependencies created by more reliable transport links and rising literacy rates, the significance of identity in smaller working-class communities, the introduction of local, national and international competition and the continued development of wagering on sporting contests. This extensive list of factors illustrates that multiple causes were at work, allowing us to formulate ideas and hypotheses not bound by monocausal explanations such as the 'Industrial Revolution'. These processes led directly to the sport's 'monetisation', with charges being made for admission – that is, 'gate-taking' – creating the phenomenon of spectatorism, with capitalist entrepreneurs not only eager to make a profit but also to allocate some of this money to attracting better players. Indeed, they soon felt obliged to do so, as without effective performers to produce winning results, their team would not attract large attendances. This became part of a self-perpetuating circle, which involved profits from attendances providing the finances to offer suitable playing resources to ensure on-field success. The sport's new-found status, plus the fact that local communities often sought and found gratification and positive identity in expressing support for their teams, gave football the possibility of attracting large crowds. This, together with a recognition by players and spectators alike that football possessed a highly agreeable 'tension balance', a game with acceptable risks that remained relatively safe but was capable of providing emotional pleasure – and, of course, disappointment – to those playing or watching, further increased its popularity. A gradual erosion of 'amateur' values, one of which was playing sport for no extrinsic reward, was represented by attitudes and structures that were 'professional' in form. However, they were never intended, deliberate processes, but were rather 'blind' or 'unplanned', the outcome of the fusion of the purposive though not necessarily pre-meditated actions of human beings interweaving over several generations. In short, a long-term sociological process.

Paying football players to take part in the game was nothing new by the early 1880s. No one can be sure when the first person received remuneration for their soccer skills, but by the 1870s, as more footballers from the industrial classes became involved, they were not averse to augmenting their often meagre incomes from their day-to-day employment with monetary incentives from their ability to play football. It should come as no surprise to learn that the very first large-scale footballing subculture, located in Sheffield and its surrounds, provided the initial reliable evidence, albeit on a limited scale, to suggest at least one individual was receiving financial recompense for playing the game. James Joseph Lang was not only gaining from his football skills, he was also a dreaded 'importation'. That is, he was coaxed from his native city – in this case Glasgow – to another area, with the sole intention of utilising him to win football matches. The action of importation was frowned upon because, at that point, the vast majority of football followers preferred that their local team used home-grown players, even to the point that those footballers might have received the occasional discreet payment. Eventually, importation, if it produced winning results, became accepted practice in the football world, but in the 1870s it provoked indignation.

Lang flourished with the Wednesday club in Sheffield, having played his first match for them on 25 November 1876, either being used over a whole season when he was resident in Sheffield – for instance 1879–80 – or simply being invited down for the occasional prestigious cup games, e.g. 6 March 1882, for the FA Cup Semi-Final draw against Blackburn Rovers and the replay nine days later. The introduction of Lang for specific, important matches probably substantiates that he was, indeed, being paid for his services. No doubt his payment included train fares, accommodation, meals and/or money for taking part in a particular match – otherwise, why would he have travelled so far in the first place? Indeed, he was leaving Glasgow, which was about to supersede any English city for the extent of its footballing subculture, but more significantly, administrators there would continue to deplore professionalism and its exponents. However, while Sheffield effectively became the first sporting environment to sustain extensive club football, it is interesting to note that, although Lang may have been what might loosely be termed the 'first professional', this process did not flourish locally.[4] The first large-scale instance of 'professionalisation' would happen far more overtly in East Lancashire, though Lang's example would become one of several isolated cases of that process in Sheffield. His career raises the question of why other Sheffield clubs did not follow Wednesday's lead in importing better players on a larger scale, though that organisation was probably already tolerating England international Billy Mosforth's tendency to accept money – albeit surreptitiously – for playing. Mosforth, however, was not a dreaded importation, and he was a popular performer on football fields in Sheffield. The city's football administrators so tenaciously opposed payment for playing, that players such as Jack Hunter, who would lead Blackburn Olympic to FA Cup glory in 1882–3, determined to 'follow the money', were forced to move elsewhere to do so. Hunter, though a Sheffield native and not an importation was, for some reason, regarded as a renegade, while Mosforth traded on his brash charisma. It might subsequently come as no surprise that it was clubs from East Lancashire, their playing strength bolstered by 'professionalisation', importation or not, which would be the first to challenge and eventually break the dominance of the southern amateurs in the FA Cup competition.

A trawl through British newspapers of the 1870s reveals very little in terms of football professionalism, though mentions abound of the practice in cricket, cycling, athletics and pedestrianism. However, the beginnings of a widespread professional football culture were commencing in East Lancashire, a region stretching from Blackburn and Darwen in the west, Clitheroe to the north, Colne in the east and southwards towards the outskirts of Bolton, much of the area following the course of the River Hyndburn. Here were incredibly close-knit communities which stood as quite separate entities, but virtually adjacent to each other. Good examples are Church and Accrington, which lie just one mile apart, with both towns developing very competitive football teams. Meaningful rivalries usually meant communities forming identities around symbols of their villages or towns, with representatives going to extraordinary lengths to outshine nearby adversaries. However, rivalry was not the only factor. Social interdependency chains, fuelled by more efficient transport links, would have been lengthening, thereby accentuating competition between an increasing number of communities. But when compared with a more mature footballing subculture such as Sheffield, East Lancashire was a quite different proposition. The key to their separate stories, sociologically at least, was, unsurprisingly, people. In Sheffield, upper-middle-class men, such as the Cleggs and William Peirce-Dix, were the most influential footballing figures in South Yorkshire and ensured that there would be no early blossoming of soccer professionalism in the steel city. In East Lancashire, a lower-middle-class leisure stratum of society, familiar with payment for sports such as pedestrianism and cricket and pressured by rivalries demanding success, more readily accepted the practice.[5] It is important that events there are studied in greater detail, as it was probable that the FA Cup, bringing as it did new attitudes to winning through growing seriousness, unintentionally served as one of the catalysts for a part of football's monetisation.

One of the earliest clubs in East Lancashire was Turton FC, just north of Bolton, which came initially under the influence of John Charles Kay (Harrow School 1868–70) and Robert Arthur Kay (Harrow School 1872–5), two brothers who lived at the local manor house of Turton Tower. Another Old Harrovian, Albert Neilson Hornby (Harrow School 1862–5; Oxford University 1865),[6] was prominent in nearby Blackburn sporting circles and would go on to captain England at cricket and rugby. At first, organised football matches in the area were played to Harrow rules, though Peter Swain notes that because of the impact and cajoling of more lower-middle-class men, such as William Thomas Dixon of Turton and

Thomas Hindle of Darwen, these were soon replaced by the laws of the FA.[7] However, the original impetus provided by Old Harrovians at least guaranteed that the preferred football form would be of the kicking and dribbling variety as opposed to a rugby-like code. As time went on, former public schoolboy influence waned, but outcomes could have been radically different had, as in Manchester, Old Rugbeians been the dominant actors.[8]

On 28 September 1878, the Lancashire FA – it could easily have been called the East Lancashire FA judging by the number of clubs from there – was formed in Darwen, this being indicative of a rapid growth in the soccer-like form of football in the area. The following clubs were the first members of the Lancashire Football Association: Astley Bridge, Blackburn Rovers, Blackburn Christ Church, Livesey United, Blackburn Park Road, Blackburn St. George's, Blackburn St. Mark's, Bolton Emmanuel, Bolton North End, Bolton Wanderers, Bolton St. George's, Bolton Rovers, Bolton St. Paul's, Church, Clough Fold, Myrtle Grove, Darwen, Lower Darwen, Darwen Grasshoppers, Darwen Rangers, Darwen Lower Chapel, Darwen St. James', Eagley, Enfield, Great Lever, Haslingden Rangers, Haslingden Grange and Turton. By the early 1880s other teams from the area could be added to this list: Accrington, Clitheroe, Egerton, Halliwell, Irwell Springs, Rossendale and Witton. It is, therefore, no exaggeration to say that, by around 1880, East Lancashire was a real hotbed of association football.[9] Lancashire clubs first entered the FA Cup in 1877–8, in the form of Darwen and Manchester, the latter having adhered to FA laws since 1875.[10] There appeared to have been little in terms of prior football contact between the two areas of Lancashire, their footballing subcultures developing largely independent of each other, with Manchester being a rugby outpost.

The following season, as covered in Chapter 3 of this book, saw the epic Darwen–Old Etonians tie which extended to three games. Significantly, it was around this time that the *Darwen Cricket and Football Times*[11] recorded the following proposed rule changes for consideration at the annual general meeting of the FA to be held on 27 February:

CHALLENGE CUP COMPETITION PROPOSED BY OLD HARROVIANS

1. That no club which does not consist entirely of amateurs, as defined by rules to be drawn up by the committee, be entitled to compete in the Challenge Cup Competition.
2. That no club which does not exact some qualification for membership be entitled to compete in the Challenge Cup Competition. The sufficiency of such qualification to be determined by the committee.
3. That no player be allowed to take part in any of the cup ties otherwise than on behalf of his regiment, university, school or local club, unless he shall have been duly elected a member of, and paid his subscriptions to such club in the preceding or some earlier season.

The proposal 'met with great disapproval' from those present and was not carried, but the timing of these suggestions is of particular significance.[12] The first Old Etonians–Darwen match was played on 13 February 1879 and the rule amendments appeared in a Darwen newspaper the day after. They might, therefore, be seen as a direct reaction to the first FA Cup encounter between those two sides, but we must remind ourselves that the Darwen club had already visited the south and defeated Remnants FC of Slough, squeezing through by the odd goal in five.[13] Southern footballers may have been shaken by this growing challenge to their playing superiority, together with the threat now being posed to their cherished amateur values. Their game was coming under threat from a section of English society who would be unable or unwilling − because of their perceived lack of a public-school education and, therefore, absence of any exposure to the supposedly superior value system present in those institutions − to uphold 'existing' and 'preferred' standards of behaviour in the game.[14]

There is little doubt that the Old Harrovians' proposals were a tilt towards strong rumours circulating at the time concerning the payment and importation of players by association clubs based in Lancashire. While the initial proposal attempted to deal with the monetary issue, the second and third propositions sought to eradicate the practice of northern clubs importing players simply for important cup ties, a process which, in many cases, ended with the player − quite often, though not always, a Scot − taking up permanent residence in the region. The infractions remained a double-edged sword − payment and importation.

★★★

The notion of 'who was the first professional footballer?' is rightly dismissed as a chimera, though among the first were two Scots other than James Lang, who were probably the direct cause of the Old Harrovian proposals. The players involved were Fergus 'Fergie' Suter and James 'Jimmy' Love, the noted 'Scotch professors' as they and other early examples from that country have been termed, in Darwen's three games against the Old Etonians; Suter will also be noted in the Blackburn Rovers 1883−4 FA Cup winning XI. That a situation existed in East Lancashire which enabled the development of professionalism in football is undeniable, this being in stark contrast to Sheffield where, as the first substantial footballing subculture, it might have been expected to thrive. Clearly, it is important that the process surrounding payment for playing requires exploration, though firstly, because Scotland provided so many of its 'exponents', a very brief examination of the situation there should be attempted.

In a nutshell, Queen's Park dominated football in Scotland during the 1870s and even beyond. The club was victorious in eight of the first 13 Scottish FA Cups, though Vale of Leven, Renton and Dumbarton enjoyed some success. Below those four clubs came teams such as Partick FC of Glasgow, not to be confused with Partick Thistle FC. The former was the older club, being founded in 1875, though when they became extinct in 1885, Thistle took over the disused facilities.[15] Partick first visited East Lancashire in January 1876 and easily beat Darwen on New Year's Day, when Peter Andrews − another Scot who would eventually find himself playing football in England − was, with three other Eastern club men, taking part as a guest.[16] But as Andy Mitchell has identified, this was not a random connection, rather William Kirkham − a Darwen native − had moved to Partick, helped to found the football club, then returned to Lancashire and instigated his former club's subsequent visits.[17] While Partick would not be classed with the likes of Queen's Park and Vale of Leven, it nevertheless established a respectable reputation for itself and was obviously organised enough to undertake no doubt financially rewarding tours to East Lancashire.

James Love is identified as representing Darwen FC in three matches – against Church on 26 October 1878, Blackburn Rovers on 2 November 1878 and Attercliffe on 9 November 1878 – although Fergus Suter's name fails to appear in newspaper reports until December. There is a possibility that Suter played his initial game for the club against Accrington, though there was no mention in the press of the time.[18] He appears to have been imported in time for the FA Cup tie with local rivals Eagley, a tie Darwen won after a replay, with Suter involved in both games played on 7 and 21 December. He would be heavily involved in Darwen's ultimately futile struggles against the Old Etonians in the FA Cup of the 1878–9 season. As well as having a close connection with the early FA Cup, Suter, like George Wilson whose story is related later in this chapter, was one of the precursors of football professionalism as well as being a bridge between the two processes of covert and overt payment. Suter's life in the game was full of controversy as, at the beginning of the 1880–1 season, he decided to throw in his lot with Blackburn Rovers, who had simply made him a better offer for his talents. As an 'Anglo' – a Scot playing football in England – he was now ignored by Scottish selectors and never received international recognition. The Scottish FA only relaxed this restriction in 1896 following six games without a win against the 'Auld Enemy' – England. Despite all this, Suter enjoyed a highly successful career as, along with fellow Scots Hugh McIntyre and Jimmy Douglas, he gained three consecutive FA Cup winner's medals with Rovers from 1883–4 to 1885–6. The connection between the two clubs and areas of Partick and Darwen effectively blazed the trail for subsequent 'Scotch professors' to make the lucrative move to Lancashire. However, while Suter prospered, poor James Love suffered an altogether different fate, joining the army but dying from fever following the battle for Alexandria, Egypt in 1882.[19]

On the field, Blackburn Rovers became the first club outside the southern amateurs to reach an FA Cup Final, losing by the only goal to Old Etonians in 1881–2. In their semi-final, the Blackburn side had disposed of Sheffield Wednesday after a replay, two games which would have made interesting viewing with on one side Fergus Suter of Rovers, and opposing him James Lang of Wednesday, both of whom had claims to be the first professional footballer.[20] The venues used for the two games were intriguing choices. The initial draw was played out at St. John's Ground, Fartown, Huddersfield, a stadium which was the home of the Huddersfield Cricket, Athletic and Football Club from 1878 to 1892 and one of the best-appointed venues in the north of England.[21] This represented the first time that an FA Cup Semi-Final had taken place at somewhere other than Kennington Oval. Indeed, following the 1882–3 semi-final between Old Etonians and Notts. County, 'The Oval' would never be used again in that capacity, but would host the final up to and including the 1891–2 season. The replay of the Wednesday–Blackburn semi-final took place at rugby-playing Manchester Football Club's ground at

Whalley Range to the south of the city centre, representing further proselytising work on behalf of the association game. The members of the FA must have been satisfied with arrangements there, as they returned the following season for the semi-final between Blackburn Olympic and Old Carthusians. The ground at Whalley Range did host other prestigious matches: when England beat Ireland by four goals to nil in a British Championship game on 28 February 1885, as well as eight England rugby international fixtures. Presumably, one of the main reasons for rugby clubs to allow soccer enthusiasts to use their facilities, must surely have been largely financial, as rivalry between the two codes still remained. However, the fact that two northern clubs were competing in 1881–2 must have had an influence on the choice of venue, together with the fact that both stadia were capable of managing large crowds.

East Lancashire romanticised

There can be little doubt that East Lancashire became a power in the English football world in the 1880s. This was, indeed, a reflection of FA Cup success, as in the nine seasons between 1882–3 and 1890–1, the cup was won six times by a side from Blackburn. However, have modern soccer historians been guilty of a fairly significant misrepresentation by promoting a romanticised, working-class ideal of perceived 'underdogs'[22] triumphing over a privileged élite, a process which has been achieved by marginally distorting the social make-up of teams from that region?

Let us first consider the Darwen side which took the Old Etonians to three games in the 1878–9 FA Cup. The names below are those that played for the East Lancashire side in the first of those matches. There were few changes over the three encounters though these have been documented both before and after Table 4.1.

There appears to be some discrepancy over a change made to the Darwen team for the first replay, which ended in another draw, this time two goals apiece. Some reports have a player called Thomas Williams replacing Tommy Marshall, whereas others say that Marshall remained in the line-up.[23] At least seven mentions have been uncovered which named Williams and three which listed Marshall. In none

Table 4.1 The Darwen line-up, with occupations, for the first game in their trilogy of matches versus Old Etonians

FA Cup Fourth Round 5	13 February 1879	Old Etonians 5 Darwen 5
John Duxbury	Gas meter inspector	
Fergus Suter	Footballer/Stonemason	
William Brindle	Paper maker	England international
William Henry Moorhouse	Loomer	
James Knowles	Book keeper, cotton mill	
Tommy Marshall	Cotton loomer	England international
James Love	Footballer	
James Gledhill	Doctor	
William Kirkham	Overlooker	
Tom Bury	Cotton weaver	
Robert Kirkham	Paper packer	

of the general reports of the match are the names of Williams or Marshall mentioned, other than in the line-ups. If guesswork were being employed by reporters, Marshall's name would be included, but from where did the surname Williams spring? There are no references to a Thomas Williams in other Darwen football reports around that time. Perhaps the last word should be with Keith Dewhurst from his book, *Underdogs*, charting the story of Darwen's cup exploits, where he states that 'on Saturday 8 March 1879, Darwen were unchanged…with Gledhill wide right and Marshall wide left'.[24]

For the second replay, which ended with a resounding victory by six goals to two for the Old Etonians, Darwen drafted in a replacement for William Kirkham in the form of William McLachlan, who was almost certainly specially imported from Partick FC in Glasgow. He was well known to the East Lancashire club which had close connections with Partick. McLachlan had actually visited with a 'Glasgow' team in the New Year of 1878 when the Scots lost 4-2 to Darwen.[25] McLachlan was a plumber/engineer who was born on 31 March 1857 and in 1881 lived on Merkland Street, Partick.

In recent times, many historians have characterised Darwen, Blackburn Olympic and Blackburn Rovers as football teams consisting solely of working-class individuals. There appear to be reasons for being slightly sceptical about the social make-up of some of the East Lancashire sides and, as a result, this process deserves more in-depth scrutiny. The Darwen side of 1878–9 has generally been described by football historians as containing players drawn exclusively from the working class. Here is a selection of their descriptions.

Bryon Butler said they were '[a] team of Lancashire mill workers'[26]; Geoffrey Green noted 'a team composed almost entirely of working lads and young men employed in the mills of that small Lancashire town'[27]; Alfred Gibson and William Pickford wrote that 'the team was comprised almost entirely of working lads and young men from the mills of that typical Lancashire town'[28]; while Morris Marples described them as '[a] humble local team of mill workers'.[29] Even 'Free Kick', the football columnist of the *Blackburn Standard* in the 1880s, emphatically spoke of their origins, emphasising that the Darwen players 'belong entirely to the working class'.[30] To a large extent, Table 4.1 generally supports these conclusions. However, in applying an absolute, these football historians have clearly been overcome with hyperbole in their haste to pigeon-hole the entire team as working class. It was not, and the existence of Dr. James Gledhill is indicative of the presence of a non-working-class participant.

Surprisingly, it was not to be Blackburn Rovers, Darwen, Nottingham Forest or even a club from Sheffield that was to be the first side outside the south to win the cup. Blackburn Olympic, in only their third tilt at the trophy – they had lost in the first round in both their previous attempts – were the slightly surprising winners. Scoring 35 goals and conceding just five, they were worthy victors, though we must consider more closely how a club which had only been in existence since 1878 could manage to win the FA Cup. The key lay in importation and surreptitious payment, though in this case, the hired help came from Sheffield/South Yorkshire rather than Scotland. The Olympic signed Jack Hunter and, along with him, George Wilson – the former driven from his native area under a cloud of

Table 4.2 The Blackburn Olympic line-up, with occupations, for the FA Cup Final, 1882–3

FA Cup Final	31 March 1883	Blackburn Olympic 2 Old Etonians 1
Thomas Hacking	Dentist[a]	
James Thomas Ward	Cotton weaver	England international
Squire Arthur Warburton	Master plumber	
Thomas Gibson	Dresser in iron foundry	
William Astley	Cotton weaver	
Jack Hunter	Footballer/Landlord	England international*
Thomas Dewhurst	Labourer in iron foundry	
Alfred Matthews	Gilder	
George Wilson	Footballer/Clerk	
James Costley	Weaver	
John Yates	Loomer	England international**

a By the 1891 UK Census, Hacking was referred to as a 'Dentist (Master)'. The occupation of each player is taken from the *Sheffield and Rotherham Independent*, 7 April 1883.
* Hunter was capped seven times while with Heeley in Sheffield before moving to Blackburn
** Yates was capped once in 1889 while with Burnley

allegations of professionalism, the latter motivated by increased financial reward, moving, it would seem, to a place with a more lenient view of payment for playing football or, at least, where administrators of clubs had found and accepted ways and means of facilitating the practice.[31] If Wilson was earning some money from football in South Yorkshire, which he probably was, he would almost certainly have earned substantially more in Blackburn.

Hunter was, by this time, an England international, having made his debut in 1878 against Scotland, though he was never capped following his move to Blackburn Olympic, being perceived as a professional outcast. He developed into what might be loosely termed as the first player/manager, a man who began to apply training and fitness regimes to football. The Olympic prepared for each cup tie and not just the final, supported by employers who even allowed their charges some time off for fitness work and whole free Saturdays when the team were involved in away fixtures. Most famously, the side trained for a whole week on the sands of Blackpool, the trip being financed as a result of collections in local mills and factories, something which epitomised the cherished identity created by the local team.[32] However, even some Lancastrians would have argued that these were hollow victories achieved by imported talent. Perhaps predictably, it is difficult to ignore such success on a national scale and not be carried along with it.

The game itself, together with other observations, makes interesting reading in the *Eton College Chronicle*, the magazine of the school:

> The match was decided at the Oval on March 31, between the Old Etonians and the Blackburn Olympic Club from Lancashire. The latter had made a considerable reputation by defeating Church, another Lancashire club who had previously beaten Darwen (the conquerors in the first round of Blackburn Rovers), and by extinguishing the chance of the Old Carthusians at Manchester in the other semi-final tie. So great was their ambition to wrest the cup from

the holders, that they introduced into football play a practice which has excited the greatest disapprobation in the South. For three weeks before the final match they went into a strict course of training, spending, so reports say, a considerable time at Blackpool, and some days at Bournemouth and Richmond. Though it may seem strange that a football eleven composed of mill-hands and working men should be able to sacrifice three weeks to train for one match, and to find the means to do so too, yet when we reflect on the thousands who attend and watch matches in Lancashire, and so swell the revenues of the Clubs, and on the enthusiasm of the employers of labour in the pursuits of successes of their countrymen it is not so surprising. To be brief the Blackburn men were in splendid condition for the match, and had spared no pains to gain victory. The Old Etonians played the same eleven as in the last previous matches, and had they only played in form approaching that which they displayed against Notts. would have won easily. No one will deny that they were the better team of the two, but it was their very confidence in this fact which probably lost them the match. Had they only been non-favourites, the result would have been different, for their play during the first part of the game was too casual, and they certainly should have gained more than one goal while fresh. As it was, this was the only point scored till half-time, when a most unfortunate accident occurred: Dunn was severely injured and had to leave the field, and shortly afterwards Goodhart was seized with cramp in both legs, and Macaulay received a nasty kick on the knee. This completed the 'rot' which had by this time set in, and the Northerners were not long in making matters even. After an hour and a half the score was equal, one goal to either side. Now came the turning point. The Association Committee had decided before the commencement of the match that an extra half hour should be played if the result was a draw. Neither side should have agreed to this, as there is no rule to force a club to play an extra half hour when only one day is fixed for a match; but the Northerners naturally did not object, knowing that their course of training would stand them in good stead, while the Old Etonians did not care to rebel against the decision of the superior body. In this fatal half hour the Olympic scored 1, the crowning point, and so gained the honour of being the first Northern Club to win the cup.[33]

It is important to challenge several misapprehensions that have arisen in connection with the Old Etonians–Blackburn Olympic match. Firstly, there is the question of southern amateur teams objecting to the methods used by Olympic in preparing for the final. There must be a modicum of truth in this as the *Eton College Chronicle* notes such disapproval from the south in general. However, certain writers, in their discriminatory use of only parts of the report, seem to have clouded the issue. Anton Rippon, for example, writes, 'The *Eton College Chronicle* said darkly, "It may seem strange that a football eleven composed of mill-hands and working men should be able to sacrifice three weeks to train for one match, and to find the means to do so"',[34] while according to Gordon Smailes, 'The *Eton Chronicle* hinted darkly that they [Olympic] were professionals'.[35] Deeper analysis of the report in the *Eton College Chronicle*, however, shows an almost grudging respect and admiration for the northern club, in particular for the direct financial support of the community in the form of paying spectators and benevolent employers, together with the 'splendid condition' of the Olympic players.

Rippon is also incorrect to suggest that 'The game went into extra-time, though there was no obligation on the part of Old Etonians to agree, especially since they had only ten men and were missing two other regular players. It was a magnanimous gesture'.[36] This was no generous act on the part of the Old Boys for, as the *Eton College Chronicle* rightly stated, both teams before kick-off had agreed upon an extra half hour. Finally, the *Eton College Chronicle* hints at over-confidence on the part of the Old Etonians, something which, because of the excellent past record of southern teams and their status as holders, is understandable. Perhaps, too, there was a hint of social superiority involved, leading to the misguided belief that the best artisans could never beat the leading aristocrats. *The Athletic News* of 21 March 1883, a Manchester-based newspaper, was left churlishly to poke fun at the upper-class Southerners' accents and at their invention of excuses for defeat. They wrote sarcastically of the 'beastly professional twaining those Owimpian few-wows had gone through that won the match'.

Blackburn Olympic's cup-winning side was certainly working class and besides a couple of imports from the Sheffield/South Yorkshire – the aforementioned Hunter and Wilson – it was made up of local players. However, of the locals, there was one interesting anomaly. Thomas Hacking, the goalkeeper, felt he was earning enough money from dentistry by 1885 that, as the game turned professional, he was able to remain an amateur and resist proposals from interested clubs, foremost of whom was Olympic. This gave him the opportunity to play for whichever club took his fancy come Saturday afternoon.[37] Of the two virtual professionals, Hunter's tale has been related extensively, but in line with much of the new material presented in this book, the story of George Wilson is less well known.

George William Wilson (born 5 May 1859 in Swinton, South Yorkshire) was not from the mainstream Sheffield footballing subculture, but hailed from the region between Sheffield and Doncaster, the industrial River Don Valley. Wilson was described as a commercial clerk in the 1881 UK Census in Swinton, where his father was part of a group of successful businessmen who set up a flourishing glassblowing company. He is occasionally listed as playing for Kilnhurst and Rawmarsh, but more particularly for Mexborough. These clubs generally played in fixtures involving other teams in the Sheffield New Football Association, formed in 1877 following the Sheffield FA's decision to prohibit from membership all clubs under two years old. The organisation would change its name to the Hallamshire FA in 1881[38] and amalgamate with the Sheffield FA at the end of the 1886–7 season to form, as is still the case in 2022, the Sheffield and Hallamshire Football Association. Wilson played for the New Association's representative side and seemed a long throw expert. He was also an able cricketer, playing mostly for his local club, Swinton, and he may have transferred his skills with his hands from that sport to football. It is worth remembering that in the early 1880s, the throw-in would have been a javelin-type effort or sling with a straight arm, not the two-handed variety of today, which was only universally agreed in late 1882 and adopted by the FA in 1883.

Wilson's first appearance in the Blackburn Olympic side came at Nottingham Forest on 14 October 1882, a game Olympic lost by a single disputed goal, succumbing to frustration or simply being bad losers by walking off just before the end. He was also present in a Lancashire Football Association Cup game at Padiham Church a week later, which Olympic won easily. Unfortunately, the newspaper report mentioned that the losers would object to Wilson's participation as he had not been a member of the Olympic club for more than two weeks;[39] the Lancashire FA awarded the tie to Olympic's opponents. Certainly, his early games for Olympic were quite controversial. The most plausible explanation for Wilson's presence in East Lancashire was that he was 'poached' by Jack Hunter, also, of course, from the Sheffield area. The *Sheffield and Rotherham Independent* noted that Wilson was 'one of the Sheffield Zulus, and when those players were debarred from playing for a season or two at Sheffield, he removed from Swinton near that town to Blackburn and joined the Olympians'.[40] The Zulus were a group of footballers, of which Hunter was arguably the leading light, playing exhibition games and pocketing the proceeds from attendance fees. These actions grossly offended the Sheffield FA who were stringently opposed to professionalism. There was undoubtedly some 'under-the-counter' payment going on in the city, especially to much sought-after performers such as England international Billy Mosforth, who also represented the Zulus.[41] These growing constraints may have encouraged Wilson to follow Hunter over the Pennines, although Wilson himself would not have felt unduly pressured by the over-zealous Sheffield FA, as he and his team Mexborough played under the auspices of the Sheffield New Association, a body seemingly less concerned with eradicating covert football professionalism. Wilson's name only appeared twice in Zulu line-ups, on Christmas Day 1880, against Hibernian in Edinburgh and on Shrove Tuesday, 1 March 1881 at Doncaster. The Sheffield FA forced eleven participants to apologise though, interestingly, the list of players only contained ten names.[42] It may be that Wilson was the 11th man and, because he was affiliated to the Sheffield New Association, he was not required formally to put pen to paper.[43]

Wilson was an unknown quantity and, in some ways, a gamble, but would in his one year with Olympic contribute as much as anyone – possibly more – to their unforgettable 1882–3 season. His importance was that he was a goal scorer, probably at that point in time an out-and-out centre forward, who would register an abundance of goals during the campaign. Wilson scored in every match of that season's FA Cup, which Olympic would go on to win, except the final. In all, he secured 11 of their 34 FA Cup goals. However, unlike Jack Hunter, who appeared to have moved permanently to East Lancashire, Wilson maintained close ties with South Yorkshire and was to be found playing for Mexborough in two games in January 1883. While one was a friendly against Rotherham, the other was an important Hallamshire cup tie against Intake, the winner of that competition in the two previous seasons. Wilson's presence was noted and his side easily beat the holders by six goals to two, with the Blackburn Olympic man netting a hat-trick. Clearly, he was 'imported' especially for that game, which took place on a Monday, warming up against Rotherham two days earlier in what proved to be a 'long weekend' sojourn. Significantly, he did not play for Mexborough on the following Saturday,[44] instead representing Olympic against Blackburn Rovers.

Revealingly, another note in the press confirmed a good deal of information on Wilson. The reporter in the *Sheffield and Rotherham Independent*,[45] quoting from an article in the *Preston Guardian*, wrote:

> George Wilson, centre forward, is a clerk. He was formerly one of the principal players of the Hallamshire (Sheffield New) Association…He was one of the Sheffield Zulus, and when those players were debarred from playing for a season or two at Sheffield, he removed from Swinton, near that town, to Blackburn, and joined the Olympians. Previous to his removal he was a half-back player, but he has proved a dashing forward. As he is a very strong player, he is not easily knocked off the ball, and he is also a good dribbler, and an unusually good shot at goal. This has been shown in the cup ties…

Surprisingly, he would turn his back on Olympic after just one season in Blackburn and it was expected that Wilson, 'the Swinton football player', would return to his native area to play for Mexborough in the following campaign.[46] He 'guested' for Olympic at the very start of the 1883–4 campaign in an exhibition game against Darwen in September, 1883.[47] The match, played at Dewsbury in Yorkshire, was designed to show 'the Rugby players the passing and dribbling of the Association game'. However, it appears that he was offered more generous terms by Preston North End where he reverted successfully to his previous position of half-back. Wilson also became the landlord of the Black-a-moor's Head public house in the town,[48] but his agreement with Preston, largely because of the obvious ties to the public house, was different to that with Olympic. His appearances for Preston were regular before Christmas 1883, but amounted to almost none in the New Year and he missed the iconic FA Cup tie against Upton Park, which was the prelude to professionalism. A clue to these events might be found in a report of an encounter with Padiham when Wilson 'did not play in anything like his usual form, his knee troubling him very much'.[49] It may have been that he was forced to take a rest from playing to recover from the injury, but the fact was that his name was not mentioned in either Preston or Mexborough in the New Year. This, together with a report of an end-of-season dinner for the former club stating that Wilson and others received medals as 'non-regular' members of the team, seems to suggest that he, for whatever reasons, did not feature as consistently as others. Importantly, his income would have been reduced, though the public house would no doubt have kept him fully employed and remunerated. Injuries incurred in football which interfered with a man's job of work would have been a problem and the area is under-researched. Certainly, in Sheffield, an accident fund was set up in 1867, to which players contributed a small sum in order to qualify for a greater amount if an injury sustained playing football prevented them from working (see the section on the Youdan Cup in Chapter 1).[50]

Wilson had also married in late October 1883, the reporter for the *Blackburn Times* tongue-in-cheek posing the question, 'Surely they [Preston North End] haven't found him a wife as well as a pub?'[51] Wilson's involvement as landlord of a public house seems to imply that he was fairly settled in Lancashire, but he returned to playing in Mexborough for the 1884–5 season, where his homecoming may have been connected with his marriage, as his new wife Hannah Hawkins had been born in Rawmarsh, South Yorkshire[52] – it would appear that Graham Phythian is incorrect to claim that Wilson married a 'Preston lass'.[53] He was not averse to helping out other teams, more particularly Wednesday, in two FA Cup encounters – continuing Wednesday's use of outstanding players for important cup ties – against Long Eaton Rangers and the defeat to Nottingham Forest.[54]

Just prior to his reappearance in Mexborough in 1884, his local club was accepted into membership of the Sheffield FA. Although Wilson had clearly forged a reputation for himself in the Hallamshire (New) FA, teams operating in that body were generally regarded as inferior to those in the Sheffield FA. The Mexborough club was, however, confident that it could win the most prestigious trophy in Sheffield football, the Challenge Cup, and with Wilson supplementing what was obviously a more than useful side, convinced it could carry it off. However, the club had to wait three seasons for its dream to become a reality. Finally, on Saturday 10 April 1886, Mexborough met Heeley at the Old Forge Ground, Newhall, Sheffield in the final of the Sheffield FA Challenge Cup in front of 2000 spectators. By his standards, Wilson had a quiet game as Mexborough prevailed by two goals to one. Interestingly, this was another personal 'final frustration' on his behalf – he was disappointing in the FA Cup Final of 1882–3 for Blackburn Olympic – despite his team's victory, making one suspect he may have been a 'fast track bully', demolishing weaker opposition but struggling against more able opponents, though his reputation may, of course, have preceded him, with adversaries marking him closely.

Despite this, he thus became one of the few men – another being his Olympic colleague Jack Hunter[55] – to win both the FA Cup and the Sheffield FA Challenge Cup. During that same season, when it might be argued that the Mexborough club had reached its zenith, it entered the FA Cup for the only time in those early years. The side drew with a strong Staveley side, one goal apiece at Kilnhurst, a few miles from Mexborough,[56] but was forced to pull out of the replay as it was required to fulfil a Sheffield FA Challenge Cup fixture. However, perhaps strangely, Wilson did not play against Staveley in what was an important game, though he was present for the Sheffield cup tie which prevented Mexborough completing the replay, as it easily defeated Owlerton.[57] In terms of payment, the probability was that he was earning extra money from football, while holding down a job in midweek, though Mexborough would not have been able to afford wages as high as those at Olympic and Preston.

Mexborough's footballing reputation petered out towards the end of the 1880s and it was, by that time, regarded as a minor club. Even Wilson deserted it and went to play for nearby Swinton, thereby returning to the place of his birth, but re-joined Mexborough in 1890–1 where he played as goalkeeper. This may have been related to a long-standing injury or simply older age creeping up on him, though it also indicated a wide-ranging skill set and certainly showed what a true all-round footballer he had become.[58] Wilson never again reached the heights of his cup-winning season with Blackburn Olympic and rarely played centre forward for an extended number of matches. There is a distinct feeling of the knee injury limiting his effectiveness with Wilson seeking to remedy this by taking up less demanding positions such as defender or goalkeeper.

More significantly, Wilson represented a fleeting conduit between the end of the amateur dominance of the FA Cup and its overt appropriation by professional forces within the game. This, of course, implies a simple transition from one philosophy to another, a watershed moment when one ideology gave way to a competing rival, which was palpably not the case. The payment of footballers had been taking place for years and amateur values would exist long after the approval of recompense, but by 1890, the dominant paradigm had changed in English football. Wilson's story, nevertheless, as well as providing information on an under-researched individual, does effectively relate the long-term processes at work in the game over the five-year period from 1880 to 1885.

If Olympic was the first northern team to win the FA Cup, no one can deny that Blackburn Rovers dominated the competition between 1883–4 and 1890–1, when it won the cup five times in those eight seasons. Four members of the 1883–4 FA Cup winning team – its first triumph in the competition – were imported Scottish professionals: Fergus Suter, Hugh McIntyre, Jimmy Douglas and John Inglis. But what of the other seven players?

The team consisted of four Scottish professionals, one ex-public schoolboy, four lower-middle-class white-collar workers and one genuine industrial worker. As well as John Hargreaves, the Malvern College link went further as John's brother Frederick William (Malvern College 1875–7) together with Doctor Haydock Greenwood (1877–8) – 'Doctor' was his actual Christian name – played regularly for Rovers in the latter half of the 1870s. By the time of the 1883–4 cup triumph, however, neither could force their way into the XI. Yet the occupations of the seven non-professionals seem to represent a stratum of society which was at least one rung above that inhabited by cotton mill workers and labourers.

It is a moot point whether the likes of Suter, McIntyre, Douglas, Inglis, Love, Hunter and Wilson should be referred to as footballers, as they were known to be involved in everyday employment. However, how much actual work they completed is open to argument. Perhaps today we might call them semi-professionals. As time went on, players such as the Rovers 'professionals' of 1884 were less likely to have been involved in part-time labours.

Table 4.3 The Blackburn Rovers line-up, with occupations, for the FA Cup Final, 1883–4

FA Cup Final	29 March 1884	Blackburn Rovers 2 Queen's Park 1
William John Herbert Arthur	Assistant to leather dealer	Goalkeeper
Fergus Suter	Footballer	
Joseph Beverley	Manufacturer's clerk	England international
Hugh McIntyre	Footballer	Scotland international
James Henry Forrest	Cotton weaver	England international
Joseph Morris Lofthouse	Licensed victualler	England international
Jimmy Douglas	Footballer	Scotland international
John Hargreaves	Solicitor	Malvern College (1875–9)
James Brown	Solicitor's clerk	England international
Joseph Edward Sowerbutts	Clerk	
John Inglis	Footballer	Scotland international

The Blackburn Rovers sides of the late 1870s and early 1880s should be described as at least lower middle class, certainly when compared with Darwen and Blackburn Olympic, who both tended, though not exclusively, to select from a more working-class base. Sociologically, this is a good example of the ready but incorrect acceptance of an absolute, as in this case, not *all* the players involved in these clubs were necessarily from one and the same social class. Drilling down into the backgrounds of those involved has revealed that none of these teams was wholly from the lower stratum of society.

★★★

The 1883–4 competition itself began with Queen's Park registering four wins by enormous margins against Crewe Alexandra by 10-0, Manchester Association by 15-0, Oswestry 7-1 and Aston Villa 6-1. It was to be Queen's Park and two Blackburn clubs, Rovers and Olympic, who emerged as favourites in the New Year. However, it came as a surprise when Upton Park went to Preston North End in the fourth round on 19 January 1884 and, in front of around 12,000 spectators, came away with a draw at one goal each after extra time had been played. Events surrounding the match itself are worth relating. The *Sporting Life* noted happenings before the game even kicked off:

> The Upton team arrived at twenty minutes past eleven on Friday evening and were met at the station by over 700 football enthusiasts, who accompanied them to their hotel giving cheer after cheer in honour of the North End's opponents, who seemed taken entirely by surprise…The home team [Preston North End] had been a week, at the pleasant seaside resort Lytham, and turned up in tip-top condition…Rumours had been afloat for some days of a protest was about to be lodged by the Upton Park Club on account of the constitution of the Preston team and a placard was freely put upon the walls asking for the public to disabuse their minds from any ill-feeling on the subject, and show to the visitors that impartial judgement for which they have become noted, and the reception they received must have proved to the Upton team that the best feeling did exist towards them.[59]

So much for northern partisanship! Captain of Upton Park was the intriguingly named Segar Richard Bastard (pronounced 'b-staar'), solicitor, England international (1880), FA Cup finalist (1878) and international match referee (England versus Wales 1879) – it was he who scored his team's equaliser in a game dominated by the Lancashire XI. The *Preston Herald* reported that 'The Upton Park team have been offered £100 by the Preston committee to play the next game [the replay] at Deepdale [Preston's home ground]'; they had already earned £81 as their half of the gate receipts from the first encounter.[60] However, despite the apparent camaraderie and goodwill, the following letter was received by the Preston secretary on Sunday, the day after the match took place.

Dear Sir,
I beg to inform that I have this morning received a protest from the Upton Park Club against your club on the ground of professionalism. It will be placed before the committee at their next meeting.
Yours truly
CW Alcock Hon. Sec.

At the next meeting of the FA on 26 January 1884, North End were disqualified from the cup, but retained their membership of the FA and would be allowed to fulfil their fixture programme. The events of the meeting seemed inconclusive, as Preston were left wondering exactly what they had done wrong.[61]

The cup remained in Blackburn for a further three years following Olympic's triumph, with Rovers recording a hat-trick of victories, the first two being against Queen's Park. For the initial cup final encounter in 1883–4, Rovers 'employed' four Scotsmen – Fergus Suter, Hugh McIntyre, Jimmy Douglas and John Inglis – and, though not being regarded as favourites, probably just about merited their victory. This was the first time that a Scottish side had reached the final, with Queen's Park confident – perhaps overconfident – after their Scottish Cup Final 'walkover' against Vale of Leven. The FA Cup Final coincided with Scotland's international match against Wales in Glasgow, with the many Scotland players in the ranks of Queen's Park opting to play for their club. The general opinion was that Queen's underperformed, with the *Fifeshire Journal* lamenting that 'They were in wretched form, and a crack Scottish club never played worse in a big match'.[62] Queen's committee was criticised for its team selection, turning down the services of Francis Watson 'Frank' Shaw, a Pollokshields Athletic player but *bona fide* member of the Queen's Park club, and those of John Leck 'Johnny' Kay, both of whom contributed to a comfortable win for their country against the Welsh,[63] the four goals to one victory being aided by a goal from Shaw and two from Kay.

The story of John 'Jock' Inglis was told graphically by his granddaughter, Eve Clucas, in an interview from the BBC Television series, 'Kicking and Screaming', part of the transcript of which appears below:

> As far as I know he first played for Glasgow Rangers in the early 1880s and he was known as a good dribbler, graceful player...he came down to Blackburn Rovers in about 1883/84 and he played for them in the FA Cup Final. He also played two international matches for Scotland, one against England – the score was 3-2 – and the other one was against Wales, and the score was 3-nothing...then he left Blackburn Rovers and went back up to Glasgow again and then he came back again and started for Preston North End... When he wasn't playing football he earned his living as a mechanic and also as a coachman to sort of eke out the pay that he wanted...He had eight children to keep and of course the wages up in Scotland then, particularly in the Clyde area where he lived, weren't very good so he came down to Blackburn Rovers because the pay was better at football than it was in Scotland... Blackburn Rovers won the FA Cup, they had a big banquet and...it was that

that started my grandfather on his drinking...when he started his football career he started drinking and he kept on drinking...and then after a painful illness he died at the age of 61 in August 1920.

The passage draws attention to the fact that Inglis had to supplement his football income with other work, the contrast with wages in Scotland and his eventual alcoholism. Inglis did, indeed, represent his country against both England (10 March 1883 at Bramall Lane, Sheffield) and Wales (12 March 1883 at the Racecourse Ground, Wrexham) while playing for Rangers in Glasgow.

So it was that the scene was set for a fairly seismic confrontation between those clubs, very largely in Lancashire, who broadly supported professionalism and those in the south, plus in particular Birmingham and Sheffield, who would prefer to eliminate the practice. As time would tell, it was the southern amateurs, administering the FA, who found or felt compelled to find a compromise solution, but events would prove to be multifaceted and, at times, tortuous.

★★★

By February 1884, attitudes in the provinces were hardening. The Sheffield FA made clear its attitude to football professionalism. In its recently re-discovered minutes for meetings of that period, its opinion was that 'it is undesirable to legalise professionalism in any shape or form'[64] and had, if anything, crystallised its view even further by December, saying, 'the legalisation of professionalism in football is inexpedient and unnecessary and can only prove injurious to the game'.[65] These statements were, firstly, an indication of the dislike which soccer officials in that city had for the practice, and, secondly, direct responses to a draining of talent to Lancashire which took place in the early 1880s, led by the presence of Jack Hunter at Blackburn Olympic, who seemed to be actively encouraging the better players from his home city to join him there.

On 28 February, the FA gathering decided that 'this meeting considers that the existence of veiled professionalism and the importation of players are serious evils calling for prompt legislation',[66] with a sub-committee appointed to consider matters. The latter body reported on 10 April 1884, recommending that professionalism should not be legalised, though many observers felt that it would be better to accept the practice in full so that payment would not be driven underground.[67] With the June Special General Meeting of the FA on 24 June 1884 limiting payment to 'necessary travelling and hotel expenses', the London-based body was still not 'grasping the nettle' and only seemed capable of proposing a partial solution to the problem.[68] Indeed, in July came the first suggestion of a split which would involve the convinced amateurs competing for a cup of their own, which was predictive of the introduction of the FA Amateur Cup in 1893.[69] In a preview of the coming 1884–5 season, an article in the *York Herald* was also supportive of an overt resolution, recommending that the FA should define the professional's 'position and status, and acknowledge his value as a very important element in the pastime', going on to note that 'With the possible exception of lawn tennis, there are recognised professionals in every English sport and pastime',[70] the latter argument being often utilised in favour of professionalism in soccer.

On 6 October 1884, the FA introduced three new rules which caused consternation in Lancashire. Rule 25 prohibited clubs who entered the FA Cup from engaging in fixtures with others who employed imported players. This clearly ruined the fixture list of many teams in Lancashire, though a solution would have been found by simply withdrawing from the cup. Rule 26 backdated the qualification period for new players to 1 September 1882, while Rule 27 required club secretaries to complete a form which included the names of players from another country or district. The first rule was the most damaging and the most controversial as it suggested that the FA had jurisdiction in matters outside the FA Cup.

Clearly this situation could not last. On 15 October 1884, at a meeting at the Bay Horse Hotel, Blackburn, 14 Lancashire clubs met opposing the measures taken by the FA[71] and by the end of the month, at the Dog and Partridge Hotel, Manchester, they had 'resolved to form an association, called the British Football Association' to rival the FA.[72] Interestingly, though no reason is given, Blackburn Rovers, Blackburn Olympic and Darwen were conspicuous by their absence. All three clubs had been closely connected to success in the FA Cup and perhaps felt an emotional attachment to the competition and the FA, the organising body. *The Athletic News* of 5 November 1884 listed 36 clubs as being in attendance, though the actual number in membership was 25.[73] The Bolton and District Charity Cup Association was also present and certain newspapers, including the *Preston Herald*, noted that Aston Villa had also sent a representative. A letter from T Bryan, treasurer of Aston Villa, in which he denied 'the assertion that Aston Villa club was represented at the meeting of the new football association in Manchester on Thursday evening. The club did not send a representative' and the person present was thought to have been 'an unauthorised member of that club located in Cottonopolis [Manchester]'.[74] Could a schism be averted or had, in fact, one already taken place?

Conclusion

It is incorrect to characterise some of those northern, particularly East Lancashire, clubs as being exclusively working class. It would seem that certain narratives have not been driven by primary sources and, as a consequence, the researcher has been somewhat mesmerised by the existing secondary material romanticising the lower orders. The existence of middle-class players – Gledhill, Hacking, Hargreaves, Hornby and Greenwood are good examples – in largely working-class teams should be seen as an illustration of relative balances in society at that time and it should come as no surprise, as skill in playing football was not solely the preserve of one particular social stratum. However, the most important message conveyed here is that one should rarely accept a bland, all-embracing statement without first checking the primary sources, even though they may, in some cases, ultimately prove to be correct. It is almost certainly fair to propose that the 'battle' for footballing hegemony was not solely between a northern horde of working-class professionals and a laid-back collection of well-educated upper-class amateurs from London. There were certain multifarious subtleties to be examined within that basic hypothesis.

Behind these machinations, there almost certainly existed an element of status rivalry[75] between the previously dominant southern amateurs and the increasingly successful northern 'professionals'. One might have believed that such a rivalry was impossible, given the extent of the social gap between the two groups. While this was no doubt the case off the pitch, on the field of play a fairly level battleground had been created, almost equality of opportunity, though imbalances still existed in terms of time absent from work, diet and money for equipment. The game was moving towards a type of meritocracy, where players were beginning to be judged on their ability rather than their perceived social status. In terms of performance and results – though perhaps not values and behaviour – membership of a particular class grouping, for once, was largely irrelevant. One contributor to *The Athlete* was in no doubt regarding the 'new arrivals', saying, 'none but gentlemen should play at the game [football], as they are the only personages who can afford to lose time and spend money on travelling',[76] which was probably true at least initially and was one of the main reasons why men working on Saturdays wanted the right to receive 'broken-time payments' for time away from work. It was financially extremely problematic for someone from the working class to challenge the soccer pre-eminence of the old boys of the south and retain his position as a pure amateur. Without at least a 'wages lost' clause, he could ill afford to absent himself from work or refuse remuneration and the passing of Rule 16 by the FA in 1882 to allow wages lost to be remunerated, legislated to make life a little easier in that respect. The rule stated:

> Any member of a club receiving remuneration or consideration of any sort above his actual expenses and any wages actually lost by any such player taking part in any match, shall be debarred from taking part in either cup, inter-association, or international contests, and any club employing such a player shall be excluded from this Association.

However, in terms of restricting the practice of payment, the 'wages lost' clause was so open to abuse that it became virtually worthless. Secretaries of clubs 'employing' players were suddenly not about to reveal all. Nor were discrepancies likely to be uncovered, as little if any written evidence was kept and players – the principal beneficiaries of the system – would have been unlikely to admit any offence.

This was not a monocausal process. The steady nationalisation of the game that resulted from the introduction of the FA Cup, the consequent undertaking of long-distance travel to away ties, the growing seriousness of competition provoked by such tournaments, together with the intense rivalries between growing, tight-knit communities in the north of England living barely a few miles from each other and the unplanned growth of spectatorism, which allowed clubs to afford to reward their players, all contributed to the march of professionalism in association football. Perhaps the strongest motivation, at least from an individual player's viewpoint, was that the chance to become a professional footballer offered working-class men an opportunity to experience a more rewarding and in many ways healthier environment – though they were, of course, exposing themselves to the physical hazards of football itself – in which to earn higher wages or supplement those they could earn in regular employment.

Two main influences were prevalent in driving football professionalism in East Lancashire. On a national scale, the FA Cup competition created a growing seriousness and the chance for nationwide acclaim. On a local level, the intense rivalry created between geographically close, tight-knit working-class communities by the expectations and need for success of the populations inhabiting those towns, also contributed. These rivalries appear to have been particularly prevalent in the industrial north and provided the local factory workers with an out-of-work focus in their 'quest for excitement', which was in direct contrast to their repetitive, production line job during the week. The unintended consequence of the accidental harnessing of local energies and pride in the form of regular and mass spectatorism at football matches was that each successful club became the recipient of large amounts of cash taken at the gate. The Blackburn Rovers versus Darwen game of November 1880 took over £250 in gate receipts, a huge sum for those times.[77] The practice of gate-taking was not restricted solely to Lancashire clubs. The FA registered receipts of £144 14s 0d for the match against Scotland in April 1879,[78] the difference being that, while this august body spent such takings on printing, stationery, refreshments and, perhaps, niceties and privileges for its officials, the likes of Blackburn Rovers and Darwen were covertly paying their players. So great was the revenue from the semi-final and subsequent replay of 1881–2 between Blackburn Rovers and Wednesday from Sheffield, that £35 each was given by the FA to the mayors of the two conurbations to divide between local charities.[79] However, any attempt by individual clubs to lift themselves morally above what amateur devotees might have termed the 'professional mire' simply led to self-inflicted ruin. The public, ever discriminating, was generally only interested in watching winners, and winners were only produced by engaging the best exponents of the game, those exponents 'moving with the money'. That is, the best players journeyed to the clubs who paid the highest wages. An administrator representing Burnley FC commented in 1885 that 'The fact of it is, the public will not go to see inferior players. During the first year we did not pay a single player, and nobody came to see us'.[80]

By 1884, opinion on importations seemed to have become even more polarised. A writer to *The Athlete* complained rather pointedly that the 'employment of the scum of the Scottish villages has tended, in no small degree, to brutalise the game [football]'.[81] To have referred to the imported Scottish professionals as 'scum' was strong language indeed, though it perhaps helps us to comprehend why so many ex-public school men either left the game now dominated by professionals and their 'win-at-all-costs', over-serious values to play against who they considered to be like-minded traditionalists, or perhaps even abandoned the association code altogether in favour of the rugby form. The FA Cup, forcing, as it did, clubs to play opponents not of their own choosing, was exacerbating that particular problem, where upper-class amateurs had to take on working-class professionals, sometimes in their own intimidating backyards. The scene was set for a confrontation between those favouring football professionalism and those who did not. But was there room for compromise?

Notes

1. *Manchester Courier and Lancashire General Advertiser*, 16 February 1885.
2. *Sheffield and Rotherham Independent*, 15 March 1886.
3. Andrew, '1883 Cup Final', 24. Andrew no doubt 'borrowed' the phrase from the description in *The Athletic News* of the semi-final of that season between Blackburn Olympic and the Old Carthusians (21 March 1883).
4. Curry, 'Playing for Money'.
5. Swain, *Emergence*, 202–4.
6. Ibid, 229. Hornby's name does not appear in Foster's *Alumni Oxonienses*.
7. Swain, *Emergence*. Swain notes that Dixon lived for two years in the early 1860s in Battersea, London where he may have encountered Charles Alcock. Subsequently, in 1874, Dixon wrote to Alcock to register his club, Turton, with the FA (See Endnote 99, Chapter Nine).
8. James, *Emergence*, 34, 49.
9. Swain, *Emergence*.
10. James, *Emergence*, 78.
11. 14 February 1879: Nos. 1, 2.
12. *Sheffield and Rotherham Independent*, 28 February 1879.
13. *Sheffield Daily Telegraph*, 31 January 1879.
14. Dunning and Sheard, *Barbarians*, 146.
15. Archer, *Jags*, 21.
16. *North British Daily Mail*, 4 January 1876. For the team lists, see the *North British Daily Mail*; for the Eastern comment see *Bell's Life*, 8 January 1876. Andrews found his way to Sheffield via Leeds as the result of being re-located with his job. See Curry, *Making of Football*, Chapter Six.
17. Andy Mitchell, on his *Scottish Sport History* website, has established a further connection between Darwen and Partick. Dr James Gledhill, a key figure in Darwen's cup run of 1878–9 (see Chapter 3 of this book), completed his medical studies at Glasgow University in the early 1880s, when he played several games for Partick.
18. Reminiscence of a former Accrington secretary in the *Lancashire Evening Post*, 4 December 1898.
19. Andy Mitchell, *Scottish Sport History*.
20. *The Athletic News*, 22 March 1882.
21. Like a number of original rugby league clubs, Huddersfield saw themselves as a multi-sports organisation, with rugby football rapidly overtaking the other sports. With thanks to Tony Collins for this information.
22. Coincidentally, though perhaps unsurprisingly, Keith Dewhurst's story of Darwen's exploits is entitled *Underdogs*.
23. The seven which named Thomas Williams were *Sporting Chronicle*, 11 March 1879, *Sheffield Daily Telegraph*, 10 March 1879, *Morning Post*, 10 March 1879, *Sporting Life*, 12 March 1879, *Daily News* (London), 10 March 1879, *Bell's Life*, 15 March 1879 and *The Field*, 15 March 1879. The four naming Thomas Marshall were *Nottinghamshire Guardian*, 14 March 1879, *Nottingham Evening Post*, 10 March 1879, *Sporting Gazette*, 15 March 1879 and *Blackburn Standard*, 15 March 1879.
24. On page 214.
25. *Bell's Life*, 5 January 1878.
26. Butler, *Giant Killers*, 14.
27. Green, *Official History of the F.A. Cup*, 24.
28. Gibson and Pickford, *Association Football*, 58.
29. Marples, *History of Football*, 170.
30. 27 November 1880.
31. Curry, *Crucible*, Chapter Four.
32. Phythian, *Shooting Stars*, Chapters Six and Eight.
33. *Eton College Chronicle*, 8 May 1883.

34 Rippon, *Soccer*, 1983: 33–4.
35 *Breedon Book of Football League Records*, 1992: 183.
36 Rippon, *Soccer*, 1983: 34.
37 Phythian, *Shooting Stars*, 69.
38 Westby, *History of Sheffield Football*, 63.
39 *The Athletic News*, 25 October 1882.
40 *Sheffield and Rotherham Independent*, 7 April 1883.
41 Curry, 'Degrading the game'.
42 Sheffield FA Minutes, 31 January 1881.
43 On 29 March 1880 (Easter Monday), Blackburn Olympic had entertained and beaten the Sheffield Zulus (*Sporting Chronicle*, 8 April 1880).
44 *South Yorkshire Times and Mexborough and Swinton Times*, 19 January 1883.
45 *Sheffield and Rotherham Independent*, 7 April 1883.
46 *South Yorkshire Times and Mexborough and Swinton Times*, 13 April 1883.
47 *Blackburn Times*, 22 September 1883.
48 *Sheffield Daily Telegraph*, 30 October 1883.
49 *Preston Herald*, 28 November 1883.
50 Personal email communication with Kevin Neill, 7 March 2022. See also *Bell's Life*, 7 December 1867, for an example of a fundraiser in Sheffield for the fund in the form of a charity match between teams representing 'Town' and 'Country'. This is an interesting subject and would benefit from further detailed research.
51 *Blackburn Times*, 27 October 1883.
52 See marriage records for 24 October 1883 and 1891 England Census.
53 Phythian, *Shooting Stars*, 56.
54 See letters in the *Sheffield Daily Telegraph* on 7 and 8 January 1885 discussing Wednesday's tendency to import players for important cup ties.
55 Hunter won the Sheffield FA Challenge Cup with Heeley in 1881–2.
56 *Sheffield and Rotherham Independent*, 3 November 1885.
57 *South Yorkshire Times and Mexborough and Swinton Times*, 13 November 1885.
58 Ibid, 14 November 1890.
59 *Sporting Life*, 21 January 1884.
60 23 January 1884. This money would probably have been a guarantee from the large crowd that would congregate at Deepdale as opposed to the smaller attendance in London.
61 *Blackburn Standard*, 2 February 1884.
62 *Fifeshire Journal*, 3 April 1884.
63 *Blackburn Standard*, 5 April 1884. Lamming says that Shaw played against Wales 'in preference to assisting Queen's Park in a cup final' (*Scottish internationalists*, 196).
64 Sheffield FA Minutes, 15 February 1884.
65 Ibid, 4 December 1884.
66 *St James's Gazette*, 29 February 1884.
67 For an example of the latter opinion, see the *Wigan Observer and District Advertiser*, 18 April 1884.
68 *Sheffield and Rotherham Independent*, 26 June 1884.
69 *Nottingham Journal*, 8 July 1884.
70 *York Herald*, 9 September 1884.
71 *Burnley Express*, 18 October 1884.
72 *Derby Mercury*, 29 October 1884.
73 *Athletic News*, 5 November 1884.
74 *The Sportsman*, 1 November 1884.
75 This phrase is usually associated with Eric Dunning and his hypothesis that there existed a good deal of competition, bordering on enmity, between the public schools of Eton and Rugby regarding their forms of football (See Curry and Dunning, *Association Football*).
76 *The Athlete*, 30 January 1884.

77 *Blackburn Standard*, 4 December 1880.
78 Green, *History of the Football Association*, 65.
79 Ibid, 66.
80 *The Athletic News*, 10 February 1885: 3.
81 *The Athlete*, 29 September 1884.

5 Importations and the coming of professionalism

By the early 1880s, professionalism in football stood at its most parlous and unedifying stage. In short, it was taking place, in some areas on a large scale, but was not yet overt in that it went undeclared, though almost everyone was aware that it was happening. The word 'shamateurism' has been coined to describe those individuals involved, a process where sports performers professed to be amateur, but were receiving financial remuneration for their efforts. The process at that time had become largely twofold – 'under-the-counter' money for playing football and the importing of individuals or even groups from other geographical areas with the sole objective of using them to strengthen the local team. The example of James Lang journeying from Glasgow to Sheffield has already been used in Chapter 4. However, the advent of the FA Cup and the entry of teams representing small, working-class communities caused events to spiral as the struggle for victory and, therefore, success became almost all-consuming, with some Lancashire sides often containing more imported Scotsmen than local players. Lancashire and the rest of the country, the latter represented by the FA, were on a collision course over professionalisation. This chapter relates those events, which, helpfully for a history of the early FA Cup, came to a head following a fixture in the competition. However, without completely pre-empting the story of those momentous proceedings, a compromise was reached and reasons for that compromise, which, we might remind ourselves, would not be found in rugby football, will be examined.

★★★

Importation, itself, was a more difficult and emotive issue than payment; moreover, it was beginning to take place on a large scale. It was quite clear that importation existed, but it would be difficult to reverse the trend as men offered the chance to play their favoured recreation and get paid for it were unlikely to refuse, even if it meant uprooting themselves and their family. However, it certainly was of concern to many in local communities, particularly some of those who resided in the East Lancashire mill towns. Views contained in a letter to *The Athletic News* from 'Fair Play' entitled 'Lancashire Football Association and Scotch Players' summed up the feelings of local communities who, despite perhaps possessing a successful team, felt that victories gained by a side largely made up of Scotsmen had a hollow ring to them:

DOI: 10.4324/9781003285595-6

> I understood when I gave my mite [presumably a small amount] towards purchasing the handsome cup [The Lancashire Football Association's trophy] that it was for Lancashire lads, and they alone. If the richer clubs can afford to pay professionals, let them do so, but when they compete for our grand trophy, let the true Lancashire lads have equal chance of winning it.[1]

The quote was a triumph for localism over universalism, but polarisation of opinion was leading increasingly to clubs resorting to extreme measures to redress their grievances, usually following defeat but occasionally after victory. Indeed, not only did they complain to their local association, but protests also became relatively commonplace following FA Cup encounters when offended, usually (though not always) defeated sides sought judgement from the parent body, the FA. Even before its FA Cup third round tie with Wednesday on 6 January 1883, Nottingham Forest lodged a protest that a Wednesday player, Arthur Malpass, had received payment for assisting another local club, Sheffield Wanderers, in a match against Bolton Wanderers on 6 November 1883. The cast list for the Sheffield team was reminiscent of a Zulu line-up (see Chapter 4 of this book) and it does not require a great leap of faith to come to the conclusion that money was involved.[2] Malpass did not take part in the first game against Forest and was also absent for the replay and, fortunately for Wednesday, he was their only man involved at Bolton and they clearly realised the possible consequences of the situation by not utilising him.

The *York Herald* carried an article on events which escalated even further after the replay. It stated:

> Considerable sensation was caused in Sheffield and district yesterday [Friday 19 January 1883] by the appearance of bills on the walls announcing that Mr. S.W. Widdowson [the Forest captain], of Nottingham would give a reward of £20 to any person or persons who can prove that W. [William] Harrison of Redcar, W. [William or Billy] Betts of Pyebank and J. [Initial should be W. for Willis] Bentley of Walkley, were not members of the Sheffield Wednesday football club before December 6 last. The reward bears upon the recent tie for the English Cup, between Sheffield Wednesday and Nottingham Forest, in which the latter were defeated by three goals to two. The Forest allege that the three men named were not *bona fide* members of the Wednesday Club, and that consequently they ought to be disqualified. The matter is under consideration by the national executive of the English association, and what course they will adopt is being strongly debated.[3]

Betts and Bentley were Sheffield men, but neither were Wednesday players in the first half of the season. In fact, although Bentley stayed with them for a couple more years, the Forest game was his debut for Wednesday.[4] Harrison, too, had a Sheffield connection. Redcar, near Middlesbrough, despite lying 100 miles away, was affiliated to the Sheffield FA and as recently as 16 December 1882, Harrison had represented the association against Lancashire in a thrilling 3-3 draw in difficult, snow-covered conditions at Bramall Lane. Harrison was an outstanding talent and held the captain's position at Redcar. Another intriguing character, he was born in Liverpool, worked as an elementary school teacher, moved to the northeast and helped found the Redcar club.[5] Although all three had tenuous Wednesday links and were, ultimately, found to be members of the club, this was sharp practice for a big game.

Old Harrovian Reginald De Courtney Welch[6] had commented on this kind of situation as early as 1881. He wrote,

> ...the majority of clubs...are ready to elect [sic] any good player who may be willing to help them in their cup matches; so that...those who play in the ordinary matches are, in the cup competition, ousted in favour of better men, connected with the locality in no other way than by some slender tie of friendship with a member of the committee...[7]

Meanwhile, *The Athletic News* noted another way Forest had used to discover wrongdoing:

> Not satisfied with that [placing bills on walls] even, they had a private detective in town last week, an officer who was extensively engaged in the notorious Peace[8] case, but he returned to Nottingham without the much craved information.[9]

Forest not only lost the replay on 13 January 1883 3-2, but was also unsuccessful in its subsequent appeal to the FA, with the national body censuring the Nottingham club for recklessness in bringing the charges against Wednesday.[10]

The situation was in danger of getting out of control. In a letter to *The Field* of 8 December 1883, 'Mancunian' listed the names of 63 footballers 'who have either been imported into the county [Lancashire], or have gone from one town to another'.[11] Fourteen were linked to Bolton Wanderers, a further ten with Halliwell, while eight were 'employed' by Preston North End. Interestingly, as well as the twin 'evils' of payment and importation, 'Mancunian' bemoaned the 'win at all costs' attitude of the importations and the increasing prevalence of betting on the outcomes of games. In terms of importation, the players mentioned did not all hail from Scotland. Contained in the list were George Wilson, who we have already met extensively in this book, from Swinton in South Yorkshire; James Beresford, about whom we will learn more later in this chapter, from Staveley, North East Derbyshire; as well as Jack Hunter and William Moss with Blackburn Olympic and Tom Buttery at Blackburn Olympic (and eventually Preston), all three of whom came from Sheffield. Also from Staveley – clearly a hotbed of the association game – were the highly rated goalkeeper Tom Hay at Bolton Wanderers; another custodian, Amos Kay at Halliwell; and William Young who followed Beresford to Church. To add to the international flavour, John 'Jack' Powell, Jackie Vaughan, Bob Roberts and Di Jones were imported by Bolton Wanderers from Wales.[12]

Of course, there was another side to this exceedingly complex coin. 'JSR' reminded readers of *The Field* of an alternative view of the situation by noting that at least 13 of the 'miscreants' had 'always lived within two miles' of their particular clubs, presumably making them innocent of importation.[13] Also mentioned in the article was the fact that West Midlands teams such as Aston Villa were guilty of similar offences to Lancashire teams. Indeed, as the struggle over professionalism continued, this particular point – that the practice was spreading to Birmingham and its surrounds – immeasurably strengthened Lancashire's case and was one of the reasons which forced the FA to act.

In London, it appeared that initially the amateur members of the FA committee were either unwilling or unable to grasp the problematic nettle that was professionalism. However, in November 1883, they finally acted. Ironically it was Darwen, much maligned in some quarters several years previously for 'employing' Fergus Suter, which complained to the FA that both Church and Accrington had paid the aforementioned James Beresford to play for them. Darwen had eliminated Church from that season's FA Cup competition in the first round after a replay, matches in which Beresford had played, and despite not directly opposing Accrington in the competition, were nevertheless near neighbours and close rivals. Beresford had played only one game for Accrington – against Rossendale on 15 September 1883[14] – and the sum of money received by the player came not from the Accrington club but from a private individual. It transpired that the treasurer and secretary, both of whom were eventually dismissed by Accrington, were aware that this action had taken place and the evidence was deemed to be sufficient by the FA to see Accrington disqualified from that season's competition. The club was also expelled from the FA and barred from fulfilling its planned fixtures, though the final sanction, about which Lancashire clubs in general felt aggrieved, was revoked. Lancashire clubs were especially disappointed in the latter punishment, as they felt that the national body was exceeding its authority. Beresford himself was banned from football for the rest of the season, though he somehow managed to guest for both Astley Bridge[15] and Bolton Wanderers[16] in May 1884.

★★★

James Beresford was an interesting character, about whom little has been written, which is surprising as he was at the centre of the FA's first real attempt to tackle professionalism. If a football historian ever required a perfect example of someone who played for a multitude of clubs, no doubt earning money along the way, then Beresford was the man. He was born in early 1860 in Staveley, where his father David was a coal miner. In the censuses of 1881 and 1891 his own occupation was also listed as a coal miner, though he no doubt subsidised this with wages gained playing football. His family lived in 'The Blocks' at Barrow Hill, which appears unwelcoming, but were actually rows of three cottages together, built to a higher standard than other examples of working-class housing of the period.

He was involved in forming a football club in Barrow Hill, an area which sprang up as a large village housing workers for the Staveley Coal and Iron Company, which soon employed over 3,000 men. Beresford is then noted as playing for Staveley, Staveley Works and Spital (a suburb of Chesterfield) in North East Derbyshire, being involved in the FA Cup for the latter club against Wednesbury Old Athletic in November 1882, when he was undoubtedly invited as a recognised talent for an important cup tie. He was ineffective during the game which Spital lost by seven goals to one. A fortnight later, reflecting the fluid nature of players representing multiple clubs at that time, Beresford was on the opposing side playing for Staveley Works as it beat Spital in the Hallamshire (New) Association Challenge Cup during a particularly rough game. In the same month he journeyed over the Pennines to join Church FC in Lancashire, the club finding him 'more profitable employment'.[17] He enjoyed four seasons from 1883–4 to 1886–7 at Church and later played 12 times and scored four goals for Blackburn Rovers in the first season of the Football League. During his time in Lancashire, Beresford epitomised an importation created by the growing seriousness of competition, partly encouraged by the establishment of the FA Cup.

Sadly, his tale did not end well. He returned to Staveley and played for the local side and again for Barrow Hill, which saw his footballing life turn full circle. On a personal note, the 1891 England Census shows him living back with his mother in Staveley, while his wife Nancy, together with their son and daughter, remained at the family home in Church. Eventually he seems to have moved to Hucknall, near Nottingham, where through his mother he had family ties. In December 1882, playing for Bestwood Church Institute in the Nottinghamshire FA Junior Cup, his professional footballing background landed him and his club in trouble. Having beaten Hucknall Portland, a protest was lodged against Beresford and Bestwood by their opponents saying the player had not been re-instated as an amateur.[18] The complaint was upheld, and it appeared that Beresford's past was harrying his sporting career. The following year, after a lengthy illness, Beresford 'died in the Nottingham Infirmary…from an attack of influenza and pneumonia', though it seems that by then he and his family had been re-united.[19]

★★★

Meanwhile, north of the border, the Scottish Football Association was being predictably harsh on those who left their country to find fame and fortune in England. The minutes of a subcommittee meeting on professionalism read as follows:

> 'A meeting of the sub-committee on professionalism of this S.F.A. was held in the rooms of 11 Carlton Place on Tuesday the 2nd of December 1884 at 8 o'clock. Mr. James McKillop, (President) in the chair. The following gentlemen were present viz:- Messrs. A Stuart, RF Harrison, A Geake, J Devlin & WJ McCulloch.
>
> The secretary was instructed to send each of the undernoted players who have left Scotland to play football in England a copy of the following letter:
> Dear Sir,
> Your name has been brought under the notice of the Sub-Committee of this association on Professionalism as having left a club belonging to their body, and that you are now playing with a club outside of their jurisdiction. They have therefore to inform you that under Rule 14 (and bye-laws pertaining thereto) of the constitution, you cannot again play with any club within their jurisdiction without their permission.
>
> John McDowell, Secretary

Table 5.1 Scottish football players based with English clubs, December 1884

Preston North End (11): John Belger (South Western), James Barnett (St, Bernard's), George Drummond (St, Bernard's), James Ferguson (Heart of Midlothian), John 'Jack' Gordon (Port Glasgow Athletic), Johnny Graham (Annbank), Alex 'Sandy' Robertson (St, Bernard's), Nick Ross (Heart of Midlothian), Jimmy Ross (Heart of Midlothian), David Russell (Stevenston Cunninghame), Samuel Thompson (Lugar Boswell)
Accrington (4): James Bonnar (Thornliebank), Robert Conway (Thornliebank), Robert 'Bob' McBeth (St, Bernard's), John Stevenson (Arthurlie)
Halliwell (7): George Bone (Kilmarnock Athletic), A Houston (Kilmarnock Athletic), Alexander Hamilton (Kilmarnock), Alexander McWhirter (Kilmarnock), James Pettigrew (Kilmarnock Athletic), David Ross (Hurlford), William Scobie (Hurlford)
Bolton Wanderers (5): James Brogan (Heart of Midlothian), James Kennedy (Third Lanark), John McKinnon (Hibernian), William Struthers (Rangers), William Steel (Arbroath)
Burnley (9): Dan Caulfield (Johnstone Athletic), Dan Friel (Vale of Leven), Peter Logan (Vale of Leven), Alex McLintock (Vale of Leven), John McAulay (Arthurlie),[20] J McRae (Vale of Leven), William Ronaldson (Heart of Midlothian), John Shields (Johnstone Athletic), Archibald Webster (Kilbarchan)
Church (2): J Connell (Mauchline), J Crawford (Mauchline)
Blackburn Rovers (4): Jimmy Douglas (Renfrew), James Harper (Beith), Hugh McIntyre (Rangers), Fergus Suter (Partick)
Preston Zingari (4): George Douglas (Heart of Midlothian), Tom Douglas (Heart of Midlothian), James Renwick (Heart of Midlothian), Jock Scotland (Heart of Midlothian)
Great Lever (6): John Goodall (Kilmarnock Athletic), David Hay (Kilmarnock Athletic), John 'Jock' Inglis (Ayr), James Lucas (Kilmarnock), David Waugh (Northern), Johnny Walkinshaw (Kilmarnock Athletic)
Padiham (3): Patrick Gallacher (Johnstone Rovers), Bill McFettridge (Thornliebank), William McConnell (Johnstone Rovers)
Aston Villa (1): Archie Hunter (Ayr)
Darwen (2): James Richmond (Kilmarnock Portland), Hugh Richmond (Kilmarnock Portland)

The *Nottingham Evening Post* of 10 December 1884 reported on this letter and also published a list of the players and clubs involved. The names of the participants and organisations appear in Table 5.1 and make interesting reading.

- 57 players were involved. Their Scottish clubs are noted in brackets.
- The 27 Scottish clubs who lost players were as follows: Heart of Midlothian (9), Kilmarnock Athletic (6), St. Bernard's (4), Vale of Leven (4), Kilmarnock (3), Arthurlie (2), Ayr (2), Hurlford (2), Johnstone Athletic (2), Johnstone Rovers (2), Kilmarnock Portland (2), Mauchline (2), Rangers (2), Thornliebank (2), Annbank (1), Arbroath (1), Beith (1), Hibernian (1), Kilbarchan (1), Lugar Boswell (1), Northern (1), Partick (1), Port Glasgow Athletic (1), Renfrew (1), South Western (1), Stevenston Cunninghame (1), Third Lanark (1).
- Heart of Midlothian was particularly devastated.
- Preston North End could literally field a team made up of Scotsmen.
- St. Bernard's was an Edinburgh-based team which would win the Scottish Cup in 1894–5. It was also found guilty by the Scottish FA of illegally paying a player in September 1890, for which it received what was thought by many to be a lengthy suspension. The club re-appeared briefly as Edinburgh Saints, but effectively did not play again for seven months.[21]

As a reiteration of this evidence, in the same month *Football Field* revealed similar data on the subject noting that no fewer than 60 Scottish born players were registered with just 11 major Lancashire sides.[22] The popularity of football north of the border meant that clubs and the national association in Scotland were earning vast amounts of money from enormous crowds – the second game of three to settle the 1876–7 Scottish Cup Final attracted at least 10,000 spectators[23] – which was rarely finding its way down to the people providing the entertainment, the players. An article in the *Glasgow Herald* questioned where these immense sums ended up, though the writer was more concerned that more deserving charitable institutions rather than the players were not receiving their fair share.[24] In the same month, no fewer than 1,500 people turned out to watch a friendly match between Third Lanark and Clydesdale at Cathkin Park, which was more a representative attendance at everyday fixtures, though still a considerable money-spinner for someone.[25]

As time passed, opinions in Lancashire hardened towards what they regarded as Scotland's rather hypocritical position. William Sudell, Preston North End's leading administrator, was quoted by the *Preston Herald* on 26 January 1887 as saying, 'professionalism exists in Scotland at the present time, just as it existed in England before it was openly recognised. I have the statement of players who have come to us from Scotland that a fixed payment is known and recognised in many Scotch clubs... Apart from all this, what is done with the enormous gate-moneys drawn by some of the first-class Scotch clubs? The Renton team [club] received £100 last Saturday, and will in all likelihood get another today. What is done with the money?...In our team we pay £1000 a year in salaries. Is our straightforward business manner not a better one than that which veils itself under the title of "amateur"?'

But perhaps the final word on the subject should lie with Jimmy Ross, a Scotsman playing a leading role for Preston North End at the time of his comments in October 1889. In a short interview with the *Staffordshire Sentinel*, he was open and forthright about Scottish football professionalism, stating that the practice was rife, especially in the Glasgow area. But he also expressed a view which was becoming more common when he noted, 'I would rather be an honest "pro", than a bogus amateur'.[26]

***

Lancashire clubs could be brazen in their approaches to players. Just before Christmas 1884, Derby County visited the north-west and played two fixtures, one against Darwen and the other against Halliwell. The letter below recorded a particularly disturbing experience:

> If any of your readers still doubt the necessity for immediate legislation *re* professionalism, let him ask for the opinion of the Derby County Football Committee. They were unwise enough to send a team into Lancashire last week and three of their men were importuned by the members of a certain local club to remain. As, however, two of them were law students, and the third a well-known Derby cricketer, it will not be surprising that they were deaf to the voice of the charmer.

It may have been either Darwen or Halliwell which made the approach as both were renowned for employing professionals, though Halliwell was probably the more active in this area. The situation in general could not go on, and at a Special General Meeting of the FA attended by around 200 delegates on 19 January 1885 – appropriately at the Freemasons' Tavern in London where the FA began life in 1863 – Charles Alcock argued that professionalism would not ruin the game and he was supported by Healey of Bolton Wanderers, Critchley from Accrington FC, William McGregor of Aston Villa (he was to be the prime mover behind the establishment of the Football League in 1888), Nicholas Lane 'Pa' Jackson of Corinthian fame and, of course, William Sudell from Preston North End. They were opposed by Charles Crump and William Jope of Birmingham, Harry Chambers and William Beardshaw from Sheffield and Thomas Lawrie of Glasgow's Queen's Park. None of the various proposals received the necessary support, so football remained in limbo.[27] To add to the consternation, the British Football Association held another meeting in Blackburn to discuss possible challenges to certain unspecified FA rules at the London body's AGM in March 1885.[28] At the latter gathering there was still no agreement and it was left to Sheffield's William Peirce Dix to suggest the need to seek compromise out of the deadlock through another subcommittee. This group circulated a set of questions to clubs and associations in April asking about professionals and their residential qualifications, selection for representative matches, involvement in the FA Cup and transfers between teams.[29] A month later it was announced in the press that the subcommittee would recommend the legalisation of professionalism in English football.[30] From a point where the general attitude was that professionalism should be stamped out, with offenders being ostracised, limited compromise was sought, with the prevailing opinion among the general public being that the worst case scenario was that the practice should be forced beneath the surface. As Jimmy Ross had opined, overt professionalism was probably preferable to covert 'shamateurism'.

And so to the final act of a lengthy drama. Another Special General Meeting was held, this time at Anderton's Hotel, London on 20 July 1885. Unusually, the voting pattern showed that 35 delegates were in favour of professionalism while 15 expressed a negative response. Delegate numbers were down on previous meetings and this may have indicated a weariness on the part of football in general over the problem. Conspiracy theorists might have seen it as a shrewd plan devised by Charles Alcock in holding such a vital gathering in the summer when many interested parties would have been away. This was reminiscent of the events at the fifth meeting of the FA on 1 December 1863, when adherents of an embryo association game had plotted to ensure that they would be in a majority when the critical vote on the nature of the game, kicking and dribbling or handling and carrying, was taken. Professionalism was essentially legalised under 'stringent conditions', including residency rules and registering of professionals annually, but perhaps the greatest slight to working-class, professional players – though they probably dismissed it as unimportant – was that they could not serve on any committee nor represent their club at any meeting of the FA. This smacked of snobbery and the minimal value that members of the FA placed on the working-class intellect and administrative ability. However, this particular ruling ensured that the real power in English football remained with the southern amateurs and, even today, a glance at the FA council conveys the overriding amateur composition of a body which is still heavily involved with decisions in the professional game.[31]

As for the British Football Association, one would have expected that, following the legalisation of professionalism, the organisation would have possessed no *raison d'être* and simply dissolved itself. That did not quite happen. Had it really possessed enough power and organisational ability to effect a real schism, or – as Dave Russell has suggested in his book chapter, 'From Evil to Expedient: The Legalization of Professionalism in English Football: 1884–5' – were they an association who never had 'the clarity of purpose demonstrated by the northern rugby clubs at the heart of the 1895 breakaway'?[32] Ultimately, things would not be plain sailing as, by September 1885 the organisation was noted as being in financial trouble.[33] Despite this, in February 1886 it was turning out a representative team from clubs which formed the British Football Association to meet Preston North End. Styled the 'Lancashire Players', they were beaten easily by ten goals to one.[34] Even as late as 1887 the association was rating a mention in the press when a proposal for the position of secretary was noted in *Cricket and Football Field*.[35] After that date there was no mention of it and so, as it was probably unsupported financially, it merely faded from the football landscape.

★★★

From 20 July 1885, the administrators of the game had accepted that players would be allowed, under 'stringent conditions', to profit from their ability at football. But however we view the professionalism debate, it is important to understand that, just as northern clubs only swept aside their southern opponents gradually, so it was with professionalism. Amateur clubs and players did not simply disappear, nor did England teams suddenly start to ignore amateur footballers; the process was one which took place over an extended period of time.

Why was it that soccer avoided what in ten years' time would be an agonising split in the sport of rugby football? Of all the theories and hypotheses surrounding the advent of professionalism in association football, Eric Dunning and Ken Sheard's explanation appears to have the most credibility.[36] Dunning and Sheard produced *Barbarians, Gentlemen and Players*, regarded as the *magnum opus* of academic studies of football – largely the rugby form – from a sociological perspective; the work was first published as early as 1979 and re-published in 2005. They believed that soccer was, at least in its early years, administered by former pupils of more upper-class – even aristocratic – establishments, such as Eton College, Harrow School, Winchester, Westminster, Shrewsbury and Charterhouse, institutions recognised as 'great' schools by the Clarendon Report of 1864, but also advocates of kicking and dribbling styles of football. This was certainly true at the FA, where men such as Charles Alcock – an Old Harrovian – along with Arthur, Lord Kinnaird and Major Francis Marindin – both Old Etonians – ruled the roost. It meant that those individuals and groups at the apex of the association game felt far more socially secure than their middle-class, provincial counterparts, such as John Charles Clegg in Sheffield and Charles Crump in Birmingham. The gap between the individuals at the FA and the working class was so great that they rarely felt threatened – apart from on the field of play – by this incursion into their leisure space. This argument effectively explains why provincial associations such as Sheffield and Birmingham were so reluctant to accept payment for playing, positioned as they were closer in social terms to working-class participants in their particular area. This proximity in economic power meant that the likes of Clegg and Crump felt threatened in a way that Alcock, Kinnaird and Marindin never did. It was also significant that southern amateurs, at least until the advent of the FA Cup, had rarely played with or against anyone from a lower social class and had not, therefore, been challenged either on or off the field of play in terms of values and behaviour differing markedly from their own. This situation was in direct contrast to the Rugby Football Union, which was administered by men who had attended far more middle-class public schools such as Rugby School itself. They inhabited social strata similar to Clegg and Crump and, in 1895, would reject the notion of payment for playing.

There are two further explanations which are worth recording. Firstly, football had cricket as an *in situ* model of how to 'control' professional players. Indeed, Charles Alcock was secretary of Surrey County Cricket Club from 1872 to 1907 and would have been aware of the successes and pitfalls. However, football professionalism was on a much grander scale and, far from being controlled largely from the outset by more upper-class administrators, the crisis created had been initiated by groups in East Lancashire who, to a certain extent, were involved in actively setting the agenda. Secondly, Dunning and Sheard also contended that

> The crisis over the legitimacy of professionalism in soccer came to a head in the middle 1880s, [which] meant that it took place towards the end of the thirty year period of relatively harmonious class relations...By contrast, the crisis over professionalism in Rugby erupted in the early 1890s, i.e. at a time when class conflict was mounting owing, on the one hand, to the maturation of the long-term changes taking place in the structure and social composition of the ruling class and, on the other, of the dawning realisation by the working class of their latent power.[37]

Dunning and Sheard would argue that industrial relations in the 1880s were, compared to the mid-1890s when the rugby split occurred, fairly amicable and, with class conflict much more overt during the latter decade, acquiescence in sport to an emerging working class may well have been construed as a step too far. However, more in-depth study reveals that there were contradictions involved in this reasoning. While 1884 saw the extension of the working-class male franchise, the same decade was noted for the growth of 'new unionism', organisations who fought for better pay and the furtherance of the Saturday half-day. The 1890s were a time of great confidence in a well-established Empire dominated by naval power, but at the same time, the suffragists – predecessors of the suffragettes – were campaigning responsibly though determinedly for the right of women to vote.[38] Tony Collins points out that the broader social context is important for understanding why it was easier for the FA to accept professionalism. He continues,

As the debate on professionalism in rugby grew in the late 1880s there was always a consciousness of the rising tide of working-class self-confidence, most obviously in the creation of unskilled unions from 1888 and the formation of the Independent Labour Party in 1893. None of this happened in the early 1880s which meant accepting professionalism in football didn't carry the same implications.[39]

The wider perspective is certainly helpful, but the examples given above present contradictions in terms of opinion regarding the political situation in the 1880s. There is, therefore, ample scope for further debate.

Dunning and Sheard additionally noted that before the 1880s, the amateur ethos existed merely as an embryonic ideal. They expanded by saying,

> It was…an amorphous, loosely articulated set of values regarding the functions of sport and the standards believed necessary for their realisation. However, with threat posed by incipient professionalisation in the North, the amateur ethos began to crystallise as a highly specific, elaborate and articulate ideology…It became…a 'collective representation', an ideational product developed by members of one collectivity in opposition to the ideas and actions of the members of another.[40]

Dunning and Sheard believed that, for the public-school élite, sport had to involve the following three attributes:

1. pursuit of the activity as an 'end in itself', i.e. simply for the pleasure afforded, with a corresponding downgrading of achievement striving, training and specialisation;
2. self-restraint and, above all, the masking of enthusiasm in victory and disappointment in defeat;
3. the norm of 'fair play', i.e. the normative equalisation of game-chances between contending sides, coupled with a stress on voluntary compliance with the rules and a chivalrous attitude of 'friendly rivalry' towards opponents.[41]

As an illustration of the complex nature of opinions at the time, Dave Russell uses the example of William Sudell, a mill manager, and Charles Crump, Chief Clerk for the Northern Division of the Great Western Railway, who he describes as being of a similar social status, but who held diametrically opposed views on football professionalism.[42] Yet Sudell, Preston North End's leading administrator, resided in an area where competition was fierce and the generally accepted way of producing large crowds who created vast receipts watching successful teams was the *modus operandi* of football businessmen. These vast crowds were also concerned with identity and generating a positive local 'personality' for their town through footballing triumphs. Crump's Stafford Road club was on an entirely different scale to Sudell's Preston North End and this, together with the fact that Crump was a committee member at the FA from 1882,[43] marks him as something of an establishment man, having been subject to arguments (initially at least) which led him to be a fervent voice against payment for playing. Although they were from a similar social stratum, Sudell represented fairly blatant commercialism, whereas Crump held onto traditional values which he felt were under attack.

For English football, the nettle had been grasped and a solution found, though teething problems would dog the game in succeeding seasons. For the moment, most people were happy, but with the benefit of hindsight, football had, perhaps unsurprisingly in a fairly staunch capitalist economy, accepted that financial might was, more times than not, about to decide matters on the field of play. It was a moot point whether the FA's administrators believed that they could still uphold their cherished public-school values and instil them in the game's participants, but they were, for the time being, satisfied that they still maintained their power base in London. They must have suspected, however, that success on the pitch was almost certainly a thing of the past.

★★★

The 1884–5 FA Cup was eventually won by Blackburn Rovers as they comfortably beat Queen's Park by two goals to nil, the latter having disposed of two Nottingham teams, County and Forest, both victories being gained following replays. The second game against Forest took place at Merchiston Castle School, Edinburgh,[44] being the first semi-final to have been played outside England and the only one to take place in Scotland.[45] Having travelled down to Derby twice for games against Nottingham opposition, Queen's were loath to trek south again and so proposed a venue in Edinburgh. When the Powderhall Stadium's playing surface was found to be too small, the head teacher of Merchiston was contacted and, apart from not interfering with the cricket square, the organisers were given *carte blanche* in terms of creating the facilities.[46] In the final, Queen's were 'by no means disgraced',[47] but fell short again.

New to the Rovers line-up and a direct replacement for Scotsman, Inglis, was Herbert Lincoln Fecitt (pronounced 'Fee-sit'),[48] a local painter and decorator, who began with junior teams in Blackburn before attracting a bigger team's attention. In the 1891 England Census he was recorded as living next to Blackburn goalkeeper Herby Arthur on Mollington Road in north Blackburn.[49] The footballers were married to the two Taylor sisters – Fecitt to Mary and Arthur to Elizabeth Ann. A further addition to Rovers' ranks was George Hawarth,[50] captain of Accrington FC, who was recruited especially for the final and rewarded Rovers with an excellent performance, being described by *The Sportsman* as 'the best man, not only of the side, but on the field'.[51] Rovers was fortunate in that Haworth had not played for Accrington against Southport in the first round and was not cup-tied,[52] a game Accrington won by three clear goals but was subsequently disqualified for playing unregistered players.[53] Interestingly, the Blackburn club had appealed directly to the British Football Association rather than the FA or even their county body for approval to use Hawarth in the final, even reputedly 'begging permission'[54] to recruit his services. This information suggests strongly that Lancashire clubs may have viewed that organisation as their governing body, though an alternative interpretation might be that this was, after all, an internal affair between teams based in that county.

Accrington themselves were thought of as potential English cup winners and would not finish the season empty-handed, as they carried off the East Lancashire Charity Cup, beating both Blackburn Rovers and Blackburn Olympic on the way. They were also successful in the Lancashire Cup on three occasions in the 1880s. Rovers, too, carried off the county cup on several occasions in the 1880s, winning it in four consecutive seasons from 1881–2. It was said that their 'performances are well known. In and out play in ordinary fixtures has always been followed by consistent success in cup ties'.[55] Despite its inconsistencies, Rovers would certainly be regarded as the best English club of that decade.

Another change in the Blackburn team in the second final with Queen's Park saw Richard John Turner replacing England international Joe Beverley, who had returned to Blackburn Olympic. Turner was an interesting character and worthy of further research, if only because his current *Wikipedia* entries for the 1884–5 and 1885–6 FA Cup Finals are so obviously incorrect and, therefore, misleading. His mini-biography states that he was Richard Rennie Turner who was born in 1882, making him much too young to have played the senior game in the 1880s. The 'real' Rovers player, Richard John Turner, was born on 20 July 1864 in Kilmarnock, Scotland, near to where his father Frederick John worked as factor or land agent for the 5th Duke of Portland on the estate around Dean Castle just outside the town. By the time of the 1881 England Census they had moved to Mansfield Woodhouse in Nottinghamshire, just outside the town of Mansfield itself, where Richard's father had been 'transferred' in 1878 to take on similar responsibilities for the Duke, this time at Welbeck Abbey and the estate's offices in Mansfield Woodhouse.[56] Richard himself attended Queen Elizabeth's Grammar School in Mansfield where he played cricket for the first XI.[57]

Richard Turner left home to settle initially in Manchester, from where he travelled to East Lancashire to play football. His reasons for living there are unclear, but an indication may lie in the fact that his father had been employed at Broughton Hall to the north-west of the city as a land agent, the post preceding his work in Scotland; Richard would, therefore, have been familiar with the area. It is also probable that Turner met his future wife Jane there, as her place of birth is noted in subsequent censuses as being Cheetham in north Manchester. The city itself was a soccer desert at this point, with the rugby code ruling the roost and Turner was forced to travel to satiate his desire to play the kicking and dribbling code. The thriving soccer subculture around East Lancashire provided him with much better opportunities.

This is reminiscent of the story of another Scot, Peter Andrews, who lived and worked in Leeds in the late 1870s but eventually journeyed to Sheffield where a soccer-like game rather than the rugby code was king. Turner himself played for Bolton Association FC in their FA Cup first round win against Bradshaw in November 1883 and was referred to as 'Turner of Manchester' when he represented them in a losing effort in the next round against local rivals Bolton Wanderers.[58] However, he was destined for greater things when, as a direct replacement for Beverley at Blackburn Rovers, he was drafted into the side for the 1884–5 season.[59] The campaign culminated in a triumph for Rovers in the cup final against Queen's Park, but Turner would return and 12 months on he claimed another

English cup winner's medal when he was in the side which defeated West Bromwich Albion after a replay.

During his time in Manchester – as was common practice at that time – Turner, as a typical gentleman amateur footballer, would also assist various other clubs, including Halliwell against Bolton Wanderers in April 1884,[60] Liverpool Ramblers who opposed Cambridge University Wanderers in January 1885[61] and Manchester Association versus Preston North End in May 1885.[62] However, a piece appeared in *The Athletic News* bringing information on Turner's relocation to pastures new. The short article read:

> RG [sic] Turner has been bagged by numerous clubs, in anticipation. The news had hardly arrived that the celebrated Blackburn Rover was coming south to study, when paragraphs appeared in the sporting dailies to the effect that Turner would play for Brentwood, the Essex champion club.
>
> A correspondent assures me that Turner likes form in preference to brute strength, and that he will play for Dulwich, a smart little team, who rely chiefly on their neat passing game. Again I am told that Turner is a Scotsman, and, of course, will help the Caledonians, in proof of which, it is said he opposed Aston Villa the other day in their opening match.[63]

Turner did, indeed, go on to play regularly for London Caledonians, who were founded by and for Scotsmen living in London, finding himself alongside Hugh McIntyre, his old Blackburn Rovers teammate and fellow FA Cup winner, against Hendon in December 1887.[64] He did, however, find time to play for Brentwood at Notts. County in October 1886, *The Athletic News* relating the presence of 'Dick Turner, the quondam Blackburn Rover'.[65]

Turner was serving on the Caledonian committee in 1890 but a year later, as recorded in the 1891 England Census, he had moved to King's Norton, Birmingham where he would work as a solicitor's clerk then solicitor at Beale and Co. From there he moved to Alderbrook Road, Solihull but there is no extant evidence that he pursued his football career in the area. Turner did remain in active practice up to his death on 29 March 1944 and in his obituary, he is credited with playing for Queen's Park (though direct confirmation has not been discovered) and earning himself the nickname 'Iron Turner'.[66] Turner is a further illustration of a middle-class player making an impact in a relatively working-class side and community. In Chapter Four some football historians were admonished for assuming that East Lancashire sides were made up solely of working-class individuals. Turner, like Gledhill, Hacking and Hargreaves before him, exemplified a continued middle-class presence in what was becoming a working-class bastion.

★★★

The classic Anglo–Scottish encounters in which Turner played were made possible by the fact that Queen's Park, already a member of the Scottish FA, was also affiliated to the Football Association. The club would enter nine out of the 14 seasons from the cup's inception in 1871–2 up to and including 1884–5 as Scotland's sole representative, except, that is, in 1875–6, when Clydesdale, who allowed South Norwood a walkover, entered. In 1885–6, as well as Queen's, the Scottish contingent would be supplemented by Third Lanark, Rangers, Partick Thistle and Heart of Midlothian, but the following campaign was to be the last for teams from north of the border. A record seven Scottish sides competed, those from 1885–6 plus Cowlairs and Renton, all of whom were affiliated to the FA. Indeed, a meeting of Honorary Secretaries of clubs in membership of the FA on 21 March 1885 included four administrators from north of the border, attending on behalf of Edinburgh, Dumbarton, Scotland and Glasgow.[67] The Scottish FA, perhaps mindful about matters of jurisdiction in the event of a dispute between clubs and realising that its clubs' continued presence in another country's cup competition undermined its own authority, decided that there would be no further entries from sides under its control into the English contest. Apart from Queen's, the Rangers club would make the greatest impact, but not until that final season of Scottish participation, when they reached the semi-final before succumbing to Aston Villa.

The 1885–6 competition saw professionals legally accepted into the fray and, just as the southern amateur era came to an end, so would the supremacy of East Lancashire. There was, however, to be one last triumph for Blackburn Rovers in the 1880s before they produced a further two victories at the beginning of the next decade. If one views the results of the 1885–6 FA Cup, the one thing which comes to the fore is the extraordinary number of disqualifications. Both Preston and Bolton produced their objections against each other, with Preston being ejected for the second time in three years after George Drummond, one of their Scotsmen, was found guilty of breaking FA residential qualifications. Bolton, after a lengthy FA investigation, was also removed over similar infractions by their Welshman, John 'Jack' Powell. Although professionalism had been legalised, there were still rules in place – 'stringent conditions' – which were all too easily infringed or circumvented, especially if vanquished opponents were looking to overturn a defeat. Some disqualifications represented teething problems with embryonic professionalism, but why should four southern amateur XIs be disqualified following the third round? Surely there was no suggestion of payment for playing. Indeed, money did not play a part – merely organisational ineptitude, bloody-mindedness and disinterest. *The Field* noted that neither Clapham Rovers (against South Reading) nor Old Harrovians (against Swifts) arrived at their pre-arranged fixtures and were disqualified. However, both Old Wykehamists and Marlow were guilty of not even attempting to arrange their tie, with the newspaper reporter noting that

> It is to be regretted that such a course had to be pursued, but it must be borne in mind that the rule on the subject is clear, and that it has over and over again been pointed out to clubs that they run a great risk in leaving the settlement of cup matches until the last available day.[68]

In other games, there were surprises when Redcar beat Middlesbrough in a local 'derby' and Notts. County lost to South Shore from Blackpool, both games being in the fifth round. Each losing team suffered a serious injury to a player, who, unfortunately being unable to carry on, prejudiced his team's chances. But, perhaps as a predictor of future events, there were two clubs from the West Midlands – West Bromwich Albion and Small Heath Alliance (the forerunners of the present-day Birmingham City) – in the semi-finals. They met each other at Aston Lower Grounds, Birmingham later renamed Villa Park and the home of Aston Villa. West Bromwich won easily by four clear goals, but things off the field turned rather unpleasant towards the end of the game.

> The partisans of the Small Heath were considerably 'riled' by the defeat of their men, and could not conceal their chagrin, but gave vent to their feeling by breaking into the enclosure [onto the field] and stopping the play, and snowballing members of the Albion team off the ground…they amused themselves by pelting occupants of all vehicles that left the ground with frozen snow.[69]

The Illustrated Sporting and Dramatic News went further and noted insightfully that this sort of behaviour was fairly commonplace 'on certain northern and midland grounds'.[70] This type of misconduct by football crowds was typical of what might be described as early 'football hooliganism'. Instead of targeting opposing fans, rowdy groups of supporters would express their anger at either the opposing team's players or, more usually, towards the referee.[71]

The final, between Blackburn Rovers and West Bromwich Albion, initially produced a 0-0 draw, with the *Pall Mall Gazette* blaming the Blackburn players' attendance at the Boat Race for their lacklustre performance.[72] Unsurprisingly, having seemingly 'exhausted' themselves by the river, the Lancashire men refused, quite legitimately, to play extra time and the match went to a replay at the Racecourse Ground, now the Derbyshire County Cricket Ground and the original home of Derby County – it would be the first time a final had been held outside the capital – where they won a disappointing match by two goals to nil. Rovers had achieved a hat-trick of cup victories, but as they collected the cup, they were naturally unaware that this would be the culmination of their successes for the time being, with the torch being passed, temporarily at least, to teams from the West Midlands.

Conclusion

There are several secondary source studies covering the move by the association game to professionalisation. This section has been included in the conclusion so that the reader is hopefully already familiar with names and key terms which have already been used by each author. The most recent in-depth analysis is attempted by Dave Russell in his essay, 'From Evil to Expedient: The Legalization of Professionalism in English Football, 1884–5', which appears in Stephen Wagg's edited book, *Myths and Milestones in the History of Sport*. In a well-balanced examination, which has already been referenced several times in this chapter, Russell reminds the reader that payment for playing was already embedded in British sport and other forms of recreation,[73] though importation and remuneration in football only became illegal in the early 1880s. Indeed, those against payments in soccer were more concerned with it being a challenge to the spirit of the game.[74] Most parts of the country were against professionalism[75] with the exception of Lancashire and, eventually, the southern amateurs,[76] though the situation in the south was complicated. Their representatives, such as Charles Alcock and, belatedly, NL Jackson of Corinthian fame, were, echoing Dunning and Sheard, secure in their social status and appeared so far removed from working-class players that they refused to perceive them as any kind of threat to their status. Russell also suggests that southern football organisations had rarely been exposed to contact with professional performers and may naively have believed themselves to be immune to their attitudes and behaviour. Their exposure was, indeed, limited.[77] He also regards the British Football Association as more of pressure group than a potential new governing body.[78] Finally, Russell notes that the number of professional soccer players was actually quite small, perhaps in early 1885 as low as 100. He believes that the prompt action of the FA probably avoided a damaging split and, once established, professionalism was 'crucial' in the game's development in becoming the premier football code in England.[79]

Indeed, during the professionalism debate, many of those in favour of monetary reward often mentioned the fact that there were professionals in cricket, the sport perhaps regarded as soccer's summer equivalent. Indeed, one such advocate of this viewpoint was Charles Alcock himself, who could not see 'why men should not... labour at football as at cricket'.[80] If southern football clubs had received little exposure to teams using professionals, this might explain their eventual support for the switch to payment for playing. However – and perhaps significantly – when 'push came to shove' and a team was directly affected by having to play against veiled professionals and importations, as Upton Park showed, they were not slow to protest. As mentioned previously, Rule 25, which involved teams being removed from the FA Cup if they played against clubs using banned players, could have been circumvented by simply dropping out of the national competition. What irked Lancashire organisations most was that the FA seemed to think it could interfere in previously agreed fixture lists which were not FA Cup ties. Lastly, the British Football Association appeared to be as much of a threat to the Lancashire FA as it was to the FA in London.

Parts of two other texts are extremely informative, with both Graham Williams' *The Code War* and Steven Tischler's *Footballers and Businessmen* both being worthy of consultation and consideration in connection with the move towards professionalism.[81] Indeed, Williams appears to have introduced a piece of rarely, if ever, quoted evidence. He brings to the attention of the reader that Upton Park, in their cup run in the 1883-4 season, which included the game against Preston North End notorious for its repercussions, imported players especially for these ties. He says that they 'had specially strengthened their team for the FA Cup ties by recruiting two players from Oxford University, and one each from Cambridge University and Sandhurst'.[82] Commenting on this possibility, Williams is especially critical of the attitude of the southern amateurs. Upton Park's supposed 'importation' of club outsiders for important cup fixtures is described as 'one law for the rich and one for the poor',[83] conveniently forgetting that Preston's players were paid while Upton Park's were almost certainly not.

Was Upton Park guilty of 'importation'? Its team against Preston lined up as follows: AJ Stanley, WJ Mangles, EA Young, N Logan, RS King, J Barnard, H Brealey, SR Bastard, N Leete, C Mitchell, AM Inglis. Of these, only Stanley, King and Mitchell – the latter an England international[84] – had not been present in the previous two rounds against Acton and Reading. Stanley, one of four goalkeepers used in as many FA Cup ties that season, and Mitchell are to be found in team lists in 1883 and were fairly regular players for the club.[85] Robert Stuart King, along with Mitchell, attended Felsted before moving on to Hertford College, Oxford starting in 1881 and only leaving in 1885, making one appearance for his country.[86] It would appear, therefore, that he was still at Oxford when the game with Preston took place and might, in those terms, be considered an 'importation'. He also appeared in the team for the next round against Blackburn Rovers. Williams is seemingly incorrect to claim several importations, though King was clearly called up from his studies at Oxford. He does seem to have been a little uncharitable in his assessment of the make-up of the Upton Park team.

Tischler gives a full introduction to the advent of professionalism, charting the course of football's development from the plebeian, through the public schools and into wider society before opening his account of professionalism partway through Chapter 2. He stresses the involvement of class consciousness in his writing, noting that '"Professional" came to be accepted as a euphemism for "working class"'[87] and notes the 'decline in the number of public-school graduates who played Association football once professionalism was legalized in 1885', which supported 'the notion that class prejudice was a significant factor in the opposition to professionalism'.[88] Tischler's strength is his preparatory comment, including an opening chapter on plebeian and schoolboy football, which primes the reader for what is to follow. However, this results in the sections on the advent of professionalism and discussions of this process only amounting to around 20 pages out of the 144.

This author would wish to suggest that, while all three studies are commendable efforts, this book, not just in the section on the professionalism process but throughout the text, delves much more deeply into the existing evidence and provides, in particular, in-depth, original factual research and writing on many of the individuals involved.

★★★

Importation and payment for playing appeared to go hand in hand in some districts. This was not inevitable, nor was it the case everywhere in English football. The two together produced controversy but also tended to breed successful teams, as entrepreneurs and communities vied with each other to achieve success – especially in our chosen topic, the FA Cup or English Cup as some, in those times, had styled it. This chapter deals more with professionalism than the cup itself, yet the two were inextricably intertwined, particularly when one considers that 'the cat was let out of the bag' in one of the contest's ties, Preston North End against Upton Park. They were also inseparably linked because the cup provided a platform for the expression of identity from northern communities, leading as it did

112 *Importations and the coming of professionalism*

to individuals and groups placing an inappropriate significance on success in what was becoming a prized national competition.

James Beresford's tale is instructive of the whole process. He was clearly a talented player and followed the path of an importation. The transfer of soccer (and cricket) talent between Staveley and East Lancashire had, indeed, become a well-trodden path, from a micro-centre of footballing excellence in North East Derbyshire, to *the* cauldron of professionalism on the other side of the Pennines.[89] There he would, of course, have joined the many Scots who had trekked down to England to earn money from something in which they excelled and enjoyed, though the process itself denuded Scotland of much of its best football talent. Conversely, Richard Turner's story is a further illustration of a middle-class individual thriving in the working-class, money-driven footballing subculture of East Lancashire.

The social status of the administrators at the FA, unlike their nervous provincial counterparts who despised the practice, enabled them to accept professionalism as they felt secure in the widest sense, that is, their overall power to legislate in the game had not been lost. Indeed, the fact that their playing careers were over may have helped them to reach their decision. Southern amateur success on the field of play was already becoming a thing of the past and they may have become resigned to northern dominance in this aspect of the sport. However, they were not ready to relinquish their hold on the organisation of football and control of the development of the game. They must have been pleased with their efforts in avoiding a schism. Unfortunately, by solving one problem – perhaps saving the game from some kind of rugby-like split – they unintentionally legitimised over-competitiveness and an over-emphasis on winning and, with it, the FA may well have created other monsters.

Notes

1 25 January 1882.
2 *Bolton Evening News*, 4 November 1882.
3 *York Herald*, 20 January 1883.
4 Dickinson, *Origins*, 109.
5 Taylor, *Association Game*, 34–5.
6 Welch won the FA Cup twice with Wanderers and was an England international. He also edited *The Harrow School Register, 1801–1900*.
7 *The Field*, 24 September 1881.
8 Charles or 'Charlie' Peace was born in Sheffield and lived his life as a burglar and murderer. He killed two policemen, one in Manchester and another in London, and the husband of a neighbour's wife in Sheffield. He was hanged at Armley gaol, Leeds in February 1879. At one point his solicitor was William Edward Clegg, the Sheffield and England footballer and administrator.
9 24 January 1883.
10 *Sheffield and Rotherham Independent*, 24 January 1883.
11 See also the unsigned letter to *The Field* of 1 December 1883, in which the writer appears, among other things, to foresee the rugby split of 1895.
12 Lewis, 'Genesis of professional football', 27–34.
13 15 December 1883.
14 *Bolton Evening News*, 28 November 1883.
15 *Manchester Courier and Lancashire General Advertiser*, 19 May 1884.

Importations and the coming of professionalism 113

16 *Walsall Observer and South Staffordshire Chronicle*, 31 May 1884. Bolton played at home against Walsall Swifts for local charities. The game took place as late as 24 May 1884 with the weather being described as 'broiling hot'.
17 *Sheffield Daily Telegraph*, 21 November 1882.
18 *Nottingham Evening Post*, 24 December 1892.
19 *Derbyshire Times and Chesterfield Herald*, 25 March 1893.
20 There is an excellent obituary to John MacAulay in the *Burnley Express* of 23 January 1937, which gives useful information on his colleagues in his footballing days and deals in brief with his journey down to Lancashire.
21 See Webb, *Scotland's Lost Clubs*, 90–3.
22 13 December 1884.
23 *Dundee Courier*, 19 March 1877.
24 10 March 1877.
25 *Glasgow Herald*, 12 March 1877.
26 26 October 1889.
27 *Sheffield Daily Telegraph*, 20 January 1885.
28 *The Sportsman*, 3 February 1885.
29 *Preston Herald*, 29 April 1885.
30 *Sheffield Daily Telegraph*, 14 May 1885.
31 Out of the 116 members of the FA Council in 2022–3, 53 are from County Associations.
32 Russell, 'From Evil to Expedient', 40.
33 *The Athletic News*, 1 September 1885.
34 *Blackburn Standard*, 20 March 1886.
35 25 June 1887.
36 Dunning and Sheard, *Barbarians*, 2005, 160–2.
37 Ibid, 2005, 163.
38 With thanks to Keri Griffiths and Maxine Tivey in the History Department of Tuxford Academy in Nottinghamshire for their valuable suggestions on this particular subject.
39 Email correspondence with Tony Collins, 26 April 2022.
40 Dunning and Sheard, *Barbarians*, 2005, 131.
41 Ibid, 132.
42 Russell, 'From Evil to Expedient', 49.
43 Green, *History of the Football Association*, 88.
44 The original site of the school was around the present Merchiston Tower, though it moved its site to a more rural location in Colinton, Edinburgh in 1930.
45 The Millennium Stadium in Cardiff, Wales was used for both semi-finals in the 2004–5 season.
46 *Glasgow Evening Post*, 28 March 1885.
47 *Sporting Life*, 6 April 1885.
48 My thanks for the correct pronunciation go to Blackburn native and my colleague at England Over-60s football, Tony Jones.
49 Fecitt Road is a current thoroughfare off Mollington Road in North Blackburn.
50 Occasionally spelt 'Howarth' (*Preston Herald*, 21 January 1885), which may have resulted from there being another Howarth from Lancashire, this one named Bob, who played for Preston North End around the same time. George also played for Preston against Corinthians in January 1885 and, confusingly, the two made their international debuts for England against Ireland on 5 February 1887.
51 11 April 1885.
52 Rule 3 of the 1871–2 FA Challenge Cup rules stated, 'No individual shall be allowed to play for more than one competing Club, but the members of each representative team may be changed during the series of matches, if thought necessary'. Betts and Ottaway provide instances in the first season when this rule may have been broken. See Chapter 1. My thanks to Tony Brown.
53 *Manchester Courier and Lancashire General Advertiser*, 13 October 1884.
54 *The Sportsman*, 4 April 1885.

114 *Importations and the coming of professionalism*

55 *Cricket and Football Field*, 3 April 1886.
56 The 5th Duke of Portland, commonly known as Lord John Bentinck, is often remembered for being a recluse and eccentric, with rumours abounding that he built a series of tunnels under Welbeck so that he could move around but not be observed.
57 *Mansfield Reporter*, 8 October 1880.
58 *The Athletic News*, 5 December 1883.
59 Ibid, 24 September 1884.
60 Ibid, 30 April 1884.
61 *Sheffield Daily Telegraph*, 9 January 1885.
62 *The Athletic News*, 19 May 1885.
63 28 September 1886.
64 *Sporting Life*, 12 December 1887.
65 5 October 1886.
66 *Birmingham Daily Post*, 30 March 1944.
67 *The Sportsman*, 23 March 1885.
68 19 December 1885.
69 *Nuneaton Advertiser*, 13 March 1886.
70 13 March 1886.
71 See Curry, 'Football Spectatorship'.
72 5 April 1886.
73 Russell, 'From Evil to Expedient', 33.
74 Ibid, 33.
75 Ibid, 34.
76 Ibid, 45.
77 Ibid, 51.
78 Ibid, 41.
79 Ibid, 52.
80 Quoted in Williams, *Code War*, 92.
81 Chapter Ten in *The Code War* and Chapter Two in *Footballers and Businessmen* are the salient sections.
82 Williams, *Code War*, 89.
83 Ibid, 89.
84 Freddi, *England Football Fact Book*, 194. Clement Mitchell attended Felsted School in Essex and eventually earned five caps.
85 *Field*, 3 March 1883 versus Civil Service; *Morning Post*, 24 October 1883 versus Royal Military Academy; *The Sportsman*, 10 January 1883 versus Barnes.
86 Freddi, *England Football Fact Book*, 178.
87 Tischler, *Footballers and Businessmen*, 43.
88 Ibid, 45.
89 See Curry, 'Spireites'.

6 West Midlands supremacy and the advent of the Football League

The 1886–7 campaign for the FA Cup was full of incidents. If watersheds were being sought, the result of a first round match in that season's competition surely provided one. Preston North End journeyed to Hampden Park, Glasgow to play Queen's Park and subsequently defeated them on 30 October 1886 with ease by three goals to nil, which represented an improvement for Queen's following the 6-1 beating handed out by Preston in a challenge match in Glasgow on 25 September 1886. The game created intense interest and over 15,000 spectators were present. Intriguingly, one newspaper report noted that Queen's had 'recruited the services of a professional trainer', which was a little surprising as they still represented and would continue to represent until 2019 one of the decaying bastions of football amateurism.[1] However, it was the raucous scenes at the end of the match following a foul by Preston's centre forward, Scotsman Jimmy Ross (who we have met briefly through his comments on veiled professionalism in Chapter Five), towards the end of the 90 minutes, which stood out. As the game finished, several Queen's players sportingly gathered round Ross to protect him, fully expecting the crowd's wrath and, as they left the field, hundreds of disappointed Scots – many brandishing sticks and umbrellas – attempted to reach the Preston player. The unhappy multitude remained outside the pavilion where the players were changing and forced them to stay inside until the mob had dispersed. As with the overzealous partisans of Small Heath Alliance in Chapter Five, this was typical of Victorian soccer 'hooliganism'.[2] Despite the presence of several hundred Preston followers, the chagrin of the 'wronged' football spectators was directed not at them but at the winning side's players, with the usual gathering of disgruntled 'fans' remaining after the game intimidating any of the opposition wanting to make a quick exit.[3]

The Preston team that day was as follows (Scottish born players in italics):

Arthur Wharton, *Nick Ross*, Bob Howarth, *Johnny Graham, Sandy Robertson, David Russell*, Fred Dewhurst, *George Drummond*, Sam Thomson, *Jimmy Ross, Jack Gordon*

The North End goalkeeper Arthur Wharton is generally recognised as the first black professional footballer. He was born in what is now Ghana and moved to England in 1882 to train as a Methodist minister. Not only was he a first-rate

DOI: 10.4324/9781003285595-7

goalkeeper, he was also a world-class sprinter and a more than useful cricketer.[4] Another interesting class anomaly was Fred Dewhurst, captain of Preston, who was an assistant master at Preston Catholic Grammar School[5] and an England international. He would be a major contributor to Preston's unbeaten league campaign in 1888–9 and victory in the FA Cup during the same season, scoring against Wolverhampton Wanderers in the 3-0 victory in the final. Dewhurst also played for the Corinthians, served as North End secretary,[6] but died at the tragically young age of 31 in 1895.

With a team consisting of more Scots than Englishmen, Preston would almost certainly have been unpopular in Glasgow for luring away many of the country's most talented footballers, with local crowds resentful of the whole process. The game itself might almost have been advertised as Scotland Amateurs (Queen's) versus Scotland Professionals (Preston), such were the numbers of Scots in the English team's line-up, with the opposing sides that day being the clearest representations of the financial polarisation of the game at that time. Some newspaper columns felt that the home crowd was reacting as much to Preston's robust 'professional' playing approach and also the fact that they were clearly one of the most overt examples of importation and commercialisation in football. The Jimmy Ross foul, which unfortunately was committed only a couple of minutes before the end of the game, would have been fresh in the minds of the miscreants, though the press roundly condemned the crowd's behaviour, commonly describing it as 'disgraceful'.[7] Interestingly, the headline of the *Glasgow Herald* report tells of 'an English player mobbed', despite the fact that Jimmy Ross was Scottish, though, of course, he played for an English club. This may be indicative of a complete loss of Scottish identity on the part of Ross, certainly in Scottish eyes, and of other Scots who journeyed south to earn wages from the game. In the eyes of the Scottish football follower, it was probably debatable which was worse – being a professional or relocating to England.

In 1886–7, their final season in the FA Cup, Scottish sides would soon redress the balance of the Queen's Park defeat in future contests, but that particular result must have come as a shock to soccer *cognoscenti* north of the border. Also in the first round, Partick Thistle beat a rapidly declining Blackburn Olympic in Lancashire, while Renton edged past Accrington with a goal three minutes from time. Cowlairs and Third Lanark were too good for lesser lights Darwen Old Wanderers and Higher Walton, respectively, while Everton allowed Rangers a walkover. The latter encounter was a strange tale. The game was played in Liverpool and Everton 'scratched', as they knew that some of their better players were ineligible in terms of being importations and, therefore, had they won, they were convinced that their opponents would appeal against the result. Rangers turned up and, with 6,000 spectators providing a healthy gate for what was essentially a friendly, the clubs went ahead with the fixture, which the away side won 1-0.[8] Most interesting of all – and a reverse to the trend of Scottish success – was the 7-1 thrashing meted out to Heart of Midlothian at Darwen. However, looking back to Table 5.1 in Chapter Five of this book, it was not that surprising, as the Edinburgh team had by that time been denuded of many of their better performers by English clubs.

This Scottish hegemony continued in the second round, with all but Third Lanark being victorious. Renton knocked out cup holders Blackburn Rovers, the latter having shown indifferent form all season, with their perennial ability to perform on the big occasion deserting them this time. However, the result may not have come as a complete surprise. The side from north of the border had won the Scottish Cup in 1884–5, been runners-up in the following season and won again in 1887–8. Of course, one way of ridding the competition of at least one Scottish team was to draw two against each other – Rangers beat Cowlairs in the third round. Eventually, Preston were too good for Renton, which left Partick Thistle and Rangers, with the former losing to Old Westminsters, though the southern amateur team did have an England international in defender Ralph Tyndall Squire (Westminster School 1876–82; Trinity Hall, Cambridge 1882–5) and two future England internationals in goalkeeper William Robert Moon (Westminster School 1883–5) and forward John Gould Veitch (Westminster School 1883–7; Trinity, Cambridge 1887–90).[9] This left Rangers to overpower the old boys in the sixth round, though the Glasgow side was reinforced from previous contests by John Forbes from Vale of Leven and Patrick Lafferty of Hibernian.[10] Forbes would come south in the late 1880s and win two FA Cups with Blackburn Rovers in 1889–90 and 1890–1. Lafferty was a former Rangers player and though it may seem that a player with close links to Hibernian – a staunchly Catholic club – could represent Rangers – a staunchly Protestant organisation – sectarian tensions were less of an issue in the 1880s.[11]

As well as professionalism and importations, the tendency to bring in talented individuals from other clubs for high-profile cup games was fairly widespread, and we have previously encountered this practice in Chapter Five with reference to the Wednesday club in Sheffield and their FA Cup ties with Nottingham Forest in January 1883. Also in the sixth round, Preston North End only sneaked past Old Carthusians after extra time, thus reinforcing the view that the old boys were not a completely spent force, though their lack of fitness, when compared to their professional opponents, did draw comment.[12] All in all, after the 1886–7 season, when the Scottish FA legislated against its clubs taking part in the 'English Cup', it must have come as a relief for Lancashire sides in particular who, because the FA operated a regionalised draw at least until the sixth round, often found themselves opposed to strong sides from north of the border in the early stages of the competition.

One name not instantly recognisable in the fifth round was Lockwood Brothers, seemingly at first glance a factory side from Sheffield. The firm was one of the leading cutlery manufacturers in the city and by 1881 employed over 400 workers. The football section was established in 1870, first appearing in press reports during the 1874–5 season in minor matches against the likes of Heeley Victoria, Broomhall and Dore. However, following this relatively encouraging beginning, after just two seasons they seemingly disappeared from view. They resurfaced in the 1879–80 season and were ultimately successful in winning three prestigious competitions: the Sheffield FA Challenge Cup and the Wharncliffe Charity Cup in 1883–4, and the Challenge Cup again in 1884–5.[13] A rare photograph of the team and administrators, accompanied by a brief history of the club, appeared in *The Sheffield Weekly Telegraph* on 31 May 1884 with the two trophies won in that season.

In 1886–7, Wednesday failed to enter the FA Cup[14] and Lockwood Brothers benefitted by gaining several of their players – some of the best in the city – for the cup contests and, consequently, were able to field the likes of Billy Mosforth, Tom Cawley, John 'Jack' Hudson and Teddy Brayshaw, all Wednesday regulars immeasurably strengthening an already effective team. Lockwood Brothers defeated Long Eaton Rangers 1-0, Cleethorpes Town 4-1 and, impressively, Nottingham Forest 2-1 and were awarded a bye in the fourth round. In the fifth round, they would meet the beaten finalists of the past two seasons, West Bromwich Albion, with the initial match at Bramall Lane being a tight affair with the visitors scraping home after extra time by the single goal scored. However, Lockwood Brothers appealed against the disallowing of what they felt had been a legitimate goal scored by them and won the right to replay the match. For the return, West Bromwich claimed a neutral venue and hostilities were recommenced at the Midland Ground, Derby.[15] The Lockwood Brothers team that day was as follows (Wednesday regulars are in italics): Brook, Salkeld, Stringer, *Hudson*, *Brayshaw*, Betts, West, Winterbottom,[16] *Mosforth*, *Cawley*, Sellars.

West Bromwich won by two goals to one, but the most interesting aspect was the make-up of the Lockwood Brothers team. In order to identify exactly how many players they had 'borrowed' from Wednesday, it is informative to compare the line-ups in this match and the one which took place less than a month later in the Sheffield FA Challenge Cup semi-final between Lockwood Brothers and Wednesday, the latter winning 4-1. Hudson, Brayshaw, Cawley and Mosforth were in the Wednesday XI, while Brooks, Salkeld, Stringer, Betts, Winterbottom, West and Sellars played for Lockwoods. Therefore, only four men were 'borrowed' from Wednesday for the replay against West Bromwich. This indicates, to a large extent, that Lockwood Brothers were, in their own right, a more than useful outfit and the reinforcement by Wednesday regulars merely made them even stronger. However, the four Wednesday men who did play in the semi-final replay were some of the best footballers in England, let alone Sheffield. Indeed, by the time of the replay, Mosforth, Brayshaw and Hudson were already internationals, while Cawley came to be regarded as a Wednesday legend and may perhaps have been unlucky not to be rewarded with a full England cap.

The end was swift for Lockwood Brothers Football Club. In the following season, 1887–8, they played Wolverhampton Wanderers at Bramall Lane in what would surely have been a closer encounter had the Sheffield side fielded anything like the line-ups regarded as commonplace in 1886–7. The score line, a victory for the visitors by a resounding eight goals to nil, was an indicator that Lockwood's glory days were at an end. Indeed, there is no mention of the club for the next decade and one can only postulate that it became defunct at the end of the 1887–8 campaign.

However, there still existed within the city's football community, the feeling that Sheffield's talent was diluted, leading to poor results in the national competition, which disappointingly continued to prevail in the city. In terms of on-field success, the Sheffield teams had lagged behind the southern amateurs, having been overtaken by Glasgow from the beginning of the 1875–6 season and now both

Lancashire and the West Midlands were moving ahead of them.[17] There was, however, a growing belief in South Yorkshire, primarily because of Lockwood Brothers' performances, that effective results against the leading teams from the rest of the country would only be achieved in two ways – by creating a team of all talents from footballers in Sheffield and through an acceptance by the Sheffield FA of professionalism. A new team, Sheffield Rovers, was formed and played its first game in April 1887, clearly being serious about challenging for honours in the near future. Although Rovers quickly fell by the wayside, one consequence was that it forced Wednesday's hand on payment for playing, with the club turning professional on 22 April 1887, a decision principally influenced by a plea from the aforementioned Tom Cawley. This action largely fashioned a club capable of making an impression in the FA Cup, as many of the better Sheffield performers were understandably not shy about accepting money for turning out on the football field. Professionalism in football was about to storm one of the sport's last bastions of amateurism – or, at least, 'shamateurism' – and now even Sheffield, perhaps the most sceptical of subcultures in this regard, had accepted that the city could not stand alone and ignore payment for playing. But did it make a difference to performances on the field? The following season saw Wednesday reach the last eight before elimination by the great Preston side, while in 1889–90 they were defeated finalists. Consecutive semi-final appearances in 1893–4 and 1894–5 were followed, in 1895–6, by an overdue FA Cup victory, as Wednesday beat Wolverhampton Wanderers to win their first 'English Cup'. Almost 40 years from the founding of the first football club in the form of Sheffield FC in 1857, the city finally had its national football trophy.

★★★

In the semi-finals of the 1886–7 FA Cup, the new power in the English game, the West Midlands, provided two teams – Aston Villa and West Bromwich Albion – who would go on to contest the final itself. While Albion defeated Preston, Villa took care of the last Scottish side in the cup, Rangers. The latter match took place at the Alexandra Ground, Crewe a venue perceived by the FA as allowing easy access by rail – the ground was adjacent to the station – with the playing surface also being first class.[18] Rangers were disappointing, despite again having the two 'imports' Forbes and Lafferty. In the other semi-final, Albion were grateful to their goalkeeper, Bob Roberts, who kept Preston at bay, though the game, at Trent Bridge, Nottingham, which West Bromwich won 3-1, was described as being 'one of the most scientific [Victorian football reporters usually employed 'scientific' to mean 'skillful'] ever witnessed'.[19] Villa had been a little fortunate in round three, having to play three replays against another West Midlands side, Wolverhampton Wanderers. However, they prevailed in their first final to leave Albion disappointed losers for the second successive year. Villa struggled to find their rhythm until the second period, but in the end were worthy winners.

The 1887–8 campaign saw the record score for the competition, which still stands in 2022, achieved by Preston North End, who beat Hyde by 26 goals to nil. Several reasons were suggested to explain the overwhelming victory: Preston was becoming so much better than everyone else, especially in 'combination' play – that is, passing; some spectators thought that the referee had played five minutes of additional time in the second half; finally, Hyde lost a man with a sprained arm in the first half, though Preston allowed a substitute as a replacement. Incredibly, some Preston supporters were reported as being disappointed with the final score, expecting at least 30 goals, and were even mildly critical that some North End men eased off in the second half![20]

The composition of the West Bromwich Albion side at this time leant heavily on English players, so much so that in the 1887–8 final, following their victory over a Preston team heavy with 'Scotch professors' (all the Albion men were English while Preston had only four, the others being six Scots and a Welsh goalkeeper) the FA President and referee of the final, Francis Marindin, was said to have asked the Albion team, 'Are you all Englishmen?' and, when their reply was in the affirmative, complimented them on their play and presented them with the match ball.[21] Apocryphal or not, the story rather sums up the simmering resentment caused by importations. *The Sportsman* seemed to confirm suspicions that the side consisting of local, English players were favoured in most quarters, noting that Albion's victory was 'all the more creditable as the whole of the team are "native born", having first seen the light within six miles of the club's headquarters'.[22] An interesting tangent to this story is that one writer, at least, offers a contrasting date to the one suggested above, with Graham Williams noting the incident as happening at the 1886–7 semi-final between Albion and Preston at Trent Bridge.[23] The discrepancy is probably irrelevant, as similar tales were utilised in encounters where largely English combinations beat those mostly made up of importations, usually – though not always – from Scotland, to re-emphasise some sort of sporting nationalism exhibited in footballing supremacy over an old enemy.

Reflecting on the initial development of football in the West Midlands involves the researcher in diverse geographical areas such as Stoke, Walsall, Wolverhampton, Stafford, West Bromwich and Wednesbury, all – at least historically – in Staffordshire, as well as in Birmingham itself. These individual communities value their separate identities very deeply. Club football in Birmingham almost certainly began when Calthorpe FC was formed in the south of the city in 1873, playing as Birmingham Clerks Association on Calthorpe Park.[24] Attitudes were decidedly middle class, with some participants being given the title of 'Mr' in the match report. However, events in Staffordshire actually preceded this as, in 1869, a factory side, Elwell's FC, began an incredible series of club formations in the town of Wednesbury, where eventually five sides involved in senior football emerged. The Elwell's team was drawn exclusively from the workforce of the Edward Elwell's foundry, which produced edge tools such as spades, shovels and hoes and, in football terms, generally gave a good account of themselves without winning much. At least four more clubs were eventually formed in the town – Wednesbury Strollers (founded 1872), Wednesbury Old Athletic (1874), Wednesbury Old Park (1875) and Wednesbury Town (1883).[25] Old Athletic was the most successful, winning the Birmingham Challenge Cup – now the Senior Cup – in 1876–7 and 1878–9, followed by the Staffordshire Senior Challenge Cup in 1879–80. The town represented a vibrant hub of the game in the late 1870s and early 1880s but became a location where the initial impetus of relative success was lost. As a centre of population, it was dwarfed by Birmingham, Wolverhampton and West Bromwich, which usually meant smaller crowds, and this inability to attract spectators limited player rewards. Diluted attendances, with so many teams in the town, also led to lower individual gates. Consequently, the better performers from Old Athletic, and many other smaller clubs, were enticed away, the most prominent of which was Albert Edward James Matthias (Jem) Bayliss, who eventually went on to captain West Bromwich Albion in the 1887-8 FA Cup Final and play for England. We have already met Stafford Road in Chapter Three, which consisted of workers from the Stafford Road Railway Works just north of the centre of Wolverhampton, but what was striking about the rise of many clubs in the region, was that they encouraged and utilised local talent. Old Athletic was founded by scholars from a local night school; Old Park was a factory team from the Patent Shaft Steel Works, the largest employer in Wednesbury; Strollers the brainchild of a local dignitary; while Town grew from a breakaway of some Old Athletic members.[26]

Continuing the local community theme, both Wolverhampton Wanderers and West Bromwich Albion also fell into this category. Wanderers' links to St. Luke's Elementary School saw them enlist numerous players into their ranks from there, while Albion drew recruits from George Salter's steel spring factory as well as Christ Church School. Indeed, in the 1885-6 FA Cup Final, Albion included seven of Salter's employees, while in 1887-8, they utilised six former pupils of Christ Church.[27] This awareness of footballing talent in the local community played a significant role in football's development in the West Midlands, which is in stark contrast to the importation approach employed in Lancashire. Little wonder that the sympathies of neutrals in general, perhaps nationalistically motivated, should be with them when they engaged with their Lancashire rivals.

The one exception was Aston Villa. There developed a strong Scottish connection at Villa — their club badge is clearly the Scottish 'lion rampant' — through players such as George Ramsay who would go on to be the club's highly successful manager for over 40 years from 1886, Archie Hunter and his brother Andy, another pair of brothers in James and Billy Lindsay, but — most importantly — their committee member, administrator, President and eventual Chairman, William McGregor. The latter has been portrayed as a visionary and this is probably true. McGregor was born in Braco, Perthshire, Scotland, moved south to Birmingham in 1870 and established a drapery business before becoming involved in the aforementioned Calthorpe FC. A teetotaller and supporter of the Temperance movement, McGregor was very much the committed Christian. However, he will be forever remembered for being the driving force behind the establishment of the Football League in 1888.

Professionalism in English football had been legalised in 1885, but with regular income needed to pay their contracted players, most clubs found it difficult to arrange a season-long series of high-profile friendlies with which to attract large paying audiences. When, as sometimes happened, these friendlies were cancelled because of other commitments, such as being forced by local associations to play cup ties, teams found themselves without a match, no spectators came through the turnstiles and organisations were unable to raise the money to pay their employees.

Consistent fixtures were required, and McGregor thought he had found the solution by inviting initially five and then 12 of the leading clubs to join a league. McGregor himself had links with baseball,[28] and he and others would have been cognisant of the flourishing leagues in that sport taking place in the United States. The Football League was, quite clearly, a blatant commercial enterprise and organisations were partly chosen on their ability to attract large crowds, but the league certainly selected its original members well. Only Accrington FC – not to be confused with Accrington Stanley – and Notts. County of the 12 chosen clubs are not playing in the main English league structure in 2022.

★★★

McGregor and the Football League leads us into the final season of our study, 1888–9, when the FA Cup would face pressure from the newly created competition for élite football clubs, all of them from the north and the Midlands. Inevitably, comparisons would be made between the two competitions and there is value in studying events which ought to be indicative of trends and hypotheses in the process.

The FA decided to revamp the FA Cup in the first season of league competition. Its plan was explained in *The Illustrated Sporting and Dramatic News*, which observed that the competition 'is now limited to thirty-two clubs – the four left in for the semi-finals in the previous spring, eighteen selected by the Association, and one from each of the ten divisions into which the country has been cut up'.[29] There were, indeed, changes to the competition rules and structure, with the task of organising the ten qualifying groups delegated for the first time to the county associations. These represented the ten divisions from which there would be one qualifier each.

In those qualifiers there were first round exits for Old Etonians, Wednesbury Old Athletic, Royal Engineers and Old Wykehamists, the latter being eliminated by Chatham, who would reach the third round, effectively the last eight. Everton, Bolton Wanderers, Stoke and Notts. County of the clubs accepted for the inaugural league season were included in the qualifiers. Because they had to face Preston on the opening day of the league, Stoke selected their reserves, Stoke Swifts, at home against Warwickshire County in the cup, and lost 2-1, while County fielded a similarly weak side against Eckington Works from near Sheffield immediately prior to their opening match in the league with Blackburn Rovers. The *Nottingham Evening Post* of 6 October 1888 explained that

> Loyalty to the League formed among twelve of the leading Northern and Midland Football Clubs, compelled Notts., who were not included amongst the sixteen selected clubs, to entrust their fixtures throughout the qualifying competition to an 11 which curiously combined the old with the new blood of the club.

Significantly, the same newspaper noted that there were 2,000 spectators present for County's victory over Eckington, but this grew to 4,000 for County's league match against Blackburn.[30]

Of the two other league teams not 'invited' into the first round proper, Everton scratched from the first qualifier against Ulster, obviously not relishing the journey across the Irish Sea or even bothering to send their reserves, though the first XI beat Aston Villa by two goals to nil in their league game. Meanwhile, Hurst scratched against Lancashire rivals Bolton Wanderers, as they would have been challenged by Bolton for including ineligible players. A friendly fixture between the two clubs ensued, which ended 0-0, with no replay required. One history records this initial encounter with Hurst scratching in the replay,[31] though the impression given that a second game was required is incorrect. The 8 October 1888 editions of both the *Leeds Mercury* and the *London Evening Standard* already have Hurst handing Bolton a walkover, which is probably accurate.

The make-up of the first round proper of the FA Cup for season 1888–9 is shown in Table 6.1.

Table 6.1 Clubs involved in the FA Cup First Round Proper, 1888–9 (32)

Original Football League members (8)	
Burnley	
Aston Villa	
Preston North End	1887–8 semi-finalist
Accrington	
Blackburn Rovers	
Wolverhampton Wanderers	
Derby County	
West Bromwich Albion	1887–8 semi-finalist
Qualifiers from geographical regions (10)	
Linfield Athletic	
Chatham	
Small Heath	
Sunderland Albion	
Old Brightonians	
South Shore	
Grimsby Town	
Sheffield Heeley	
Notts. County	Original Football League member
Wrexham	
Invited clubs (14)	
Bootle	
Walsall Town Swifts	
Old Westminsters	
Swifts	
Nottingham Forest	
Witton	
Halliwell	
Crewe Alexandra	1887–8 semi-finalist
Old Carthusians	
Derby Junction	1887–8 semi-finalist
The Wednesday	
Notts. Rangers	
Birmingham St. George's	
Long Eaton Rangers	

124 *West Midlands supremacy and the advent of the Football League*

The league had selected its 12 clubs, but the FA had no need to take those choices into account; indeed, they may have deliberately picked others simply to be regarded as independent. The national governing body had been informed that league games would take place in the first half of the season, thus leaving the time after Christmas for County Cups, the FA Cup and various Charity Cups – in fact, the first league games took place on 8 September 1888 and the last one on 20 April 1889. The FA, therefore, chose clubs to pass straight into the first round proper on a number of criteria, the first of which was those that possessed the better overall records from the 1887–8 season. However, we should not be so naive as to think that there were no other reasons. Selecting Nottingham Forest and not Notts. County may well have been based on the former's continued commitment to amateurism, and while Old Carthusians had reached the last eight of the 1887–8 FA Cup with Swifts in round four, Old Westminsters had lost heavily to the Old Etonians in the third round in that season. Crewe Alexandra was fairly straightforward – they had been semi-finalists in 1887–8 and also had a good relationship with the FA as they had already provided the venue for one semi-final and would go on to host two more.

Notts. County played its reserve team again in the second qualifying round of the cup in a game with local rivals Beeston St. John's which, as with the match

Table 6.2 Clashes between cup and league, 1888–9

6 October 1888	**FA Cup First qualifying round**
	Notts. County 4 Eckington Works 1
	Stoke Swifts 1 Warwickshire County 2
	Ulster v Everton (Walkover for Ulster)
	Hurst v Bolton Wanderers (Walkover for Bolton Wanderers)
	Football League Match Day 5
	Burnley 4 Bolton Wanderers 1
	Everton 2 Aston Villa 0
	Notts. County 3 Blackburn Rovers 3
	Preston North End 7 Stoke 0
27 October 1888	**FA Cup Second qualifying round**
	Notts. County 4 Beeston St. John's 2
	West Manchester 1 Bolton Wanderers 0 Match declared void
	Football League Match Day 8
	Notts. County 6 Burnley 1
	No league fixture for Bolton Wanderers
3 November 1888	**FA Cup Second qualifying round replay**
	Bolton Wanderers 9 West Manchester 0
	Football League Match Day 9
	Everton 2 Bolton Wanderers 1
17 November 1888	**FA Cup Third qualifying round**
	Notts. County 2 Derby Midland 1
	Linfield Athletic 4 Bolton Wanderers 0
	Football League Match Day 12
	Bolton Wanderers 1 West Bromwich Albion 2
8 December 1888	**FA Cup Fourth qualifying round**
	Staveley 1 Notts. County 3
	Football League Match Day 15
	Notts. County 2 Aston Villa 4

with Eckington Works, preceded a first team league encounter, this time with Burnley. Two thousand were in attendance for the cup tie with this figure doubling by the time the league encounter began. Bolton surprisingly lost to a single goal to West Manchester but objected, as the match, having gone to extra time, was alleged to have been stopped six minutes before the end of the additional half hour.[32] Bolton were awarded a replay, which they easily won 9-0. In both games, Bolton played its second string, while at the same time as the replay, the first team lost to Everton in the league. Bolton's reserves were sent to Ireland in the third qualifier, where they were comprehensively beaten by Linfield Athletic.

County prioritised the FA Cup on 8 December 1888, which was the first time in that campaign that any club had decided to follow that course, though the strength of Staveley on its own ground was sufficient reason to do so. Staveley was a strong side, usually very physical and with an excellent home record and – furthermore – the encounter, 'so far as Staveley was concerned, was considered the match of the season'.[33] That campaign they would reach the Sheffield Challenge Cup Final only to lose to Rotherham Town.[34] County was described as utilising Notts. Rangers men against Aston Villa[35] in its league fixture which clashed with the Staveley FA Cup tie, though Shaw was the only name in common with Rangers' FA Cup first round tie with Wednesday in February 1889.[36] Interestingly, on a very wet and soggy day, 2,000 watched the cup match in the rain at Staveley, while just 1,500 saw County lose to Aston Villa in the league. The general public illustrated that they did not particularly care whether the match was for league or cup, what mattered was the standard of players involved and the likelihood of seeing good football together with a competitive game. Therefore, a forever discriminating supporter base soon realised that County was selecting its first team at Staveley and, consequently, that was where the larger crowd appeared. Over 11 home league games in season 1888-9, County attracted 44,000 spectators at an average of 4,000 per game. In four home cup matches during the same campaign, 8,500 onlookers came through the gate at an average of 2,125, significantly lower than league crowds.

Although there were league matches on subsequent days when rounds of the FA Cup were being played in 1888-9, they did not result in a clash for any of the competing clubs. Importantly, this tells us a great deal about how the original Football League viewed the FA Cup. It had issued instructions to its members to prioritise league matches over cup ties and it seems to indicate that some antipathy had remained over the struggle to legalise professionalism. However, Notts. County ignored this directive when playing Staveley and Aston Villa on the same Saturday prioritising the cup match, though there did not appear to have been any action taken against the club for disregarding the ruling. The league's decision certainly devalued the status of the FA Cup, with several of the better clubs selecting reserve sides, though the problem only arose in the qualifying competition. The two competing bodies appeared to have found a solution in the second season, 1889-90. All 12 league clubs were exempt from qualifying and went straight through to the first round proper. This did not take place until 18 January 1890, giving the league free rein before Christmas. Although several league games were played on cup dates, no team was involved in both competitions on the same occasion.

The 1888–9 FA Cup became a contest between Lancashire and the West Midlands. However, there was a surprise packet in Chatham FC who played at the army owned pitch at 'The Lines' where they regularly attracted crowds of approaching 10,000.[37] Unfortunately, there were no gates to take admission money and club officials were reported as 'going round with the box' in the crowd for 'donations', but the problem would only be solved by obtaining an enclosed ground.[38] These large, uncontrolled crowds were the main reason why the FA passed a rule stating that grounds must be enclosed to host ties in the FA Cup. In 1888, Rule 26 of the competition read as follows: *A club not having a private ground, and which, having the choice, decides to play its Cup Tie on an enclosed ground, in which gate money can be charged, shall pay the whole cost of the ground.* This effectively meant that the club with choice of ground could play on an open space if it so chose. However, by 1889 Rule 26 had become: *A club not having a private ground shall provide a private or enclosed ground to which gate money can be charged for Cup Ties free of all charge to the visiting Club, or play on its opponents' ground.* It was clear that clubs without an enclosed ground could still enter the competition but would have to play elsewhere.[39]

The other side in and around Chatham was the Royal Engineers, ensuring that the area's FA Cup pedigree was beyond doubt. However, there seems to be little indication in reports and team lists that there was any link between the town team and the 'Sappers'. Chatham's greatest moment came when it knocked Nottingham Forest out of the cup after a titanic struggle over three games. However, although Chatham was obviously a good team – it won the Kent Cup, known as the Kent County Badge, in each season of the competition's three-year existence – there were no noteworthy individuals in its ranks. Chatham met its match in the form of cup holders West Bromwich Albion, whose players were royally welcomed to Kent on the Friday before the game with 'coloured fire and a torch light procession'.[40] The number of people present at the fixture was thought to be around 16,000, an enormous crowd for what was a relatively provincial setting. Unfortunately, the home team was easily beaten by ten goals to one, though there may have been extenuating circumstances. The Chatham side had finally beaten Nottingham Forest in their trilogy of games on the Thursday before they faced West Bromwich Albion on the Saturday and this would probably have contributed to their heavy defeat. The semi-finals were literally Lancashire against the West Midlands, as Preston North End beat West Bromwich Albion and Wolverhampton Wanderers overcame Blackburn Rovers.

***

To bookend perfectly the story of the early FA Cup and its inconsistencies of social class, comes the tale of an amateur goalkeeper who thrived among the many professionals in this final season of our study. Dr Robert Herbert Mills-Roberts played in goal for Preston North End in all their cup games in that campaign without conceding a goal, though only made two appearances out of 22 in the league, where James Trainer was the regular custodian. Both of them were Welsh, with Mills-Roberts gaining eight caps for his country while Trainer was awarded 20.

The two league fixtures where Mills-Roberts took over goalkeeping duties took place on 15 December 1888 in the 2-2 draw at Burnley and on 9 February 1889 in the 2-0 win at Aston Villa.

Mills-Roberts was born in Penmachno, North Wales on 5 August 1862 and in his prime stood 5 feet 8 1/2 inches (1.74 m) tall. He was educated at Friar's School in Bangor and captained the school football XI there in 1878. From there he went to University College, Aberystwyth and captained both the rugby and football teams in 1881. By 1882 he moved to London to St. Thomas's Hospital until 1887, where he qualified as a surgeon (MRCS) and physician (LRCP) and attended to the secretarial work of the football section.[41]

Mills-Roberts was a typical gentleman amateur and aided multiple clubs and representative sides during his career. He had played for Middlesex in 1883[42] and the Surrey County XI in October 1884,[43] together with being selected for London against Sheffield on 29 Nov 1884 at Kennington Oval in a 1-1 draw. His affiliation for the latter game was listed as Guy's Hospital in the *York Herald* on 1 December 1884, Barnes in *The Sportsman* of 27 November 1884 and St. Thomas's Hospital in the latter's 1 December 1884 issue. The first mention is probably a mistake, but the skills of Mills-Roberts were undoubtedly in demand and in the following year he was in action for Brentwood as they hosted Oxford University.[44] *The Field* listed him as linked with Merionethshire when noting his selection for Wales against Scotland[45] and he even appears to have swapped codes, as the *Northampton Mercury* wrote on 6 March 1886 when, having been 'knocked out of the Football Association Cup, [Mills-Roberts] is having a turn at the Rugby game'. United Hospitals, for whom he was secretary, versus Cambridge University[46] was followed by the *Sporting Life* of 24 February 1887 recognising his place in the Wales XI versus England while playing his club football for Bangor and, shortly afterwards, he was seen keeping goal for Casuals in a London Charity Cup match.[47] Finally, *The Sportsman* of 4 February 1888 listed him as Bangor and Corinthians for a game for Wales against England.

Mills-Roberts moved to the West Midlands where he served as house surgeon at Birmingham General Hospital, maintaining his football career with an appearance for The Provincials,[48] while continuing at Preston. Twelve months later he was to be found playing golf and cricket in Gloucestershire, where he was employed as a house surgeon in Stroud.[49] For a Preston game against Bootle in 1889, Mills-Roberts had to leave Stroud at the unearthly hour of 5 am, such was his devotion to the North End cause.[50] He was involved with other clubs such as Crusaders, Warwickshire County, Mitchell St. George's (Birmingham) and the Birmingham FA, but his fascinating life did not stop there. He served in two conflicts – the Boer War and the First World War – before passing away on 27 November 1935 in Bournemouth.[51]

The preceding paragraphs seem to be merely repetitive renderings of different clubs in a footballer's career. However, what they illustrate, which is relevant to our study, is that there was still a place for the gentleman amateur (though not a whole team of them) to make a mark among hardened, single-minded professional players. In just the same way as southern amateur teams did not simply disappear following Blackburn Olympic's 1882–3 FA Cup triumph, so too did talented amateur footballers remain in the sport for some time to come. Mills-Roberts' love of sport – and of football in particular – was clear and he was one of the last amateur players to win the cup, with Robert Topham for Wolverhampton Wanderers in 1892–3 being a later example.

The final in 1888–9 was a one-sided affair. North End already led Wolverhampton Wanderers by two clear goals at half-time and went on to lift the 1888–9 FA Cup without conceding in any of their five ties. The club had won the inaugural league title without suffering a defeat and, during the season as a whole, 'had played 69 matches, of which nine were drawn, nine lost, and 51 won...201 goals scored against 74'.[52] Table 6.3 lists their defeats and it is surely more than interesting that five of the nine should have come at the hands of Scottish combinations, with four of those being in Glasgow. The reverses, it should be stated, were suffered in friendly encounters, eight of the nine being away from home, and apart from the Bolton match, were fairly close in terms of the scoreline.

So the wheel had almost turned full circle and, specifically in the FA Cup but also on a wider front, the élite level of association football had passed, by a series of extraordinary events, from the privileged section of English society to the professional part, represented by a relatively well recompensed set of association footballers.

Conclusion

While many Lancashire-based football clubs were now filled with players from other parts of Britain (mainly Scotland), teams in other areas of the country – notably Wolverhampton Wanderers and West Bromwich Albion – bucked the trend by utilising links in their local communities. Both strategies achieved success. The footballing landscape was changing elsewhere, with Scottish teams finally concluding their association with the FA Cup, ending their days without a victory in the competition. Names from the past were stirring, as Sheffield realised that the city had to accept full-blown professionalism if it was to produce a team capable of challenging Lancashire and the West Midlands. A potted biography of a middle-class player active and effective in an increasingly professional domain is presented in the form of Dr Robert Herbert Mills-Roberts, who gained a cup winners medal with Preston North End in the 1888–9 final.

Had the real romance of the FA Cup disappeared with the coming of professionalism and the beginning of the Football League? Had the cup begun to lose some of its lustre and was already taking second place to the perceived importance of the league? Had the southern amateurs, turning up just before the start of a game, not taking the whole process very seriously, provided the *joie de vivre* and real allure of sport, something which all but disappeared when serious-minded professionals filled their stead? From the 1888–9 season, the cup still had a presence and a special place in many hearts, but that seemed to stem from the upset, the giant-killing by a lower league team of some élite Goliath, which still continues to this day. With the expansion of the UEFA Champions League to allow the entry of two clubs – champions and runners-up – from eight domestic leagues in 1997–8 and, subsequently in 1999–2000, four teams from Europe's top national leagues (at

Table 6.3 Defeats suffered by Preston North End in the 1888–9 season

Date	Opponents	Score	Venue	Newspaper reference
12 September 1888	Glasgow Select	2-3	Glasgow	*Lancashire Evening Post* 13 September 1888
4 October 1888	Third Lanark	2-4	Glasgow	*Lancashire Evening Post* 05 October 1888
10 December 1888	Sheffield Wednesday	1-2	Sheffield	*Nottingham Evening Post* 10 December 1888
31 December 1888	Cambuslang	0-2	Preston	*Sheffield Daily Telegraph* 1 January 1889
23 February 1889	Newton Heath*	0-1	Newton Heath	*Preston Herald* 27 February 1889
9 March 1889	Corinthians	0-2	Kennington Oval	*Sheffield and Rotherham Independent* 11 March 1889
6 April 1889	Bolton Wanderers	1-5	Bolton	*Sheffield Evening Telegraph* 6 April 1889
27 April 1889	Queen's Park	1-2	Glasgow	*Nottingham Evening Post* 27 April 1889
29 April 1889	Sunderland	1-4	Sunderland	*Sheffield and Rotherham Independent* 30 April 1889
25 May 1889	Celtic	1-2	Glasgow	*Dundee Courier* 27 May 1889

* The game against Newton Heath was abandoned 'seven or eight minutes from the finish' because of continued crowd incursions onto the pitch (*Cricket and Football Field*, 23 February 1889.). The *Preston Herald* of 27 February 1889 made several observations:
- The game was 'unsatisfactory'.
- The gate of around 12,000 produced takings of £250, half of which went to Preston North End.
- Newton Heath was at full strength, even preventing Jack Doughty from playing for Wales against England at Stoke on the same day. North End played a weakened eleven, with at least five regulars out. Two were on duty for England against Wales (John Goodall and Fred Dewhurst) with James Trainer in goal for the Welsh. Two others, Sammy Thomson and Bob Howarth, were away on business. Clearly there were contrasting attitudes to releasing players for international appearances, but the fact that Newton Heath kept Doughty probably indicated that they were treating the game against Preston more seriously than their opponents. For them, business also obviously took precedence over international friendlies.
- The Newton Heath players, as befitted their robust reputation, were 'inclined to be rough'. This assessment is reiterated in my article on Victorian football spectators' behaviour in matches between Sheffield Wednesday and Newton Heath. The Lancashire side had 'a man sent off and Wednesday players were attacked by home supporters at half and full time' in a fixture in April 1890 at Newton Heath.[53]

that point it was Italy, Germany and Spain), the FA Cup fell further down the priorities of England's leading clubs. Yet the FA Cup still retains an importance in terms of the fixture list today – the day of the third round, when clubs from the highest divisions become involved, despite other distractions, remains as anticipated as ever, though crowds tend to be on the disappointing side. However, there can be no hiding the fact that the onset of the Football League had an effect on the FA Cup in terms of team selection and attendances. But perhaps the final word should lay with the reporter in the *Daily News* (London) as he wrote on Preston's 1888–9 triumph in the FA Cup. He noted,

> Preston have at length secured possession of the much-coveted Challenge Cup. It is only right that the trophy, which carries with it *the championship of Association football* [my italics], should fall to the celebrated North End eleven, who for several years past have been distinctly the best side in the kingdom.[54]

At least, in his mind, the cup was still considered more prestigious than the league, but for how much longer?

Notes

1. *The Umpire*, 31 October 1886.
2. See Curry, 'Football Spectatorship'.
3. *Glasgow Herald*, 1 November 1886.
4. Vasili, *First Black Footballer*.
5. *Preston Chronicle*, 14 February 1885.
6. *Lancashire Evening Post*, 7 January 1891.
7. *The Sportsman*, 1 November 1886 and *Dundee Courier*, 5 November 1886.
8. *Liverpool Mercury*, 1 November 1886. Thanks to Tony Brown for providing the initial explanation.
9. Both Squire and Veitch won 'blues' for soccer at Cambridge.
10. *Sheffield Daily Telegraph*, 21 February 1887.
11. Email communication with Andy Mitchell, 26 April 2022.
12. *Morning Post*, 3 March 1887.
13. Westby, *History of Sheffield Football*, 161–2.
14. Wednesday was not the only club excluded because its entry was late. Ten other teams did not find their way into the first round draw. They were, Romford, Lancing Old Boys, Hurst, Bury, Stafford Union, Eckington Works, Stafford Rangers, Walsall Swifts, Wellington Town and Aston Shakespeare (*Birmingham Daily Post*, 7 September 1886).
15. Home of the Derby Midland club, which began life in 1881, but folded just a decade later. However, apart from one resounding victory over Nottingham Forest in 1889–90, they had little success in the FA Cup.
16. Harry Winterbottom is generally regarded as a Wednesday man, but a scan of team lists in the 1886–7 season reveals that he played the vast majority of it in Lockwood Brothers' colours.
17. Curry, *Making of Association Football*, Chapter Five.
18. *The Field*, 12 March 1887. The Alexandra Ground was close to Crewe's home today, Gresty Road, but closed in 1898 to provide land for the expansion of the railway station.
19. *Lancashire Evening Post*, 7 March 1887.

20 *Preston Herald*, 19 October 1887.
21 Pawson, *100 Years of the FA Cup*, 71.
22 28 March 1888.
23 Williams, *Code War*, 98.
24 *Midland Examiner and Times*, 19 December 1874. The 1874 example is of a match against yet another Wednesbury club, though this particular one had no separate designation.
25 In the course of research, there have been mentions of several other Wednesbury clubs, notably Wednesbury Athletic and Wednesbury St. James.
26 There can be no better reference on this subject than Mike Bradbury's *Lost Teams of the Midlands*.
27 Morris, *West Bromwich Albion*, 3–5 and 22.
28 Szymanski and Zimbalist, *National Pastime*, 43–4.
29 13 October 1888.
30 *Nottingham Evening Post*, 6 October 1888.
31 Brown, *FA Challenge Cup*; Smailes, *Breedon Book of Football League Records*.
32 *York Herald*, 3 November 1888.
33 *Sheffield Daily Telegraph*, 10 December 1888.
34 See Curry, 'Spireites'.
35 *Lancashire Evening Post* and *Nottingham Evening Post*, 8 December 1888.
36 *Sheffield and Rotherham Independent*, 1 February 1889.
37 Ibid, 18 February 1889, when 8,000 attended the second round FA Cup tie against Nottingham Forest.
38 *Sheerness Times Guardian*, 17 November 1888.
39 My thanks to Tony Brown for this information.
40 *Sheerness Times Guardian*, 9 March 1889.
41 *Preston Herald*, 24 March 1888.
42 *The Sportsman*, 30 October 1883.
43 Ibid, 16 October 1884.
44 *Morning Post*, 2 December 1885.
45 28 March 1885.
46 *The Field*, 12 February 1887.
47 *Morning Post*, 28 March 1887.
48 *Birmingham Mail*, 11 April 1888.
49 *Gloucester Journal*, 16 February and 3 August 1889.
50 *Preston Herald*, 6 February 1889.
51 For a full biography of Mills-Roberts and, indeed, all the Preston players of the time, see *Preston Herald*, 24 March 1888.
52 *Preston Herald*, 14 September 1889.
53 Curry, 'Football Spectatorship', 198.
54 1 April 1889.

Conclusion

This conclusion reflects the methodology employed during a period of over 30 years in research and writing by the author on the early sociology and history of association football. While in this case, events in the FA Cup provided the more specific canvas, the subject matter itself evolved over that period of time in a deliberate attempt to 'follow the evidence' rather than find uncontested answers to certain pre-determined questions. The latter approach has not been the aim of this writer. Rather, posited hypotheses should not necessarily be proved or disproved, they simply need to be *tested*, theories advanced and, perhaps most importantly, the body of knowledge hopefully increased. As expressed throughout this book, the key concept explores the inter-relationship between social class and power.

★★★

There was always something intangible about the FA Cup, though some might argue that its romanticism began when working-class underdogs began to challenge the collective *status quo* as expressed on the field of play and, at the same time, contest that which existed in the rest of society. Those fantasies continued through to the early 1990s before the UEFA Champions League appeared but, for some people, that nostalgia endures to this day. That magic does still exist because the format of the competition – sudden death – appeals to human beings seeking excitement in relatively unexciting societies.[1] It was, along with the promotion of international fixtures, one of the innovations which probably saved the FA, an organisation that had been floundering around somewhat aimlessly and unproductively for nearly ten years. The suggestion that both ideas should have been largely the work of one man, Charles Alcock, goes against the teachings of many academics who reject the 'great man' theory of history. Figurational sociologists are not so inflexible and believe that everyone involved in such processes is important, though some are more important than others, allowing us to advocate the work of plainly 'more important' individuals such as Alcock.

The years from 1871 to 1889 represent a supplement to the 'making of association football' as a modern sport.[2] Although the game had largely been established by 1877 when common laws for its playing were accepted in England, the 'completed' version of football was only really created following its professionalisation and organisation into the structure of an élite league. These were, of course,

DOI: 10.4324/9781003285595-8

adjustments to a fundamentally refined and rational recreation, which possessed a national governing body organising an English cup competition and international fixtures, was codified nationwide and exhibited a playing form appealing to players and spectators alike. While it was continuing to shake off the differences with its rugby rival and beginning to outstrip it as an accepted way of playing football, the only blot on the landscape was a failure to develop a reasonable infrastructure in terms of purpose-built facilities, instead using existing fields of play usually employed as cricket grounds in the summer months. Kennington Oval in London, Bramall Lane in Sheffield and Trent Bridge in Nottingham are examples of this practice. Football was growing in popularity to the point where it would develop beyond all recognition.

★★★

What, therefore, has been accomplished in the preceding chapters of this book? The following appear to be the most salient points.

1. Part of the title of this book notes a specific dichotomy but, in a sense, the phrase 'privileged to professionals' is a little misleading. The handover of power might be said to have conveniently taken place at a single watershed, when Blackburn Olympic beat Old Etonians in the 1882–3 FA Cup Final. This isolated event has tended to cloud the issue of the transference of supremacy on the field of play from the footballing aristocrats and upper-middle-class to their working-class counterparts. This cannot be viewed as another simple, straightforward division. For instance, Richard Turner, a middle-class Scotsman brought up in England, would 'assist' Blackburn Rovers successfully in two FA Cup Finals. Furthermore, old boy teams did not suddenly disappear following the 1883 final, rather they continued to have some impact on future FA Cups. However, the 1881–2 season would be their final triumph.

2. The FA Cup can be regarded as something of a time capsule for the increasing social and economic power of the working class in England towards the end of the 19th century. But in football, this must be tempered by the knowledge that the London élite retained the real power over the game's development by firstly imposing stringent conditions on professionalism (though these were often circumvented) and secondly by excluding professionals from the administrative process. Their playing careers over, the members of the FA were determined to cling onto their cherished sport in the committee room.

3. The format and idea for the FA Cup almost certainly emanated from Harrow School via Charles Alcock. There is some speculation surrounding possible diffusion from Sheffield, but only because the Youdan and Cromwell Cups preceded the FA Cup by several years. However, it is highly doubtful that socially élite individuals such as Alcock and others at the FA would have mimicked provincial practices in South Yorkshire when they had their own school experiences on which to draw.

4. More evidence has been discovered that the game was diffused directly by old boys returning home, with the case of Edward George Farquharson at

the Panthers club in Dorset being particularly instructive of this process. This represents the traditional hypothesis for football's spread to the wider society and, while this was not the only way in which its early development took place, it was, between the mid-1850s and at least 1870, the most common.[3]

5   A significant part of the text is perfectly positioned for Norbert Elias's insistence that researchers should not accept absolutes. The social composition of, in particular, northern and Midlands football teams in the 1870s and 1880s has been oversimplified as wholly working class, probably as part of a celebration of a supposedly rich lower orders subculture. However, from Elias's perspective, the historical sociologist's approach would be to delve more deeply and drill down into the available primary sources to test existing hypotheses. In our case, one hypothesis was that the East Lancashire clubs of Darwen, Blackburn Rovers and Blackburn Olympic, performing at their zenith in the FA Cup, consisted solely of players from working-class occupations. In one instance, it was accurate – Darwen's side, other than the two 'Scotch professors', appeared wholly working class. However, those of Blackburn Rovers and Blackburn Olympic, especially the former, were not. What was, perhaps, of more interest was the fact that, although upper-middle-class players were often found in predominantly working-class line-ups, this was rarely the case in reverse. The only consistent examples of this in the early days were to be found in Sheffield, where lower-class footballers such as Billy Mosforth and Jack Hunter played with the Clegg brothers and their associates. However, they were only 'allowed' to represent clubs such as Wednesday and Heeley, together with the Sheffield FA side, because of their undoubted ability, though there was no question of ever being asked by the socially élite Sheffield FC. The upper-middle strata of mid-to-late Victorian footballing society preferred to remain aloof.

6   The analysis of the above hypothesis represents the most controversial and provocative suggestion in the whole book. In proposing that early clubs from East Lancashire have been characterised by many historians as being wholly working class, it also suggests that, in a phrase, the subculture has been over-romanticised. Their participants have been placed on a class-related pedestal, which advocates a simple division between working-class and upper-middle-class football teams. This was not the case as there were, as has been well documented in this book, several decidedly middle-class individuals in East Lancashire teams and, indeed, elsewhere. Perhaps there is some justification in criticising this proposal as the numbers of middle-class performers in working-class settings were small, but they *did* exist.

7   The establishment of the FA Cup gave the association form a much-needed impetus in its rivalry with the rugby code. The latter's eschewing of competitive contests made their sport less attractive to excitement-seeking individuals and teams. Perhaps it was something of a gamble on the part of Alcock and the FA, as there was no guarantee or inevitability that the football-playing fraternity would accept a more serious way of playing. That they did was one of the turning points – international matches were the other, though rugby

embraced them as much as soccer – for association football's acceptance as the preferred code in England. The fact that soccer was more simplified and, apart from offside, much easier to understand, also aided its popularity.

8   There was absolutely no doubt that the advent of the Football League immediately affected the FA Cup. Reading newspaper reports and studying data on, for instance, attendances, the change was tangible. A new footballing élite along with differing priorities had been established and, in real terms, the FA Cup had to take an immediate back seat. The better teams competed in the league and the financial and performance gap between those and any outsiders grew year by year.

9   Appendix 2 shows that the FA Cup took time to become popular with potentially interested parties. In fact, there was a consistent but lukewarm response from southern amateur sides during the whole of our period of study, with entries never really growing at any great rate. Indeed, from a peak of 41 in 1880–1 and 1881–2, numbers actually dropped to 33 in 1887–8. It eventually increased its popularity in the north, especially following the 1879–80 season when clubs in the West Midlands and East Lancashire, where victory in the competition represented a triumph in what was probably deemed something of a class struggle, entered in increasing amounts.

Ways forward

There appear to be many different tangents which researchers could follow from areas touched upon in this book, some representing a bigger picture than simply the FA Cup. They include:

What were the exact make-ups in terms of nationality of teams involved in the FA Cup? The 1880–1 Old Carthusians cup-winning team had a majority of their players who were not born in the British Isles. Later in that decade, did English-dominated XIs such as West Bromwich Albion outnumber mainly Scottish clubs such as Preston? More pointedly, where were other footballers born who played in the competition? How many Welsh or Irish were involved and were there others from countries further afield? Did the influx of 'Scotch professors' influence results in the cup and the league?

Why was the Youdan Cup organised in its particular format? It certainly resembled those structures used in several English public schools, notably Harrow, suggesting diffusion from one of them. However, it is well known that Sheffield's early football subculture was barely influenced by former public schoolboys, so this is unlikely. Nevertheless, the use of byes for 'odd teams' is somewhat tantalising.

There is little known about James Powell, the man thought to have been largely responsible for the first draft of the rules for the FA Cup. Apart from being Honorary Secretary of Barnes FC in 1870[4] and no doubt one of Ebenezer Cobb Morley's acolytes, he is something of a mystery man. The strangest thing about him was that he was never listed in any football XIs, leaving one to believe that, apart from a few average athletics performances,[5] he was more of an able administrator.

Conclusion

The question of what happened to the British Football Association as the 1880s wore on is an interesting one. As noted in the text, lack of consistent financial backing probably hastened the organisation's end and, to a large extent, it had surely achieved its major objective when professionalism in football was legalised. Yet the fact that Blackburn Rovers appealed to the BFA rather than the FA for George Hawarth of Accrington to play for them in the 1884–5 FA Cup Final against Queen's Park shows that allegiance had been split because of their existence. The BFA must have wielded considerable power, especially in Lancashire, around that time.

Donington Grammar School near Spalding in Lincolnshire was the most obscure entrant for the inaugural FA Cup competition, yet no link has been established between employees or pupils there at the time and any member of the FA in London. Nor did any reports of the school's football activities appear in the press. One of the members of staff – the head, an assistant teacher or the gym master – was probably responsible, but, for now, it remains one of the cup's unanswered questions.

The appearance of Hugh McIntyre in London on the same London Caledonians side as Richard Turner in 1887 came as something of a surprise. Caledonians were a confirmed amateur outfit (they won the FA Amateur Cup in 1922–3) while McIntyre was an inveterate professional. The two do not seem to have been a good match.

There has been very little research attempted into the early development of football in and around Birmingham, apart from Molyneux's university thesis on physical recreation in the area in the mid-to-late 50s and Benkwitz and Molnar's more recent offering.[6] However, as the latter authors themselves admit, 'particular heed is paid to the working classes' involvement in football, as previous literature has often focused on the middle classes and their influence on and participation in organized sport'.[7] This rather sets a limited agenda, anchored as it is by the work of Marxist and 'New Left' academic, Raymond Williams. However, it is important not to be too critical as the latter article does, at least, represent a beginning. What is now required is an article on the very early processes involved, looking at the people concerned with those initial years, eschewing class distinctions in an attempt to discover possible trends and changes in the social backgrounds of players and administrators.

Expanding from there could see more research on the vast urban areas around Birmingham, particularly in the old county of Staffordshire. Stafford Road is an obvious first step, but the footballing phenomenon of Wednesbury and the plethora of club sides from that town deserves further attention.

Finally, the sporting links between North East Derbyshire (specifically Staveley) and East Lancashire – with the former almost acting as a footballing and cricketing nursery for the latter – is another way forward.

***

The Football Association Challenge Cup is the oldest association football competition in the world. That fact alone, together with the realisation that, apart from two world wars, it has had a continued existence in the English football calendar, should make it worthy of study. It even survived the 'Covid' pandemic to complete its programme during the 2019–20 and 2020–1 seasons. Of course, our examination starts much earlier and studies the first 18 campaigns when the cup transformed from being a pleasurable pastime for mainly southern, upper-middle-class ex-public schoolboys to providing, before the beginning of the Football League, the pinnacle of footballing glory for mainly working-class professionals representing nationally ambitious communities from Lancashire and the West Midlands. This book gives the reader new insights into the opening stanzas in the hope that those unique perspectives will create a greater understanding of the meaning of the FA Cup in today's highly commercialised football world.

Notes

1. Elias and Dunning, *Quest*.
2. See Curry, *Making of Association Football*.
3. See, for instance, Curry, 'Early football in Lincolnshire', where the example of Old Harrovian Noel Allix returning to Ancaster in Lincolnshire is quoted.
4. *The Field*, 5 March 1870.
5. For instance, he was ninth in the 1200 yards Flat Race Handicap (open) at Barnes FC athletic sports in March 1869 (*The Sportsman*, 20 March 1869).
6. Molyneux, 'Development of Physical Recreation'; Benkwitz & Molnar, 'Emergence and development of association football'.
7. Benkwitz & Molnar, 'Emergence and development of association football', 1027.

Appendix 1
Football Association Challenge Cup Finals, 1871–2 to 1888–9

Season, teams, result, scorers, kick off	Date played	Venue	Referee Umpires	Attendance
1871–2 Wanderers 1 Royal Engineers 0 W: Betts 3.05 pm	16 March 1872	Kennington Oval	Alfred Stair (Upton Park) JH Giffard (Civil Service) J Kirkpatrick (Civil Service)	2,000
1872–3 Wanderers 2 Oxford University 0 W: Kinnaird, Wollaston 11.30 am	29 March 1873	Lillie Bridge	Alfred Stair (Upton Park) JH Clark (Maidenhead) JR Dasent (Gitanos)	3,000
1873–4 Oxford University 2 Royal Engineers 0 OU: Mackarness, Patton 3.15 pm	14 March 1874	Kennington Oval	Alfred Stair (Upton Park) A Morton (Crystal Palace) CHR Wollaston (Wanderers)	2,000
1874–5 Royal Engineers 1 Old Etonians 1 (aet) RE: Renny-Tailyour OE: Bonsor 3.35 pm	13 March 1875	Kennington Oval	Charles Alcock (Wanderers) JR Dasent (Gitanos) JH Giffard (Civil Service)	3,000
1874–5 Replay Royal Engineers 2 Old Etonians 0 RE: Renny-Tailyour 2 3.05 pm	16 March 1875	Kennington Oval	Charles Alcock (Wanderers) JR Dasent (Gitanos) JH Giffard (Civil Service)	3,000
1875–6 Wanderers 1 Old Etonians 1 (aet) OE: Edwards	11 March 1876	Kennington Oval	Walter Buchanan (Clapham Rovers) RAMM Ogilvie (Clapham Rovers)	3,500

(Continued)

(Continued)

Season, teams, result, scorers, kick off	Date played	Venue	Referee Umpires	Attendance
OE: Bonsor			WH White (South Norwood)	
1875–6 Replay Wanderers 3 Old Etonians 0 OE: Wollaston, Hughes 2 3.30 pm	18 March 1876	Kennington Oval	William Rawson (Oxford University) RAMM Ogilvie (Clapham Rovers) AH Savage (Crystal Palace)	3,500
1876–7 Wanderers 2 Oxford University 1 (aet) W: Kenrick, Lindsay OU: Kinnaird (o.g.) 3.15 pm	24 March 1877	Kennington Oval	Sidney Wright (Great Marlow) BG Jarrett (Cambridge University) C Warner (Upton Park)	3,000
1877–8 Wanderers 3 Royal Engineers 1 W: Kenrick 2, Kinnaird RE: Morris 3.40 pm	23 March 1878	Kennington Oval	Segar Bastard (Upton Park) BG Jarrett (Old Harrovians) C Warner (Upton Park)	4,500
1878–9 Old Etonians 1 Clapham Rovers 0 OE: Clerke 3.27 pm	29 March 1879	Kennington Oval	Charles Alcock (Wanderers) SR Bastard (Upton Park) CE Leeds (South Norwood)	5,000
1879–80 Clapham Rovers 1 Oxford University 0 CR: Lloyd-Jones 3.15 pm	10 April 1880	Kennington Oval	Francis Marindin (Old Etonians) CW Alcock (Wanderers) R Barker (Herts. Rangers)	6,000
1880–1 Old Carthusians 3 Old Etonians 0 OC: Wynyard, Parry, Tod 3.45 pm	9 April 1881	Kennington Oval	William Peirce Dix (Sheffield FA) EH Bambridge (Swifts) CHR Wollaston (Wanderers)	4,500
1881–2 Old Etonians 1 Blackburn Rovers 0 OE: Anderson	25 March 1882	Kennington Oval	Charles Clegg (Sheffield FA) C Crump (Birmingham and District FA)	6,500

(Continued)

(Continued)

Season, teams, result, scorers, kick off	Date played	Venue	Referee Umpires	Attendance
3.05 pm			CHR Wollaston (Wanderers)	
1882–3				
Blackburn Olympic 2 Old Etonians 1 (aet)	31 March 1883	Kennington Oval	Charles Crump (Birmingham and District FA)	8,000
BO: Matthews, Costley			MP Betts (Old Harrovians)	
OE: Goodhart			W Peirce Dix (Sheffield FA)	
3.34 pm				
1883–4				
Blackburn Rovers 2 Queen's Park 1	29 March 1884	Kennington Oval	Francis Marindin (Royal Engineers)	12,000
BR: Douglas, Forrest			CHR Wollaston (Wanderers)	
QP: Christie			C Crump (Birmingham and District FA)	
1884–5				
Blackburn Rovers 2 Queen's Park 0	4 April 1885	Kennington Oval	Francis Marindin (Royal Engineers)	12,500
BR: Forrest, Brown			W Peirce Dix (Sheffield FA)	
			CHR Wollaston (Wanderers)	
1885–6				
Blackburn Rovers 0	3 April 1886	Kennington Oval	Francis Marindin (Royal Engineers)	15,000
West Bromwich Albion 0			JC Clegg (Sheffield FA)	
			P Morton (Old Harrovians)	
1885–6 Replay				
Blackburn Rovers 2	10 April 1886	Racecourse Ground Derby	Francis Marindin (Royal Engineers)	12,000
West Bromwich Albion 0			MP Betts (Old Harrovians)	
BR: Brown, Sowerbutts			JC Clegg (Sheffield FA)	
1886–7				
Aston Villa 2 West Bromwich Albion 0	2 April 1887	Kennington Oval	Francis Marindin (Royal Engineers)	15,500
AV: Hunter, Hodgetts			RC Gregson (Lancashire FA)	
			JC Clegg (Sheffield FA)	
1887–8				
West Bromwich Albion 2	24 March 1888	Kennington Oval	Francis Marindin (Royal Engineers)	19,000

(Continued)

(Continued)

Season, teams, result, scorers, kick off	Date played	Venue	Referee Umpires	Attendance
Preston North End 1 WBA: Woodhall, Bayliss PNE: Dewhurst			MP Betts (Old Harrovians) JC Clegg (Sheffield FA)	
1888–9				
Preston North End 3 Wolverhampton Wanderers 0 PNE: Dewhurst, Ross, Thomson	30 March 1889	Kennington Oval	Francis Marindin (Royal Engineers) Lord Kinnaird (Old Etonians) JC Clegg (Sheffield FA)	27,000

Without doubt, the most detailed book on the subject of the first 12 seasons of FA Cup finals is Keith Warsop's *The Early F.A. Cup Finals and the Southern Amateurs*. This table tries to condense much of that information into a more manageable framework.

Appendix 2

Football Association Challenge Cup entrants by region, 1871–2 to 1887–8

	Total entries	South	Midlands	North	Scotland Wales Ireland
1871–2	(15)	13	1	0	1
1872–3	(15)	14	0	0	1
1873–4	(28)	26	1	1	0
1874–5	(29)	27	1	1	0
1875–6	(32)	29	1	1	1
1876–7	(37)	32	2	1	2
1877–8	(43)	35	3	3	2
1878–9	(43)	35	4	4	0
1879–80	(54)	38	8	7	1
1880–1	(62)	41	11	9	1
1881–2	(73)	41	14	17	1
1882–3	(84)	35	19	27	3
1883–4	(100)	31	28	37	4
1884–5	(114)	37	39	32	6
1885–6	(130)	36	45	39	10
1886–7	(124)	34	43	34	13
1887–8	(149)	33	56	53	7

First qualifying round

| 1888–9 | (92) | 22 | 26 | 42 | 2 |

Second qualifying round additions

| 1888–9 | (34) | 5 | 15 | 8 | 6 |

There were 34 new clubs in the second qualifying round, plus the 46 who were successful from the first qualifying round, this made 80 in total.

First round proper after regional qualifying

| 1888–9 | (22) | 3 | 11 | 8 | 0 |

There were two new clubs in the first round proper, plus the ten who were successful from the four qualifying rounds, this made 32 in total.

Comments

The main table includes the seasons from the first FA Cup competition to contain the last contest when there were no qualifying rounds. It illustrates at a glance the increase in representation of provincial clubs over the cup's first 17 seasons.

Appendix 2

The clubs were involved by region in the first round proper in 1888–9 after the initial use of regional qualifying rounds.

The north and Midlands as separate entities only began to overhaul the south's total of participating clubs by the last season in the table, 1887–8. The south's numbers remained healthy and consistent throughout the period of study.

Lancashire's entry increased from two in 1877–8 to 29 a decade later in 1887–8. The West Midlands grew similarly over that period from none to 29.

As well as Lancashire driven by East Lancashire, and the West Midlands led by the Birmingham conurbation and Staffordshire, the other areas with relatively large representations were Nottinghamshire (largely Nottingham), Derbyshire (largely Derby), Lincolnshire (widespread – Lincoln, but also Grantham, Spilsby, Horncastle, Gainsborough and Grimsby/Cleethorpes), Sheffield and, eventually, the north-east of England. The first four regions – Nottinghamshire, Derbyshire, Lincolnshire and Sheffield – represented the 'old guard' in that they were at the forefront of early club formation and were well set to enter the initial contests.

Scottish clubs were banned by their governing body from entering the FA Cup from the 1887–8 season.

The total entry dropped by six from the previous season in 1886–7 as a result of a reduction of that number from Lancashire.

Appendix 3

Tertiary education of southern amateur FA Cup finalists, 1871–2 to 1882–3

Cambridge	30		
Trinity	22	*King's*	4
Trinity Hall	2	*Magdalene*	1
St. John's	1		
Oxford	56		
Trinity	8	*University*	8
Balliol	6	*Christ Church*	7
Exeter	5	*Brasenose*	4
New	4	*Oriel*	3
Hertford	2	*Keble*	2
Merton	2	*St. John's*	2
Magdalen	1	*Pembroke*	1
Queen's	1		
Did not attend university	41		
Royal Military Academy, Woolwich	33		
		Total players	159

Includes both of John Eyre's (Oxford University AFC) colleges – Keble and Christ Church.
Oxford provides far more examples because their team reached four finals, while Cambridge never achieved that distinction.
Trinity College, Cambridge maintains its reputation as a centre for football and general sports diffusion. See Graham Curry, 'The Trinity Connection: An analysis of the role of members of Cambridge University in the development of football in the mid-nineteenth century', *The Sports Historian*, 22. 2 (2002): 46–73.
Royal Engineers reached four cup finals with all but one of their players (William Merriman) attending the Royal Military Academy, Woolwich.

Appendix 4
Schools of southern amateur FA Cup finalists, 1871–2 to 1882–3

Eton	48	Charterhouse	15
Winchester	12	Harrow	11
Westminster	11	Cheltenham	7
Lancing	5	Malvern	3
Marlborough	3	Wellington	3
Brentwood	2	Brighton	2
Cheam School	2	Forest	2
Highgate	2	Mill Hill	2
Repton	2	Rugby	2
Shrewsbury	2	Addiscombe College	1
Aldin House, Slough	1	Blackheath Proprietary	1
Bradfield College	1	Bruce Castle, London	1
Clifton College	1	Diocesan, Rondebosch, South Africa	1
Edinburgh Academy	1	Epsom School	1
Felsted	1	Haileybury College	1
Kensington School	1	King's College School	1
King's School, Rochester	1	Loretto College	1
Reading School	1	Royal Academy, Gosport	1
RMC Sandhurst	1	Sherborne	1
Shifnal Grammar	1	Somerset College, Bath	1
Streatham School	1	Trent College	1
Trinity College, Glenalmond	1	Uppingham	1
Wallace's, Cheltenham	1	Woodcote House, Windlesham	1
Privately educated	4	Unknown (Vincent Edward Weston)	1
Royal Military Academy, Woolwich	33		

Newspapers, periodicals etc.

Bell's Life.
Birmingham Daily Post.
Birmingham Mail.
Blackburn Standard.
Blackburn Times.
Bolton Evening News.
Bridport News.
Burnley Express.
Cricket and Football Field.
Daily News (London).
Darwen Cricket and Football Times.
Derby Mercury.
Derbyshire Times and Chesterfield Herald.
Dundee Courier.
England Census, 1871, 1881, 1891, 1901.
Eton College Chronicle.
Fifeshire Journal.
Football Field.
Glasgow Evening Citizen.
Glasgow Evening Post.
Glasgow Herald.
Gloucester Journal.
Hertfordshire Express and General Advertiser.
Illustrated Sporting News and Theatrical and Musical Review.
Lancashire Evening Post.
Leeds Mercury.
Lincolnshire Chronicle.
Liverpool Mercury.
Lloyd's Weekly Newspaper.
London Daily News.
London Evening Standard.
Manchester Courier and Lancashire General Advertiser.
Mansfield Reporter.

Midland Examiner and Times.
Morning Advertiser.
Morning Post.
North British Daily Mail.
Northampton Mercury.
Nottingham Evening Post.
Nottinghamshire Guardian.
Nottingham Journal.
Nuneaton Advertiser.
Pall Mall Gazette.
Penny Illustrated Paper.
Preston Chronicle.
Preston Herald.
Reading Mercury.
Salisbury and Winchester Journal.
Sheerness Times Guardian.
Sheffield Daily Telegraph.
Sheffield Evening Telegraph.
Sheffield FA Minutes.
Sheffield and Rotherham Independent.
South London Chronicle.
Southern Times and Dorset County Herald.
South Yorkshire Times and Mexborough and Swinton Times.
Sporting Chronicle.
Sporting Gazette.
Sporting Life.
St James's Gazette.
The Athlete.
The Athletic News.
The Field.
The Illustrated Sporting and Dramatic News.
The Sportsman.
The Umpire.
Walsall Observer and South Staffordshire Chronicle.
Wigan Observer and District Advertiser.
Windsor and Eton Express.
York Herald.

Secondary sources

Alcock, Charles W. (Ed.). *The Football Annual.* London: Virtue & Co., 1871.

Andrew, Christopher. '1883 Cup Final: "Patricians v Plebeians"'. *History Today,* 33, 3 (5 May 1983): 21–24.

Archer, Ian. *The Jags: The Centenary History of Partick Thistle Football Club.* Glasgow: Molendinar Press, 1976.

Bailey, Malcolm. *From Cloisters to Cup Finals: A History of Charterhouse Football*. Shrewsbury: Quress, 2009.

Bancroft, James W. *The Early Years of the FA Cup: How the British Army Helped Establish the World's First Football Tournament*. Barnsley: Frontline Books, 2021.

BBC Television series 'Kicking and Screaming', first screened in 1995.

Benkwitz, Adam and Gyozo Molnar. 'The Emergence and Development of Association Football: Influential Sociocultural Factors in Victorian Birmingham'. *Soccer & Society*, 18, 7 (2017): 1027–1044.

Booth, Keith. *The Father of Modern Sport: The Life and Times of Charles W. Alcock*. Manchester: Parrs Wood Press, 2002.

Bradbury, Mike. *Lost Teams of the Midlands*. Bloomington, Indiana: Xlibris, 2013.

Bradbury, Mike. *Lost Teams of the North*. Hednesford: SRPM Limited, 2016.

Bradbury, Mike. *Lost Teams of the South*. Willenhall: Black Country Research, 2019.

Brown, Anthony. (2020) 'Cecil Reid: Local Hero'. Available at https://hitchintownfc.club/phpbb/viewtopic.php?p=11865#p11865 (Accessed: 4 January 2021).

Brown, Tony. *The Official History of Notts. County: 1862–1995*. Harefield: Yore Publications, 1996.

Brown, Tony. *The FA Challenge Cup 1871/2 to 2011/12*. Nottingham: Soccerdata, 2011a.

Brown, Tony. *The Football Association 1863–1883: A Source Book*. Nottingham: Soccerdata, 2011b.

Brown, Tony. *The FA Challenge Cup Complete Results (2020 Edition)*. Nottingham: SoccerData, 2020.

Butler, Bryon. *The Giant Killers*. London: Pelham Books, 1982.

Cavallini, Rob. *The Wanderers F.C.: 'Five Times F.A. Cup Winners'*. Worcester Park, Surrey: Dog 'n' Duck, 2005.

Cavallini, Rob. *A History of Clapham Rovers Football Club 1869–1914*. Bury: Dog 'n' Duck, 2021.

Chester, Ian. *Charles Alcock and the Little Tin Idol: The Story of the Birth of Football and the First Ever FA Cup* (150th Anniversary Edition). Independently published, 2020.

Collins, Tony. *A Social History of English Rugby Union*. London: Routledge, 2009.

Curry, G. 'Playing for Money: James J. Lang and Emergent Soccer Professionalism in Sheffield'. *Soccer & Society*, 5, 3 (2004): 336–355.

Curry, Graham. 'Football Spectatorship in Mid-to-Late Victorian Sheffield'. *Soccer & Society*, 8, 2/3 (April/July 2007): 185–204.

Curry, Graham. 'Degrading the Game: The Story of the Sheffield Zulus'. *Soccer History*, 24 (2009): 31–35.

Curry, Graham. *A Crucible of Modern Sport: The Early Development of Football in Sheffield*. Hauppauge, New York: Nova Science Publishers Inc., 2018a.

Curry, Graham. 'Stunted Growth: The Early Development of Football in Derby and South Derbyshire'. *Soccer & Society*, 19, 1 (2018b): 24–34.

Curry, Graham. 'Up'Ards, Down'Ards and Derbies: Figurational Reflections on Intense Enmity in Pre-modern English football'. *Soccer & Society*, 19, 5–6 (2018c): 645–656.

Curry, Graham. 'A Review of Early Football in Lincolnshire: County Town, Market Towns and Grammar Schools'. In Curry, Graham (Ed.), *The Early Development of Football: Contemporary Debates*. Abingdon: Routledge, (2019a), 97–118.

Curry, Graham. 'Early Football in and Around Shrewsbury: Soccer in the Sticks'. In Curry, Graham (Ed.), *The Early Development of Football: Contemporary Debates*. Abingdon: Routledge, (2019b), 154–173.

Curry, Graham. 'Football in the Capital: A Local Study with National Consequences'. *Soccer & Society*, 20, 3 (2019c): 512–527.

Curry, Graham. *The Making of Association Football: Two Decades Which Created the Modern Game*. Newcastle upon Tyne: Cambridge Scholars, 2020.

Curry, Graham. 'Spireites, Spital and Clodhoppers: Early Football in North East Derbyshire'. *Soccer & Society*, 22, 6 (2021): 550–570.

Curry, Graham and Eric Dunning. *Association Football: A study in figurational sociology*. Abingdon: Routledge, 2015.

Curry, Graham and Eric Dunning. 'The "Origins of Football Debate" and the Early Development of the Game in Nottinghamshire'. *Soccer & Society*, 18, 7 (2017): 866–879.

Dewhurst, Keith. *Underdogs: The Unlikely Story of Football's First FA Cup Heroes*. London: Yellow Jersey Press., 2012.

Dickinson, Jason. *The Origins of Sheffield Wednesday*. Stroud: Amberley, 2015.

Dunning, Eric and Jason Hughes. *Norbert Elias and Modern Sociology*. London: Bloomsbury, 2013.

Dunning, Eric and Kenneth Sheard. *Barbarians, Gentlemen and Players: A Sociological Study of the Development of Rugby Football*. Oxford: Martin Robertson, 1979. Reprinted with an afterword on 'The Continuing Commercialization and Professionalization of Rugby Union', 247–286. London: Routledge, 2005.

Elias, Norbert. *The Civilising Process: The History of Manners*. Oxford: Blackwell, 2000.

Elias, Norbert and Eric Dunning. *Quest for Excitement: Sport and Leisure in the Civilising Process*. Cambridge: Blackwell, 1986.

Elias, Norbert and John Lloyd Scotson. *The Established and the Outsiders*. London: Cass, 1965. Re-published by Sage (London) in 1994.

Fabian, Aubrey Howard and Geoffrey Green, *Association Football*. London: Caxton Publishing Co., 1960.

FCR 3 (Sheffield Football Club Records 3).

Football Association Minutes.

Foster, Joseph. *Alumni Oxonienses: The Members of the University of Oxford, 1715–1886: Their Parentage, Birthplace and Year of Birth, with a Record of their Degrees* (4 Volumes). Oxford: Parker and Co., 1888.

Gibson, Alfred and William Pickford. *Association Football and the Men Who Made It* (4 Volumes). London: Caxton, 1906.

Goldblatt, David. *The Ball is Round: A Global History of Football*. London: Penguin, 2007.

Green, Geoffrey. *The History of the Football Association*. London: The Naldrett Press, 1953.

Green, Geoffrey. *The Official History of the F.A. Cup*. London: Heinemann, 1960.

Harvey, Adrian. *Football: The First Hundred Years. The Untold Story*. Abingdon: Routledge, 2005.

Holzmeister, James R. 'The 1883 F.A. Cup Final: Working Class Representation, Professionalism and the Development and the Development of Modern Football in England'. *Soccer & Society*, 18, 2–3 (2017): 218–229.

James, Gary. *The Emergence of Footballing Cultures: Manchester, 1840–1919*. Manchester: Manchester University Press, 2019.

Joannou, Paul and Alan Candlish, 'The Early Development of a Football Hotbed: The Onset of the Game in Tyne and Wear, 1877–1882'. *Soccer & Society*, 19, 1 (2018): 107–122.

Kerrigan, Colm. *East London: A Hotbed of Football, 1867–1918*. Upminster: 3–2 Books, 2008.

Lamming, Douglas. *A Scottish Soccer Internationalists' Who's Who: 1872-1986*. Beverley: Hutton Press, 1987.

Lewis, Robert William. 'The Genesis of Professional Football: Bolton-Blackburn-Darwen, the Centre of Innovation 1878–85'. *The International Journal of the History of Sport*, 14, 1 (1997): 27–34.

Marples, Morris. *A History of Football*. London: Secker & Warburg, 1954.

Marshall, Frank. *Football: The Rugby Union Game*. London: Cassell and Company Limited, 1895.

Mason, Tony. *Association Football and English Society: 1863–1915*. Brighton: The Harvester Press, 1980.

Masson, David. 'The Life and Poetry of Keats'. In Masson, David (Ed.). *Macmillan's Magazine*, 3 (November 1860–April 1861): 1–16. Cambridge: Macmillan & Co.

Metcalf, Mark. *The Origins of the Football League: The First Season*. Stroud: Amberley Publishing, 2013.

Midwinter, Eric. *Parish to Planet: How Football Came to Rule the World*. Studley, Warwickshire: Know the Score, 2007.

Mitchell, Andy. *First Elevens: The Birth of International Football and the Men Who Made It Happen*. Scotland: Andy Mitchell Media, 2012.

Mitchell, Andy. www.scottishsporthistory.com.

Molyneux, Denis David. 'The Development of Physical Recreation in the Birmingham District from 1871 to 1892', MA thesis, University of Birmingham, 1957.

Morris, Peter. *West Bromwich Albion: 1879–1965*. London: The Sportsman's Book Club, 1966.

Morris, Terry. *Vain Games of No Value? A Social History of Association Football in Britain During its First Long Century*. Bloomington, Indiana: AuthorHouse, 2016.

Pawson, Tony. *100 Years of the FA Cup: The Official Centenary History*. London: Heinemann, 1972.

Phythian, Graham. *Shooting Stars: The Brief and Glorious History of Blackburn Olympic FC 1878-1889*. Nottingham: SoccerData, 2007.

Rippon, Anton. *Soccer: The Road to Crisis*. Ashbourne, Derbyshire: Moorland Publishing, 1983.

Robinson, Richard. *History of the Queen's Park Football Club 1867–1917*. Glasgow: Hay, Nisbet and Co. Ltd., 1920.

Russell, Dave. 'From Evil to Expedient: The Legalization of Professionalism in English Football: 1884-5'. In Wagg, Stephen (Ed.). *Myths and Milestones in the History of Sport*. Basingstoke: Palgrave MacMillan, 2011, 32–56.

Smailes, Gordon. *The Breedon Book of Football League Records*. Derby: Breedon Books, 1992.

Smart, John Blythe. *The Wow Factor*. Freshwater, England: Blythe Smart Publications, 2003.

Stapylton, Henry Edward Chetwynd. *Second Series of Eton School Lists comprising the years between 1853 and 1892, with notes and index*. Eton: R. Ingalton Drake, 1900.

Swain, Peter. *The Emergence of Football: Sport, Culture and Society in the Nineteenth Century*. Abingdon: Routledge, 2020.

Szymanski, Stefan and Andrew Zimbalist. *National Pastime: How Americans Play Baseball and the Rest of the World Plays Soccer*. Washington, DC: Brookings Institution Press, 2006.

Tabner, Brian. *Through the Turnstiles*. Harefield: Yore Publications, 1992.

Taylor, Matthew. *The Association Game: A History of British Football*. Harlow: Pearson Education Limited, 2008.

Vasili, Phil. *The First Black Footballer: Arthur Wharton, 1865–1930. An Absence of Memory*. London: Frank Cass, 1998.

Venn, John and John Archibald Venn. *Alumni Cantabrigienses* (6 volumes). Cambridge: Cambridge University Press, 1940.

Wainewright, John Bannerman. *Winchester College Register*. Winchester: P. and G. Wells, 1907.

Wallis, Peter John. *The Sheffield Collegiate School: 1836-1885 – a Biographical Register*. Sheffield: Sheffield Local History Collection, Sheffield Library, 1953.

Warsop, Keith. *The Early F.A. Cup Finals and the Southern Amateurs*. Nottingham: SoccerData, 2004.

Webb, Jeff. *Scotland's Lost Clubs: Giving the Names You've Heard, the Story They Own*. Worthing: Pitch Publishing, 2021.

Welbourne, David J. *Donington School and the first F.A. Cup Competition, 1872*. 1972.

Welch, Reginald Courtenay. *The Harrow School Register, 1801-1900*. London: Longmans, Green and Co., 1894.

Westby, Martin. *A History of Sheffield Football 1857-1889 '...speed, science and bottom'*. Second Edition. Bournemouth: England's Oldest Football Clubs, 2018.

White's Directory of Lincolnshire, 1871.

Williams, Graham. *The Code War: English Football Under the Historical Spotlight*. Harefield: Yore Publications, 1994.

Wright, Don. *Forever Forest: The Official 150th Anniversary History of the Original Reds*. Stroud: Amberley, 2015.

Young, Percy Marshall. *A History of British Football*. London: Stanley Paul, 1968.

Index

Pages in **bold** refer tables, and pages followed by n refer notes.

A History of Clapham Rovers 8
Alcock, Charles W. 9, 12–13, 19, 22, 24, 26, 58, 61, 102–103, 132
Allport, Douglas 35
Amateur Athletic Club 52
Andrew, Christopher 69
Andrews, Peter 106
Association Football and English Society 3
Astley Bridge 73
Athletic News of 21 March 1883 80

Baker, Alfred Joseph 13
Bambridge, Edward Charles 69
Bambridge, Ernest Henry 51
Bambridge, George Frederick 51
Bambridge, William Samuel 51
Barker, Robert 36–37
Barnes Football Club 35
Beresford, James 68, 96–98
Birkett, Louis 39
Blackburn Christ Church 73
Blackburn Olympic 68–70, 77
Blackburn Rovers 27, 68, 77, 105, 109, 117
Blackburn Standard 77
Bolton Wanderers 95–96
Booth, Keith 8, 14
Bourdieu, Pierre 7
bourgeoisie 5
Bowen, Edward Ernest 29
Bradbury, Mike 8
Brayshaw, Teddy 118
British Football Association 70, 88, 101–102, 105, 110, 136
Brixton Football Club 26
Brymer, John George 55
Butler, Bryon 77
Buttery, Tom 96

Cavallini, Rob 8
Cawley, Tom 118
Charles Alcock and the Little Tin Idol 8
Charles, Edward 51
Chequers 24
Chester, Ian 8
civilising process 6, 10n11
Civil Service and Royal Engineers 33–34
Civil Service club 33, 37
Clapham Common Club (CCC) 25–26, 38, 40
Clapham Rovers 38–40, 49, 61
Clegg, John Charles 102
Clegg, William Edward 25
Clutton, Ralph William 32
Cockerell, John 24
Corinthians Football Club 56
Crake, William Parry 23, 29
Cricket and Football Field 102
Cromwell Cup 15
Crump, Charles 65, 101–102
Crystal Palace 34–35
Curry, Graham 7, 10n12, 20n4, 45n2, 92n41, 130n17, 137n2
Cursham, Arthur William 56

Darwen Cricket and Football Times 73
Desborough, Lawrence Vivian 35
Dewhurst, Fred 115–116
Dixon, William Thomas 72
Donington Grammar School 27, 136
Douglas, Jimmy 75
Drummond, George 115
Dunning, Eric 2–3, 5, 8, 20, 102–104

East Lancashire: 1878–9 FA Cup 76; FA Cup Final, 1882–3 **78**; FA Cup Final, 1883–4 **84**; FA Cup Final of 1882–3 83;

football professionalism 87; Queen's Park 85–87
1872–3 competition 50–52
1873–4 to 1877–8 52–63
1885–6 season 68
Elias, Norbert 4, 8, 20
Elias's theory of civilising processes 6
English Cup 27, 49, 95, 106–107, 111, 117, 119, 133
Erskine, Albany Mar Stuart 36
Erskine, Robert 24
Eton College Chronicle 78–80

FA Cup *see* Football Association Challenge Cup
Farquharson, Edward George 133
Football Annual of 1871 40
Football Association (FA) 11
Football Association Challenge Cup 1; advent of the Football League 135; began as a London-based competition 30; Blackburn Olympic beat Old Etonians in the 1882–3 final 133; Chesterfield only entered from 1892–3 25; clashes between cup and league, 1888–9 **124**; closing stages of the inaugural 40–42; Clubs involved in the **123**; competition in the first round 97; 'Covid' pandemic 137; 1871–2 final 29; 1872–3 25; 1872–3 competition 50–52; 1873–4 to 1877–8 52–63; 1880–1 60; 1884–5 105–107; 1884–5 final against Queen's Park 136; 1886–7 campaign for 115; 1886–7, Wednesday failed to enter 118; entrants by region, 1871–2 to 1887–8 142–143; establishment of the 98, 134–135; finals, 1871–2 to 1888–9 138–141; initial FA Cup draw, 1871–2 **23**; Lancashire clubs 100–102; list of winners from the 1882–3 69; localism over universalism 95; meeting on professionalism 98–99; newspaper reports 22; origins of 12–16; Preston North End 115–116; Preston team 115; proposed by Old Harrovians 73–76; rules for the 135; semi-finals of the 1886–7 119–122; tertiary education of southern amateur finalists, 1871–2 to 1882–3 144; Wanderers v Royal Engineers 42–43
Football: Our Winter Game 13
football professionalism 4, 61, 72, 75, 81, 87, 90, 100, 103–104
Football: The Association Game 14
Football: The First Hundred Years 2
Forest Football Club 12, 28, 30, 49

Gibson, Alfred 77
Giffard, John Hardinge 36, 41
Gledhill, James 77
Goodyer, Arthur Copeland 57
Gordon, Jack 115
Goulden, William 31
Graham, Johnny 115
Graham, Robert George 35
Green, Geoffrey 2, 8

Hampstead Heathens club 36–37
Harrow Chequers 22–23, 29, 32, 36–37, 40, 43
Harrow School 20, 32, 50
Harvey, Adrian 2–3
Hay, Tom 96
Heron, Hubert 55
Hindle, Thomas 73
Hitchin club 32, 43
Holroyd, Mark 59
Holzmeister, James R. 3–4
Holzmeister R., James 3
hooliganism 109, 115
Hornby, Albert Neilson 72
Howarth, Bob 115
Hudson, John 'Jack' 118
Hunter, Jack 4, 96

Industrial Revolution 70

Jones, Di 96
Jope, William 101

Kay, John Charles 72
Kay, Robert Arthur 72
Kennedy, Gilbert George 24
Kinnaird, Arthur 55
Kirkham, William 74, 77
Kirkpatrick, James 23

laissez-faire 19
Lancashire Football Association 73, 81, 94
Lausanne club 24
Leopold, Arthur 51
Livesey United 73
Lloyd, Theodore 35
Lockwood Brothers Football Club 118
Love, James 57
Lucas, William Tindall 32

Macmillan's Magazine 36
Maidenhead Football Club 31
Malpass, Arthur 95
Manchester Football Club 75

Marshall, Tommy 76
Mason, Tony 3
Masson, David 36
McGregor, William 122
McIntyre, Scots Hugh 75, 136
McLachlan, William 77
Merriman, William 34
Metcalf, Mark 8
Midwinter, Eric 7
Mills-Roberts, Robert Herbert 126–127
Mitchell, Andy 74
Moon, William Robert 117
Morley, Ebenezer Cobb 13, 35
Morris, Terry 8
Mosforth, Billy 71, 118
Moss, William 96

Nottingham Forest 57–58

Old Carthusians 49, 61
Old Etonians 49, 61, 122
Old Harrovians 30
Old Wykehamists 122
Ottaway, Cuthbert John 23, 31
Oxford University 49

Parry, Edward Hagarty 68
Peirce-Dix, William 72
Pember, Arthur 13
Pickford, William 77
Powell, James 23, 135
Preston Catholic Grammar School 116
professionalisation 72

Queen's Park Football Club 27, 55, 74, 105

Rawson, William John 28
Reid, Cecil Frederick 32
Richards, Lewis Matthew 63
Roberts, Bob 96
Robertson, Sandy 115
Ross, Jimmy 115
Ross, Nick 115
Royal Engineers 32–33, 49, 122
Rugby Football Union (RFU) 24
Russell, David 115

Scottish Football Association 98
shamateurism 94, 101, 119
Sheard, Kenneth 2–3, 7
Sheffield and Hallamshire Football Association 80
Sheffield clubs 71
Sheffield Collegiate School 56

Sheffield FA Challenge Cup competition 55
Sheffield Football Club 16, 18
Sheffield Rovers 119
Sheffield Wanderers 95
Siordet, John Louis 35
Small Heath Alliance 115
Small Houses 15
Smith, Arthur Hubert 57, 59
Smith, Robert 43
Smith, Stuart George 55
Sorby, Henry Clifton 56
Stair, Alfred 23, 41
Strang, James 55
Suter, Fergus 57

Taylor, Matthew 3
The Athletic News 94, 96
The Early F.A. Cup Finals and the Southern Amateurs 2
The Father of Modern Sport: The Life and Times of Charles W. Alcock 8
The Football Association 1863–1883: A Source Book 2
The History of the Football Association 8
The Illustrated Sporting and Dramatic News 109, 122
The Official History of the F.A. Cup 2
The Origins of the Football League: The First Season 8
The Pickwick Papers 36
The Sportsman 7, 14, 22, 37, 42, 45, 46n14, 61, 105, 120
Thomson, Sam 115
Tod, Alexander Hay 63
Turner, James 35
Turner, Richard Rennie 106–107, 136

UEFA Champions League 1, 132
Upton Park club 35–36
Urwick, Frederick 35

Vaughan, Jackie 96
Veitch, John Gould 117

Wace, Henry 55
Walters, Arthur Melmoth 68
Warsop, Keith 2
Wawn, George Twizell 13
Wednesbury Old Athletic 122
Welch, Reginald Courtenay 23
West Bromwich Albion 109, 121
Wharton, Arthur 115
Widdowson, Sam Weller 57–58
Williams, Raymond 136

Williams, Thomas 76–77
Willis, Robert Watson 13, 35
Wilson, George 4, 82, 96
Wilson, George William 80
Wimbledon Men's Singles title 52
Windsor Home Park 24
Windsor Home Park Football Club 50–51
Wolverhampton Wanderers 121

working-class origins 3–4, 9, 21, 32
Wylie, John 55

York Herald 95
Youdan Cup 135
Youdan, Thomas 16
Young, Percy 7